MACAULAY

—

EXTRAITS DES ESSAIS

MACAULAY

EXTRAITS DES ESSAIS

AVEC

UNE INTRODUCTION, DES NOTES

ET

un lexique de tous les noms propres contenus dans l'ouvrage
avec la prononciation figurée

PAR

Jules GUIRAUD

AGRÉGÉ DE L'UNIVERSITÉ, PROFESSEUR D'ANGLAIS
AU LYCÉE VOLTAIRE

PARIS

LIBRAIRIE CLASSIQUE EUGÈNE BELIN

BELIN FRÈRES

RUE DE VAUGIRARD, 52

Toutes nos éditions sont revêtues de notre griffe.

SAINT-CLOUD. — IMPRIMERIE BELIN FRÈRES.

INTRODUCTION

Thomas Babington, Lord MACAULAY, naquit à Rothley-Temple, dans le comté de Leicester, le 25 octobre 1800. Dès son enfance, il se fit remarquer par une mémoire prodigieuse, outil précieux pour un futur historien. Après de brillantes études à l'Université de Cambridge, il se fit recevoir avocat. Il débuta bientôt dans la littérature par son *Essai* sur Milton publié par la revue d'Edimbourg, *The Edinburgh Review*, en 1825. Cinq ans plus tard il entrait dans la vie politique comme membre de la Chambre des Communes, et, en 1834, il était nommé membre du Conseil suprême de l'Inde. A ses deux ans et demi de séjour dans ce pays, nous devons ses *Essais* sur Clive et sur Warren Hastings, si pittoresques et si documentés. De retour en Angleterre, il partagea sa vie entre la politique et la littérature. A plusieurs reprises député d'Edimbourg, il prononça un certain nombre de discours dont le recueil constitue une partie intéressante de son œuvre. Mais il donnait le meilleur de son temps à ses *Essais* et à son *Histoire d'Angleterre*, qu'il n'avait malheureusement pas achevée quand il mourut, le 28 décembre 1859.

Historien, critique, orateur, homme d'État, poète, Macaulay n'est peut-être pas le plus original, mais il est à coup sûr un des plus séduisants parmi les écrivains de l'Angleterre moderne. Son *Histoire d'Angleterre*, fruit d'un long labeur et d'une vaste érudition, est d'une lecture aussi attrayante que celle d'un roman. Ses *Essais*, biographiques ou critiques, où il porte des jugements avec la hauteur de vue d'un philosophe et la délicatesse d'un artiste, sont des modèles de style, de bon sens et de clarté; de profondeur aussi, bien que sous ce rapport, la lucidité des idées et du langage ait pu faire illusion sur son compte. L'auteur de l'*Essai sur Machiavel* ne saurait, sans injustice, être accusé de s'arrêter à la surface des choses. On a dit de lui qu'il était moins anglais que français. Oui, s'il suffit d'être clair pour être français. Mais cela suffit-il? L'esprit élargi par d'immenses lectures, par la connaissance des littératures anciennes et modernes, Macaulay a sans doute presque perdu le goût de terroir si prononcé chez des écrivains de culture plus restreinte comme Dickens ou Carlyle; mais, malgré tout, chez Macaulay, le fond demeure anglais. Il nous semble que seul un Anglais, et un Anglais du dix-neuvième siècle, accoutumé aux débats de la Chambre des Communes, ait pu écrire le plaidoyer politique qu'est l'*Essai sur les incapacités civiles des Juifs*. Et cet admirable *Essai* sur Bunyan, pourrait-il, plus que le *Pilgrim's Progress* lui-même, être l'œuvre d'un homme né et élevé dans un autre milieu que le milieu anglo-saxon? — Macaulay est un Anglais qui a l'esprit clair comme un Français. Voilà, si l'on ne veut se payer de mots, ce que l'on devrait se borner à dire.

ŒUVRES DE MACAULAY

Lays of Ancient Rome, 1842.

A History of England from the Accession of James the second, 1848, 1855, 1861 (inachevée).

Critical and Historical Essays contributed to the *Edinburgh Review* :

Milton, 1825.
Machiavelli, 1827.
Hallam's Constitutional History, 1828.
Southey's Colloquies on Society, 1830.
Mr. Robert Montgomery's Poems, 1830.
Civil Disabilities of the Jews, 1831.
Moore's Life of Lord Byron, 1831.
Samuel Johnson, 1831.
John Bunyan, 1830.
John Hampden, 1831.
Burleigh and his Times, 1832.
War of the succession in Spain, 1833.
Horace Walpole, 1833.
William Pitt, Earl of Chatham, 1834.
Sir James Mackintosh's History of the Revolution, 1835.
Lord Bacon, 1837.
Sir William Temple, 1838.
Gladstone on Church and State, 1839.
Lord Clive, 1840.
Ranke's History of the Popes, 1840.
The Comic Dramatists of the Restoration, 1841.

Lord Holland, 1841.
Warren Hastings, 1841.
Madame d'Arblay, 1843.
The Life and Writings of Addison, 1843.
The Earl of Chatham, 1844.
Etc.

Dans l'*Encyclopædia Britannica*, biographies de :

William Pitt.
Oliver Goldsmith.
Etc.

PREMIÈRE PARTIE

RÉCITS, BIOGRAPHIES, DESCRIPTIONS, PORTRAITS

Londres en 1642[1].

The city of London was indeed the fastness of public liberty, and was, in those times, a place of at least as much importance as Paris during the French Revolution. The city, properly so called[2], now consists in a great measure of immense warehouses and counting-houses, which are frequented by traders and their clerks during the day, and left in almost total solitude during the night. It was then closely inhabited by three hundred thousand persons, to whom it was not merely a place of business, but a place of constant residence. This great capital had as complete a civil and military organization as if it had been an independent republic. Each citizen had his company; and the companies, which now seem to exist only for the sake of epicures[3] and of antiquaries, were then formidable brotherhoods, the members of which were almost as closely bound together as the members of a Highland[4] clan. How strong these artificial ties were, the numerous and valuable legacies anciently bequeathed by citizens to their corporations abundantly prove. The municipal offices were filled by the most opulent and respectable merchants of the kingdom. The pomp of the magistracy of the capital was inferior only to that which

---

1. Extrait de l'*Essai sur John Hampden*.

2. *Properly so called*, proprement dite.

3. Allusion aux banquets que don-nent ces célèbres *compagnies* ou *guilds*.

4. *Highland*, des montagnes (d'Ecosse).

surrounded the person of the sovereign. The London-
ers loved their city with that patriotic love which is
found only in small communities, like those of ancient
Greece, or like those which arose in Italy during the
middle ages. The numbers, the intelligence, the
wealth of the citizens, the democratical form of their
local government, and their vicinity to the Court and
to the Parliament, made them one of the most formidable bodies in the kingdom. Even as soldiers they were
not to be despised. In an age in which war is a profession, there is something ludicrous in the idea of batta-
lions composed of apprentices and shopkeepers, and
officered by aldermen [1]. But, in the early part of the
seventeenth century, there was no standing army in
the island; and the militia of the metropolis was not
inferior in training to the militia of other places. A city
which could furnish many thousands of armed men,
abounding in natural courage, and not absolutely un-
tinctured with military discipline, was a formidable
auxiliary in times of internal dissension. On several
occasions during the civil war, the trainbands [2] of
London distinguished themselves highly; and at the
battle of Newbury [3] in particular, they repelled the fiery
onset of Rupert [4], and saved the army of the Parliament from destruction.

Le Bengale et ses habitants [5].

Of the provinces which had been subject to the House
of Tamerlane, the wealthiest was Bengal. No part of
India possessed such natural advantages, both for agri-
culture and for commerce. The Ganges, rushing

1. *Aldermen*, sorte de conseillers municipaux parmi lesquels on choisit le Lord Mayor.

2. *Trainbands* est synonyme de *militia*.

3. En 1644. Newbury est dans le comté de Berks.

4. Le prince Rupert, neveu de Charles Ier commandait la cavalerie pendant la guerre entre le roi et le Parlement.

5. Extrait de l'*Essai sur Clive*.

through a hundred channels to the sea, has formed a
vast plain of rich mould which, even under the tropical
sky, rivals the verdure of an English April. The rice
fields yield an increase such as is elsewhere unknown.
Spices, sugar, vegetable oils, are produced with mar-
vellous exuberance. The rivers afford an inexhaustible
supply of fish. The desolate islands along the seacoast, overgrown by noxious vegetation, and swarming
with deer and tigers, supply the cultivated districts with
abundance of salt. The great stream which fertilises
the soil is, at the same time, the chief highway of East-
ern commerce. On its banks, and on those of its tribu-
tary waters, are the wealthiest marts, the most splendid
capitals, and the most sacred shrines of India. The
tyranny of man had for ages struggled in vain against
the overflowing bounty of nature. In spite of the
Mussulman despot, and of the Mahratta freebooter,
Bengal was known through the East as the garden of
Eden, as the rich kingdom. Its population multiplied
exceedingly. Distant provinces were nourished from
the overflowing of its granaries; and the noble ladies
of London and Paris were clothed in the delicate produce
of its looms. The race by whom this rich tract was
peopled, enervated by a soft climate and accustomed to
peaceful avocations, bore the same relation to other
Asiatics which the Asiatics generally bear to the bold
and energetic children of Europe. The Castilians have a
proverb that in Valencia the earth is water and the men
women; and the description is at least equally appli-
cable to the vast plain of the Lower Ganges.....

The physical organization of the Bengalee[1] is feeble
even to effeminacy. He lives in a constant vapour bath.
His pursuits are sedentary, his limbs delicate, his movements languid. During many ages he has been trampled upon by men of bolder and more hardy breeds.
Courage, independence, veracity, are qualities to which

1. Ce passage est extrait de l'*Essai sur Warren Hastings*.

his constitution and his situation are equally unfavourable. His mind bears a singular analogy to his body.
It is weak even to helplessness, for purposes of [1] manly
resistance; but its suppleness and its tact move the
children of [2] sterner climates to admiration not unmin-
gled with contempt. All those arts which are the
natural defence of the weak are more familiar to this
subtle race than to the Ionian of the time of Juvenal, or
to the Jew of the dark ages [3]. What the horns are to
the buffalo, what the paw is to the tiger, what the sting
is to the bee, what beauty, according to the old Greek
song, is to woman, deceit is to the Bengalee. Large
promises, smooth excuses, elaborate tissues of circum-
stantial falsehood, chicanery, perjury, forgery, are the
weapons, offensive and defensive, of the people of the
Lower Ganges. All those millions [4] do not furnish one
sepoy to the armies of the Company [5]. But as usurers,
as money-changers, as sharp legal practitioners [6], no
class of human beings can bear a comparison with them.
With all his softness, the Bengalee is by no means pla-
cable in his enmities or prone to pity. The pertinacity
with which he adheres to his purposes yields only to the
immediate pressure of fear. Nor does he lack a certain
kind of courage which is often wanting in his masters.
To inevitable evils he is sometimes found to oppose a
passive fortitude, such as the Stoics attributed to their
ideal sage. An European warrior who rushes on a bat-
tery of cannon with a loud hurrah will sometimes shriek
under the surgeon's knife, and fall into an agony of
despair at the sentence of death. But the Bengalee who
would see his country overrun, his house laid in ashes,
his children murdered or dishonoured, without having

1. *For purposes of* (pour des objets
de), quand il s'agit de.
2. *Children of* (enfants de), gens
nés dans.
3. *The dark ages* (les siècles obs-
curs), le moyen âge.
4. Sous-entendu : *of people*.

5. C'est-à-dire *the East India Company*, la Compagnie des Indes Orientales, fondée en 1600. Elle fit la conquête de l'Inde, et en conserva le
gouvernement jusqu'en 1858.
6. *Legal practitioners* (praticiens
du droit), praticiens.

the spirit to strike one blow, has yet been known to endure torture with the firmness of Mucius, and to mount the scaffold with the steady step and even pulse of Algernon Sydney.

The Black Hole of Calcutta [1].

The great province of Bengal, together with Orissa and Bahar, had long been governed by a viceroy, whom the English called Aliverdy Khan [2], and who, like the other viceroys of the Mogul, had become virtually independent. He died in 1756, and the sovereignty descended to his grandson, a youth under twenty years of age, who bore the name of Surajah Dowlah. Oriental despots are perhaps the worst class of human beings; and this unhappy boy was one of the worst specimens of his class. His understanding was naturally feeble, and his temper naturally unamiable. His education had been such as would have enervated even a vigorous intellect and perverted even a generous disposition. He was unreasonable, because nobody ever dared to reason with him, and selfish, because he had never been made to feel himself dependent on the goodwill of others. Early debauchery had unnerved his body and his mind. He indulged immoderately in the use of ardent spirits, which inflamed his weak brain almost to madness. His chosen companions were flatterers, sprung from the dregs of the people, and recommended by nothing but buffoonery and servility. It is said that he had arrived at that last stage of human depravity, when cruelty becomes pleasing for its own sake, when the sight of pain, as pain, where no advantage is to be gained, no offence punished, no danger averted, is an agreeable excitement. It had early been his amusement to tor-

1. Extrait de l'*Essai sur Clive.* | 2. *Khan* est un mot d'origine tartare qui signifie *prince.*

ture beasts and birds; and, when he grew up, he enjoyed with still keener relish the misery of his fellow-creatures.

From a child[1] Surajah Dowlah had hated the English. It was his whim to do so; and his whims were never opposed. He had also formed a very exaggerated notion[2] of the wealth which might be obtained by plundering them; and his feeble and uncultivated mind was incapable of perceiving that the riches of Calcutta, had they even been greater than he imagined, would not compensate him for what he must lose, if the European trade, of which Bengal was a chief seat[3], should be driven by his violence to some other quarter. Pretexts for a quarrel were readily found. The English, in expectation of a war with France, had begun to fortify their settlement without special permission from the Nabob[4]. A rich native, whom he longed to plunder, had taken refuge at Calcutta, and had not been delivered up. On such grounds as these[5] Surajah Dowlah marched with a great army against Fort William[6].

The servants of the Company[7] at Madras had been forced by Dupleix to become statesmen and soldiers. Those in Bengal were still mere traders, and were terrified and bewildered by the approaching danger. The governor, who had heard much of Surajah Dowlah's cruelty, was frightened out of his wits[8], jumped into a boat, and took refuge in the nearest ship. The military commandant thought that he could not do better than follow so good an example. The fort was taken after a feeble resistance; and great numbers of the English fell into the hands of the conquerors. The Nabob seated

1. *From a child* (= from *the time when he was* a child), dès son enfance.

2. *He had... formed a... notion*, il s'était fait une idée.

3. *Seat*, centre.

4. *The Nabob*, c'est-à-dire Surajah Dowlah qui était Nabab (gouverneur ou vice-roi) du Bengale.

5. *On such grounds as these* (sur de tels motifs que ceux-ci), pour des motifs de cette sorte.

6. Fort que les Anglais avaient élevé au sud de Calcutta.

7. *The Company*, c'est-à-dire *the East India Company*. Voy. note 5, page 12.

8. *Was frightened out of his wits* (fut effrayé hors de son esprit), perdit la tête.

himself with regal pomp in the principal hall of the factory, and ordered Mr. Holwell, the first in rank among the prisoners, to be brought before him. His Highness abused [1] the insolence of the English, and grumbled at the smallness of the treasure which he had found; but promised to spare their lives, and retired to rest.

Then was committed that great crime, memorable for its singular atrocity, memorable for the tremendous retribution by which it was followed. The English captives were left at the mercy of the guards, and the guards determined to secure [2] them for the night in the prison of the garrison, a chamber known by the fearful name of the Black Hole. Even for a single European malefactor, that dungeon would, in such a climate, have been too close and narrow. The space was only twenty feet square. The air-holes were small and obstructed. It was the summer solstice, the season when the fierce heat of Bengal can scarcely be rendered tolerable to natives of England by lofty halls and by the constant waving of fans. The number of the prisoners was one hundred and forty-six. When they were ordered to enter the cell, they imagined that the soldiers were joking; and, being in high spirits [3] on account of the promise of the Nabob to spare their lives, they laughed and jested at the absurdity of the notion [4]. They soon discovered their mistake. They expostulated; they entreated; but in vain. The guards threatened to cut down all who hesitated. The captives were driven into the cell at the point of the sword, and the door was instantly shut and locked upon them.

Nothing in history or fiction, not even the story which

---

1. *Abused* (injuria), parla en termes injurieux de.

2. *Secure* (mettre en sûreté), enfermer.

3. *In high spirits*, de bonne humeur. Ici *spirits* a le sens d'*esprits animaux*, « fluide imaginaire qu'on supposait formé dans le cœur et dans le cerveau et distribué par le moyen des nerfs dans toutes les parties du corps. » (LITTRÉ.) — La vigueur, la verve, la gaité, l'entrain, étaient considérés comme le résultat de la présence, chez quelqu'un, d'une grande quantité d'esprits animaux.

4. *The notion* = *this notion*, cette idée.

Ugolino told in the sea of everlasting ice [1], after he had wiped his bloody lips on the scalp of his murderer, approaches the horrors which were recounted by the few survivors of that night. They cried for mercy. They strove to burst the door. Holwell who, even in that extremity, retained some presence of mind, offered large bribes to the gaolers. But the answer was that nothing could be done without the Nabob's orders, that the Nabob was asleep, and that he would be angry if anybody woke him. Then the prisoners went mad with despair. They trampled each other down, fought for the places at the windows, fought for the pittance of water with which the cruel mercy of the murderers mocked their agonies, raved, prayed, blasphemed, implored the guards to fire among them. The gaolers in the mean time held lights to the bars, and shouted with laughter at the frantic struggles of their victims. At length the tumult died away in low gaspings and moanings. The day broke. The Nabob had slept off [2] his debauch, and permitted the door to be opened. But it was some time before the soldiers could make a lane for the survivors, by piling up on each side the heaps of corpses on which the burning climate had already begun to do its loathsome work. When at length a passage was made, twenty-three ghastly figures, such as their own mothers would not have known, staggered one by one out of the charnel-house. A pit was instantly dug. The dead bodies, a hundred and twenty-three in number, were flung into it promiscuously, and covered up.

But these things, which, after the lapse of more than eighty years, cannot be told or read without horror, awakened neither remorse nor pity in the bosom of the

1. Allusion à un épisode bien connu de l'*Enfer* de Dante où sont racontées les souffrances du comte *Ugolino della Gherardesca* qui, victime d'une conspiration, fut enfermé avec ses fils et ses neveux dans une tour où ils moururent de faim.

2. *Slept off*, cuvé. — L'adverbe *off* exprime l'action de faire disparaitre, dissiper ; — le verbe *to sleep* indique le moyen employé. La traduction littérale serait : *dissipé par le sommeil*

savage Nabob. He inflicted no punishment on the murderers. He showed no tenderness to the survivors.
Some of them, indeed, from whom nothing was to be
got, were suffered to depart; but those from whom it
was thought that any thing could be extorted were
treated with execrable cruelty. Holwell, unable to walk,
was carried before the tyrant, who reproached him,
threatened him, and sent him up[1] the country in irons,
together with some other gentlemen who were suspected
of knowing more than they chose to tell about the
treasures of the Company. These persons, still bowed
down by the sufferings of that great agony, were lodged
in miserable sheds, and fed only with grain and water,
till at length the intercessions of the female relations[2]
of the Nabob procured their release. One Englishwoman
had survived that night. She was placed in the harem
of the Prince at Moorshedabad.

Les Nababs[3].

The great events which had taken place in India had
called into existence a new class of Englishmen, to whom
their countrymen gave the name of Nabobs[4]. These
persons had generally sprung from families neither ancient nor opulent; they had generally been sent at an
early age to the East; and they had there acquired large
fortunes, which they had brought back to their native
land. It was natural that, not having had much opportunity of mixing with the best society, they should
exhibit some of the awkwardness and some of the pom-
posity of upstarts. It was natural that, during their
sojourn in Asia, they should have acquired some tastes
and habits surprising, if not disgusting[5], to persons who

1. *Up*, au fond de.
2. *Female relations*, parentes.
3. Extrait de l'*Essai sur Clive*.

4. Le sens ordinaire de *nabab* est *gouverneur* ou *vice-roi*. Voy. note 4, page 14.
5. *Disgusting*, choquants.

never had quitted Europe. It was natural that, having enjoyed great consideration in the East, they should not be disposed to sink into obscurity at home ; and as they had money, and had not birth or high connexion, it was natural that they should display a little obtrusively the single advantage which they possessed. Wherever they settled there was a kind of feud between them and the old nobility and gentry, similar to that which raged in France between the farmer-general and the marquis. This enmity to the aristocracy long continued to distinguish the servants of the Company[1]. More than twenty years after the time of which we are now speaking, Burke pronounced that among the Jacobins[2] might be reckoned " the East Indians[3] almost to a man[4], who cannot bear to find that their present importance does not bear a proportion to[5] their wealth."

The Nabobs soon became a most unpopular class of men. Some of them had in the East displayed eminent talents, and rendered great services to the state ; but at home their talents were not shown to advantage, and their services were little known. That they had sprung from obscurity, that they had acquired great wealth, that they exhibited it insolently, that they spent it extravagantly, that they raised the price of every thing in their neighbourhood, from fresh eggs to rotten boroughs[6], that their liveries outshone those of dukes, that their coaches were finer than that of the Lord Mayor[7], that the examples of their large and ill-governed households corrupted half the servants in the country, that some of them, with

---

1. *The Company*, c'est-à-dire *the East India Company*. — Voy. note 5, page 12.

2. Le nom de *Jacobins* fut donné en Angleterre à ceux dont les opinions politiques présentaient quelque analogie avec les opinions de Robespierre et de ses amis.

3. *The East Indians*, les colons des Indes orientales.

4. *Almost to a man* (presque à un homme [près]), presque tous.

5. *Does not bear a proportion to,* n'est pas proportionnée à.

6. *Rotten boroughs*, bourgs pourris, nom donné à certaines localités qui, jusqu'à la réforme électorale de 1832, envoyaient des députés au Parlement, alors que la population, réduite à une poignée d'habitants dans la plupart des cas, avait même parfois complètement disparu. Le propriétaire de la région étant, en réalité, l'unique électeur, disposait des sièges à son gré.

7. *The Lord Mayor*, le maire de la cité de Londres.

all their magnificence, could not catch the tone of good
society, but, in spite of the stud and the crowd of menials,
of the plate and the Dresden china [1] of the venison and
the Burgundy, were still low [2] men; these were things
which excited, both in the class from which they had
sprung and in the class into which they attempted to
force themselves, the bitter aversion which is the effect of
mingled envy and contempt.   But when it was also ru-
moured that the fortune which had enabled its possessor
to eclipse the Lord-Lieutenant [3] on the race-ground, or to
carry the county [4] against the head of a house as old as Domesday Book [5], had been accumulated by violating public
faith, by deposing legitimate princes, by reducing whole
provinces to beggary, all the higher and better as well as
all the low and evil parts of human nature were stirred
against the wretch who had obtained by guilt and dishon-
our the riches which he now lavished with arrogant and
inelegant profusion.   The unfortunate Nabob seemed to
be made up of those foibles against which comedy has
pointed the most merciless ridicule, and of those crimes
which have thrown the deepest gloom over tragedy, of
Turcaret and Nero, of Monsieur Jourdain and Richard
the Third. A tempest of execration and derision, such
as can be compared only to that outbreak of public
feeling against the Puritans which took place at the
time of the Restoration [6], burst on the servants of the
Company.   The humane man was horror-struck at the
way in which they had got their money, the thrifty man
at the way in which they spent it.   The dilettante sneered
at their want of taste.   The maccaroni [7] black-balled

1. *Dresden china* (porcelaine de
Dresde), porcelaine de Saxe.

2. *Low*, vulgaires.

3. *The Lord-Lieutenant*, premier
magistrat d'un comté, est, dans l'administration anglaise, à peu près
l'équivalent de notre préfet.

4. *To carry the county* (emporter,
gagner le comté dans une lutte électorale) se faire élire député du comté.

5. *Domesday Book*, ou *Doomsday
Book* (étymologie incertaine), ca-
dastre rédigé du temps de Guillaume
le Conquérant dont l'original peut se
voir aux archives de Londres.

6. Voy., plus loin, le morceau
intitulé : *La Corruption et les Puritains*.

7. *The maccaroni*. Les jeunes élé-
gants de cette époque s'appelaient
maccaroni, parce qu'un certain
nombre d'entre eux, ayant voyagé

them [1] as vulgar fellows. Writers the most unlike in sentiment and style, methodists [2] and libertines, philosophers and buffoons, were for once on the same side. It is hardly too much to say that, during a space of about thirty years, the whole lighter literature of England was coloured [3] by the feelings which we have described.

Burke [4].

The zeal of Burke was still fiercer [5]; but it was far purer. Men unable to understand the elevation of his mind have tried to find out some discreditable motive for the vehemence and pertinacity which he showeed on this occasion. But they have altogether failed. . . . . The plain truth is that Hastings had committed some great crimes, and that the thought of those crimes made the blood of Burke boil in his veins. For Burke was a man in whom compassion for suffering, and hatred of injustice and tyranny, were as strong as in Las Casas or Clarkson. And although in him, as in Las Casas and in Clarkson, these noble feelings were alloyed with the infirmity which belongs to human nature, he is, like them, entitled to this great praise, that he devoted years of intense labour to the service of a people with whom he had neither blood nor language, neither religion nor manners in common, and from whom no requital, no thanks, no applause could be expected.

en Italie, avaient introduit en Angleterre l'usage du plat national de la péninsule, et avaient fondé un *club du macaroni*.

1. *Black-balled them* (*black ball*, boule noire, est ici employé comme verbe; c'est notre néologisme *blacbouler*), — votait contre eux (quand ils voulaient devenir membres du club).

2. *Methodists*. Vers le milieu du dix-huitième siècle, alors que l'esprit religieux semblait moribond en Angleterre, quelques étudiants d'Oxford prirent l'initiative d'un mouvement de renaissance du christianisme. Ils se distinguaient par un grand enthousiasme et par une austère régularité de vie qui leur valut le surnom de *Methodists*. Les plus célèbres furent *Whitfield* et les deux frères Charles et John *Wesley*.

3. *Coloured*, caractérisée.

4. Extrait de l'*Essai sur Warren Hastings*).

5. *Fiercer*, plus violent (que celui de Philip Francis qui fut un des plus redoutables adversaires de Warren Hastings.

His knowledge of India was such as few, even of those Europeans who have passed many years in that country, have attained, and such as certainly was never attained by any public man who had not quitted Europe. He had studied the history, the laws, and the usages of the East with an industry such as is seldom found united to so much genius and so much sensibility. Others have perhaps been equally laborious, and have collected an equal mass of materials. But the manner in which Burke brought his higher powers of intellect to work on statements of facts, and on tables of figures, was peculiar to himself. In every part of those huge bales of Indian information[1] which repelled almost all other readers, his mind, at once philosophical and poetical, found something to instruct or to delight. His reason analysed and digested those vast and shapeless masses; his imagination animated and coloured them. Out of darkness, and confusion, he formed a multitude of ingenious theories and vivid pictures. He had, in the highest degree, that noble faculty whereby man is able to live in the past and in the future, in the distant and in the unreal. India and its inhabitants were not to him, as to most Englishmen, mere names and abstractions, but a real country and a real people. The burning sun, the strange vegetation of the palm and the cocoa tree, the rice-field, the tank, the huge trees, older than the Mogul empire, under which the village crowds assemble, the thatched roof of the peasant's hut, the rich tracery of the mosque where the imaum[2] prays with his face to Mecca, the drums, and banners, and gaudy idols, the devotee swinging in the air[3], the graceful maiden, with the pitcher on

---

1. *Indian information*, renseignements sur l'Inde.

2. *Imaum* (s'écrit aussi *imam* et *iman*), — *iman*, prêtre de la religion mahométane.

3. « En quel pays d'Europe trouverait-on des malheureux qui, pour une récompense médiocre, se fissent tournoyer en l'air avec vitesse, suspendus à une corde par deux crochets en fer passés comme des hameçons dans les chairs du dos? Chaque année, à une des fêtes religieuses du printemps, des gens de bonne volonté se soumettent à ce supplice, payés par des hommes riches et hypocrites, qui prétendent faire leur salut par des mortifications de la chair d'autrui. » Victor JACQUEMONT, *Voyage dans l'Inde.*

her head, descending the steps to the river-side, the black faces, the long beards, the yellow streaks of sect[1], the turbans and the flowing robes, the spears and the silver maces, the elephants with their canopies of state, the gorgeous palanquin of the prince, and the close litter of the noble lady, — all those things were to him as the objects amidst which his own life had been passed, as the objects which lay on the road between Beaconsfield[2] and St. James's Street[3]. All India was present to the eye of his mind, from the halls where suitors laid gold and perfumes at the feet of sovereigns to the wild moor where the gipsy camp was pitched, from the bazars, humming like bee-hives with the crowd of buyers and sellers, to the jungle where the lonely courier shakes his bunch of iron rings to scare away the hyænas. Oppression in Bengal was to him the same thing as oppression in the streets of London.

Samuel Crisp[4].

His name, well known, near a century ago, in the most splendid circles of London, has long been forgotten. His history is, however, so interesting and instructive, that it tempts us to venture on a digression.

Long before Frances Burney was born, Mr. Crisp had made his entrance into the world, with every advantage. He was well connected[5] and well educated. His face and figure[6] were conspicuously handsome; his manners were polished; his fortune was easy; his character was without stain; he lived in the best society; he had read much; he talked well; his taste in literature, music, painting, ar-

----

1. *Of sect*, qui distinguent les sectes.

2. Burke habitait cette ville, située dans le comté de Buckingham, à vingt-cinq milles de Londres.

3. *St-James's Street*, importante rue de Londres, qui va de *Piccadilly* à *Pall Mall*, et où se trouvent plusieurs clubs célèbres.

4. Extrait de l'*Essai* sur Mme d'Arblay.

5. *Well connected*, de bonne famille.

6. *Figure*, tournure.

chitecture, sculpture was held in high esteem. Nothing that the world can give seemed to be wanting to his happiness and respectability, except that he should understand the limits of his powers, and should not throw away distinctions which were within his reach in the pursuit of distinctions which were unattainable.

" It is an uncontrolled[1] truth," says Swift, " that no man ever made an ill figure who understood his own talents, nor a good one who mistook them. " Every day brings with it fresh illustrations of this weighty saying; but the best commentary that we remember is the history of Samuel Crisp. Men like him have their proper place, and it is a most important one, in the Commonwealth of Letters. It is by the judgment of such men that the rank of authors is finally determined. It is neither to the multitude, nor to the few who are gifted with great creative genius, that we are to look for sound critical decisions. The multitude, unacquainted with the best models, are captivated by whatever stuns and dazzles them. They deserted Mrs. Siddons to run after Master Betty; and they now prefer, we have no doubt, Jack Sheppard to Van Artevelde. A man of great original genius, on the other hand[2], a man who has attained to mastery in some high walk[3] of art, is by no means to be implicitly trusted as a judge of the performances of others. The erroneous decisions pronounced by such men are without number. It is commonly supposed that jealousy makes them unjust. But a more creditable explanation may easily be found. The very excellence of a work shows that some of the faculties of the author have been developed at the expense of the rest; for it is not given to the human intellect to expand itself widely in all directions at once, and to be at the same time gigantic and well proportioned. Whoever becomes preeminent in any art, nay, in any style of art, generally does so by devo-

---

1. *Uncontrolled*, irréfutée.
2. *On the other hand*, d'autre part.

3. *Walk* (voic), branche.

ting himself with intense and exclusive enthusiasm to the pursuit of one kind of excellence. His perception of other kinds of excellence is therefore too often impaired. Out of his own department[1] he praises and blames at random, and is far less to be trusted than the mere connoisseur, who produces nothing, and whose business is only to judge and enjoy. One painter[2] is distinguished by his exquisite finishing. He toils day after day to bring the veins of a cabbage leaf, the folds of a lace veil, the wrinkles of an old woman's face, nearer and nearer to perfection. In the time which he employs on a square foot of canvas, a master[3] of a different order covers the walls of a palace with gods burying giants under mountains, or makes the cupola of a church alive with seraphim[4] and martyrs. The more fervent[5] the passion of each of these artists for his art, the higher the merit of each in his own line[6], the more unlikely it is that they will justly appreciate each other. Many persons who never handled a pencil[7] probably do far more justice to Michael Angelo than would have been done by Gerard Douw, and far more justice to Gerard Douw than would have been done by Michael Angelo.

It is the same with literature. Thousands, who have no spark of the genius of Dryden or Wordsworth, do to Dryden the justice which has never been done by Wordsworth, and to Wordsworth the justice which, we suspect, would never have been done by Dryden. Gray, Johnson, Richardson, Fielding, are all highly esteemed by the great body of intelligent and well informed men. But Gray could see no merit in Rasselas; and Johnson could see no merit in the Bard[8]. Fielding thought Richardson a sol-

---

1. *Department*, branche, spécialité.
2. Macaulay a en vue *Gérard Dow* que, d'ailleurs, il nomme un peu plus loin.
3. C'est-à-dire *Michel-Ange*.
4. *Seraphim*, pluriel hébraïque de *seraph*.
5. *The more fervent*, sous-entendu : *is*. De même plus loin après *the higher*.

6. *Line*, branche, spécialité. Cf. plus haut *walk* et *department* employés dans le même sens.
7. *Pencil*, pinceau.
8. *The Bard*, le Barde, Ode de Gray publiée en 1757. Dans sa biographie de Gray (*The Lives of the English Poets*), Johnson, après une critique acerbe du poème, daigne cependant ajouter : " *To say that he has no*

emn prig; and Richardson perpetually expressed contempt and disgust for Fielding's lowness[1].

Mr. Crisp seems, as far as we can judge, to have been a man eminently qualified for the useful office of a connoisseur. His talents and knowledge fitted him to appreciate justly almost every species of intellectual superiority. As an adviser he was inestimable. Nay, he might probably have held a respectable rank as a writer, if he would have confined himself to some department of literature in which nothing more than sense, taste, and reading was required. Unhappily he set his heart on being a great poet, wrote a tragedy in five acts on the death of Virginia, and offered it to Garrick, who was his personal friend. Garrick read, shook his head, and expressed a doubt whether it would be wise in Mr. Crisp to stake a reputation, which stood high, on the success of such a piece. But the author, blinded by ambition, set in motion a machinery such as none could long resist. His intercessors were the most eloquent man and the most lovely woman of that generation. Pitt was induced to read Virginia, and to pronounce it excellent. Lady Coventry, with fingers which might have furnished a model to sculptors, forced the manuscript into the reluctant hand of the manager; and, in the year 1754, the play was brought forward.

Nothing that skill or friendship could do was omitted. Garrick wrote both prologue and epilogue. The zealous friends of the author filled every box; and, by their strenuous exertions, the life of the play was prolonged during ten nights. But, though there was no clamorous reprobation, it was universally felt that the attempt had failed. When Virginia was printed, the public disappointement was even greater than at the representation. The critics, the Monthly Reviewers[2] in particular, fell on

beauties would be unjust ". Mais ces beautés, il se garde bien de les indiquer.

1. *Lowness*, vulgarité.

2. *The Monthly Reviewers*, les critiques des *monthly reviews* (revues mensuelles).

plot, characters, and diction without mercy, but, we fear, not without justice. We have never met with a copy [1] of the play; but, if we may judge from the scene which is extracted in the Gentleman's Magazine [2], and which does not appear to have been malevolently selected, we should say that nothing but the acting of Garrick, and the partiality of the audience, could have saved so feeble and unnatural a drama from instant damnation.

The ambition of the poet was still unsubdued. When the London season [3] closed, he applied himself vigorously to the work of removing blemishes. He does not seem to have suspected, what we are strongly inclined to suspect, that the whole piece was one [4] blemish, and that the passages which were meant to be fine, were, in truth, bursts of that tame extravagance into which writers fall, when they set themselves to be sublime and pathetic in spite of nature. He omitted, added, retouched, and flattered himself with hopes of a complete success in the following year; but in the following year, Garrick showed no disposition to bring the amended tragedy on the stage. Solicitation and remonstrance were tried in vain. Lady Coventry, drooping under that malady which seems ever to select what is loveliest for its prey, could render no assistance. The manager's language was civilly evasive; but his resolution was inflexible.

Crisp had committed a great error; but he had escaped with a very slight penance. His play had not been hooted from the boards. It had, on the contrary, been better received than many very estimable performances have been, than Johnson's Irene, for example, or Goldsmith's Good-natured Man [5]. Had Crisp been wise, he

---

1. *Copy*, exemplaire.
2. *The Gentleman's Magazine.* Voy. au lexique l'article *Cave*.
3. *The London season*, la saison de Londres (c'est-à-dire la partie de l'année où la haute société est à Londres, et où les théâtres sont ouverts, où se donnent les bals, etc.) s'étendait alors du mois d'octobre au mois de mai. De nos jours, elle se trouve limitée aux mois de mai, juin et juillet.

4. *One*, une seule et grande.

5. La comédie de Goldsmith est de 1768.

would have thought himself happy in having purchased self-knowledge so cheap. He would have relinquished, without vain repinings, the hope of poetical distinction, and would have turned to the many sources of happiness which he still possessed. Had he been, on the other hand, an unfeeling and unblushing dunce, he would have gone on writing scores of bad tragedies in defiance of censure and derision. But he had too much sense to risk a second defeat, yet too little sense to bear his first defeat like a man. The fatal delusion that he was a great dramatist, had taken firm possession of his mind. His failure he attributed to every cause except the true one. He complained of the ill will of Garrick, who appears to have done for the play every thing that ability and zeal could do, and who, from selfish motives, would, of course, have been well pleased if Virginia had been as successful as the Beggar's Opera[1]. Nay, Crisp complained of the languor[2] of the friends whose partiality had given him three benefit nights[3] to which he .had no claim. He complained of the injustice of the spectators when, in truth, he ought to have been grateful for their unexampled patience. He lost his temper and spirits, and became a cynic and a hater of mankind. From London he retired to Hampton, and from Hampton to a solitary and long deserted mansion, built on a common[4] in one of the wildest tracts of Surrey. No road, not even a sheepwalk, connected his lonely dwelling with the abodes of men. The place of his retreat was strictly concealed from his old associates. In the spring he sometimes emerged, and was seen at exhibitions and concerts in London. But he soon disappeared, and hid himself, with no society but his books, in his dreary hermitage. He survived his failure about thirty years. A new generation sprang up around him. No memory

1. *The Beggar's Opera*, l'opéra du Gueux, de John Gay, est une comédie satirique qui eut, au dix-huitième siècle, un immense succès; elle fut jouée pour la première fois en 1727.

2. *Languor*, mollesse.

3. *Three benefit nights*, trois représentations à [son] bénéfice.

4. *Common*, terrain communal.

of his bad verses remained among men. His very name was forgotten. How completely the world had lost sight of him, will appear from a single circumstance. We looked for him in a copious Dictionary of Dramatic Authors published while he was still alive, and we found only that Mr. Henry Crisp, of the Custom House, had written a play called Virginia acted in 1754. To the last [1], however, the unhappy man continued to brood over the injustice of the manager and the pit, and tried to convince himself and others that he had missed the highest literary honours, only because he had omitted some fine passages in compliance with Garrick's judgment. Alas, for human nature, that [2] the wounds of vanity should smart and bleed so much longer than the wounds of affection! Few people, we believe, whose nearest friends and relations died in 1754, had any acute feeling of the loss in 1782. Dear sisters, and favourite daughters, and brides snatched away before the honeymoon was passed, had been forgotten, or were remembered only with a tranquil regret. But Samuel Crisp was still mourning for his tragedy, like Rachel weeping for her children [3], and would not be comforted. "Never", such was his language twenty-eight years after his disaster, "never give up or alter a tittle unless it perfectly coincides with your own inward feelings. I can say this to my sorrow and my cost. But mum!" Soon after these words were written, his life, a life which might have been eminently useful and happy, ended in the same gloom in which, during more than a quarter of a century, it had been passed. We have thought it worth while to rescue from oblivion this curious fragment of literary history. It seems to us at once ludicrous, melancholy, and full of instruction.

---

1. *To the last* (sous-entendu : *moment*), jusqu'à la fin.

2. *Alas, for human nature, that...* (hélas, pour la nature humaine, que...) hélas, pauvre nature humaine, faut-il que...

3. *Rachel weeping for her children.* Allusion biblique : " *Rachel weeping for her children refused to be comforted for her children, because they were not.* " JEREMIAH, XXXI, 15.

Boswell et Johnson[1].

The Life of Johnson is assuredly a great, a very great
work.   Homer is not more decidedly the first of heroic
poets, Shakspeare is not more decidedly the first of dramatists, Demosthenes is not more decidedly the first of
orators, than Boswell is the first of biographers.   He has
no second.   He has distanced all his competitors so
decidedly that it is not worth while to place them.
Eclipse[2] is first, and the rest[3] nowhere[4].

We are not sure that there is in the whole history of
the human intellect so strange a phænomenon as this
book.   Many of the greatest men that ever lived have
written biography.   Boswell was one of the smallest
men that ever lived, and he has beaten them all.   He
was, if we are to give any credit to his own account or
to the united testimony of all who knew him, a man of
the meanest and feeblest intellect.   Johnson described
him as a fellow who had missed his only chance of
immortality by not having been alive when the Dunciad
was written.   Beauclerk used his name as a proverbial
expression for a bore.   He was the laughing-stock of the
whole of that brilliant society which has owed to him
the greater part of its fame.   He was always laying
himself at the feet of some eminent man, and begging
to be spit upon and trampled upon.   He was always
earning some ridiculous nickname, and then " binding
it as a crown unto him "[5], not merely in metaphor, but
literally.   He exhibited himself, at the Shakspeare
Jubilee[6], to all the crowd which filled Stratford-on-
Avon, with a placard round his hat bearing the inscrip-

---

1. Extrait de l'*Essai sur la Vie de
Johnson*, par Boswell.
2. *Eclipse*, célèbre cheval de course
du temps de Johnson.
3. *The rest*, les autres.
4. *Nowhere*, terme de courses (nulle
part), *non placés*.

5. Allusion biblique : " *My desire
is... that mine adversary had written
a book. Surely I would take it upon
my shoulder, and bind it as a crown
to me.* " Job, xxxi, 35, 36.
6. Jubilé qui eut lieu le 6 septembre 1769, organisé par Garrick.

tion of Corsica Boswell[1]. In his Tour[2], he proclaimed to all the world that at Edinburgh he was known by the appellation of Paoli Boswell[3]. Servile and impertinent, shallow and pedantic, a bigot and a sot, bloated with family pride, and eternally blustering about the dignity of a born gentleman, yet stooping to be a talebearer, an eavesdropper, a common butt in the taverns of London, so curious to know every body who was talked about[4], that, Tory and high Churchman[5] as he was, he manœuvred, we have been told, for an introduction to[6] Tom Paine, so vain of the most childish distinctions, that when he had been to court, he drove to the office where his book was printing[7] without changing his clothes, and summoned all the printer's devils to admire his new ruffles and sword; such was this man, and such he was content and proud to be. Every thing which another man would have hidden, every thing the publication of which would have made another man hang himself, was matter of gay and clamorous exultation to his weak and diseased mind. What silly things he said, what bitter retorts he provoked, how at one place he was troubled with evil presentiments which came to nothing, how at another place, on waking from a drunken[8] doze, he read the prayer-book[9] and took a hair of the dog that had bitten him[10], how he went to see men hanged and came away

---

1. *Corsica Boswell*, parce qu'il était l'auteur d'un livre intitulé *Account of Corsica* (1768) et d'*Essays in Favour of the Corsicans*. C'est le 15 août 1768 que la Corse, qui appartenait aux Génois, fut réunie à la France.

2. C'est-à-dire le *Journal of a Tour to the Hebrides with Dr. Johnson* (1785).

3. Le célèbre héros corse, après avoir lutté contre les Génois, essaya en vain de résister à la domination française. et se réfugia en Angleterre. En 1766, Boswell, lors de son voyage en Corse, avait été l'hôte de Paoli.

4. *Who was talked about*, dont on parlait.

5. *High Churchman* (homme de la haute Eglise), anglican avancé, c'est-à-dire partisan extrême des membres de l'Eglise anglicane dont les opinions en matière liturgique se rapprochent le plus de celles des catholiques.

6. *For an introduction to*, pour être présenté à.

7. *His book was printing*, on était en train d'imprimer son livre. *Printing = being printed*.

8. *Drunken*, d'ivresse.

9. *The prayer-book* est le livre de prières et le rituel de l'Eglise anglicane.

10. *And took a hair of the dog that had bitten him* (et prit un poil du chien qui l'avait mordu), allusion à une croyance populaire suivant la-

maudlin, how he added five hundred pounds to the fortune of one of his babies because she was not scared at Johnson's ugly face, how he was frightened out of his wits[1] at sea, and how the sailors quieted him as they would have quieted a child, how tipsy he was one evening and how much his merriment annoyed the ladies, how impertinent he was to the Duchess of Argyle and with what stately contempt she put down his impertinence, how his father and the very wife of his bosom laughed and fretted at his fooleries; all these things he proclaimed to all the world, as if they had been subjects for pride and ostentatious rejoicing. All the caprices of his temper, all the illusions of his vanity, all his hypochondriac whimsies, all his castles in the air[2], he displayed with a cool self-complacency, a perfect unconsciousness that he was making a fool of himself[3], to which it is impossible to find a parallel in the whole history of mankind. He has used many people ill; but assuredly he has used nobody so ill as himself.

That such a man should have written one of the best books in the world is strange enough. But this is not all. Many persons who have conducted themselves foolishly in active life, and whose conversation has indicated no superior powers of mind, have left us valuable works. Goldsmith was very justly described by one of his contemporaries as an inspired idiot, and by another as a being,

" Who wrote like an angel, and talked like poor Poll "[4].

La Fontaine was in society a mere simpleton. His blunders would not come in amiss[5] among the stories

quelle un poil du chien qui vous a mordu suffit pour guérir la blessure; au figuré l'expression s'emploie dans le sens de : boire un coup, pour dissiper les effets d'une débauche.

1. *Was frightened out of his wits* (fut effrayé hors de son esprit), perdit la tête de frayeur.

2. *Castles in the air*, châteaux en Espagne.

3. *He was making a fool of himself*, il se rendait ridicule.

4. *Poll*, diminutif de *Polly*, qui est déjà un diminutif de *Mary*, Marie. *Poll* est, comme *Jacquot* en français, le nom qu'on donne communément aux perroquets.

5. *Would not come in amiss* (n'entreraient pas mal à propos), ne seraient pas déplacées.

of Hierocles. But these men attained literary eminence in spite of their weaknesses. Boswell attained it by reason of his weaknesses. If he had not been a great fool, he would never have been a great writer. Without all the qualities which made him the jest and the torment of those among whom he lived, without the officiousness, the inquisitiveness, the effrontery, the toad-eating[1], the insensibility to all reproof, he never could have produced so excellent a book. He was a slave proud of his servitude, a Paul Pry, convinced that his own curiosity and garrulity were virtues, an unsafe companion who never scrupled to repay the most liberal hospitality by the basest violation of confidence, a man without delicacy, without shame, without sense enough to know when he was hurting the feelings of others or when he was exposing himself to derision; and because he was all this, he has, in an important department of literature, immeasurably surpassed such writers as Tacitus, Clarendon, Alfieri, and his own idol Johnson.

Of the talents which ordinarily raise men to eminence as writers, Boswell had absolutely none. There is not in all his books a single remark of his own[2] on literature, politics, religion, or society, which is not either commonplace or absurd. His dissertations on hereditary gentility, on the slave-trade, and on the entailing of landed estates[3], may serve as examples. To say that these passages are sophistical would be to pay them an extravagant compliment. They have no pretence to argument, or even to meaning. He has reported innumerable observations made by himself in the course of conversation. Of those observations we do not re-

---

1. *Toad-eating*, courtisanerie. Ce mot vient de *toad-eater* (mangeur de crapauds), synonyme de *courtisan*, *vil flatteur*, et d'étymologie incertaine. On y a vu une corruption d'un mot espagnol. C'est plutôt simplement une façon pittoresque de désigner un personnage si vil qu'il est prêt, pour faire sa cour à un puissant, à manger le reptile le plus dégoûtant. D'ailleurs on dit en français *avaler un crapaud*, *avaler une couleuvre* pour dire : faire quelque chose de répugnant ou de désagréable.

2. *Of his own*. à lui, personnelle.

3. *To entail an estate* (terme du droit anglais), limiter les conditions de transmission d'une propriété.

member one which is above the intellectual capacity of a boy of fifteen. He has printed many of his own letters, and in these letters he is always ranting or twaddling. Logic, eloquence, wit, taste, all those things which are generally considered as making a book valuable, were utterly wanting[1] to him. He had, indeed, a quick observation and a retentive memory. These qualities, if he had been a man of sense and virtue, would scarcely of themselves have sufficed to make him conspicuous; but because he was a dunce, a parasite, and a coxcomb, they have made him immortal.

Those parts of his book which, considered abstractedly, are most utterly worthless, are delightful when we read them as illustrations of the character of the writer. Bad in themselves, they are good dramatically, like the nonsense of Justice Shallow, the clipped English of Dr. Caius, or the misplaced consonants of Fluellen[2]. Of all confessors[3], Boswell is the most candid[4]. Other men who have pretended to lay open their own hearts, Rousseau, for example, and Lord Byron, have evidently written with a constant view to effect, and are to be then most distrusted when they seem to be most sincere. There is scarcely any man who would not rather accuse himself of great crimes and of dark and tempestuous passions than proclaim all his little vanities and wild fancies. It would be easier to find a person who would avow actions like those of Cæsar Borgia or Danton, than one who would publish a day-dream like those of Alnaschar[5] and Mal-

---

1. *Were... wanting* (manquaient), faisaient défaut.

2. *Justice Shallow* (le juge S.) et *Dr. Caius* (le docteur C.), personnages comiques des *Merry Wives of Windsor* de Shakespeare. *Caius*, qui est français, supprime souvent, en parlant anglais, des terminaisons ou des lettres; ainsi il dit : " He has *save* his soul, *dat* (= that) he is *no* (= not) come. " — *Fluellen*, personnage de *Henry V* de Shakespeare, prononce l'anglais avec l'accent gallois, qui a quelque analogie avec l'accent allemand; il dit *peard* pour *beard*, *falorous* pour *valorous*.

3. *Confessors*, auteurs de confessions.

4. *Candid*, sincère.

5. *Alnaschar*, personnage d'un conte des *Mille et une Nuits*. Il emploie tout l'argent d'un héritage à acheter de la verrerie pour la revendre. Installé au marché, il se laisse aller à sa rêverie, fait, par l'imagination, une fortune colossale qui le rend

volio[1]. Those weaknesses which most men keep covered up in the most secret places of the mind, not to be
disclosed to the eye of friendship or of love, were precisely the weaknesses which Boswell paraded before all
the world. He was perfectly frank, because the
weakness of his understanding and the tumult of his
spirits prevented him from knowing when he made
himself ridiculous. His book resembles nothing so
much as the conversation of the inmates of the Palace
of Truth.

His fame is great; and it will, we have no doubt, be
lasting; but it is fame of a peculiar kind, and indeed
marvellously resembles infamy. We remember no other
case in which the world has made so great a distinction
between a book and its author. In general, the book
and the author are considered as one. To admire the
book is to admire the author. The case of Boswell is
an exception, we think the only exception, to this rule.
His work is universally allowed to be interesting, instructive, eminently original : yet it has brought him
nothing but contempt. All the world reads it : all the
world delights in it : yet we do not remember ever to
have read or ever to have heard any expression of respect and amiration for the man to whom we owe so
much instruction and amusement. While edition after
edition of his book was coming forth, his son, as Mr.
Croker tells us, was ashamed of it, and hated to hear it
mentioned. This feeling was natural and reasonable.
Sir Alexander[2] saw that, in proportion to the celebrity
of the work, was the degradation of the author. The
very editors of this unfortunate gentleman's books have
forgotten their allegiance, and, like those Puritan
casuists who took arms by the authority of the king

insolent, et. d'un brusque mouvement du pied, il renverse et met en
morceaux toute sa marchandise. C'est
une variante de *Perrette et le Pot au
lait*.
- 1. *Malvolio*, personnage de la comédie de Shakespeare *The Twelfth
Night*; il s'imagine que la princesse
Olivia, dont il est l'intendant, s'est
éprise de lui, et sa conduite, jusqu'alors grave et raisonnable, devient
celle d'un homme qui a perdu la tête.
2. *Sir Alexander Boswell*, le fils de
Boswell.

against his person, have attacked the writer while doing homage to the writings. Mr. Croker, for example, has published two thousand five hundred notes on the life of Johnson, and yet scarcely ever mentions the biographer whose performance he has taken such pains to illustrate without some expression of contempt.

An ill-natured man Boswell certainly was not. Yet the malignity of the most malignant satirist could scarcely cut deeper than his thoughtless loquacity. Having himself no sensibility to derision and contempt, he took it for granted that all others were equally callous. He was not ashamed to exhibit himself to the whole world as a common[1] spy, a common tattler, a humble companion without the excuse of poverty, and to tell a hundred stories of his own pertness and folly, and of the insults which his pertness and folly brought upon him. It was natural that he should show little discretion in cases in which the feelings or the honour of others might be concerned. No man, surely, ever published such stories respecting persons whom he professed to love and revere. He would infallibly have made his hero as contemptible as he has made himself, had not his hero really possessed some moral and intellectual qualities of a very high order. The best proof that Johnson was really an extraordinary man is that his character, instead of being degraded, has, on the whole, been decidedly raised by a work in which all his vices and weaknesses are exposed more unsparingly than they ever were exposed by Churchill or by Kenrick.

Johnson grown old, Johnson in the fulness of his fame and in the enjoyment of a competent fortune, is better known to us than any other man in history. Every thing about him[2], his coat, his wig, his figure, his face, his scrofula, his St. Vitus's dance[3], his rolling walk, his blinking eye, the outward signs which too clearly

---

1. *Common*, vulgaire.
2. *Everything about him*, tout ce qui le concerne.

3. *St. Vitus's dance*, danse de Saint-Guy.

marked his approbation of his dinner[1], his insatiable appetite for fish-sauce and veal-pie with plums, his inextinguishable thirst for tea, his trick of touching the posts as he walked, his mysterious practice of treasuring up scraps of orange-peel, his morning slumbers, his midnight disputations, his contortions, his mutterings, his gruntings, his puffings, his vigorous, acute, and ready eloquence, his sarcastic wit, his vehemence, his insolence, his fits of tempestuous rage, his queer inmates, the cat Hodge and the negro Frank, all are as familiar to us as the objects by which we have been surrounded from childhood. But we have no minute information respecting those years of Johnson's life during which his character and his manners became immutably fixed. We know him, not as he was known to the men of his own generation, but as he was known to men whose father he might have been. That celebrated club[2] of which he was the most distinguished member contained few persons who could remember a time when his fame was not fully established and his habits completely formed. . . . .

Johnson came up to London[3] precisely at the time when the condition of a man of letters was most miserable and degraded. It was a dark night between two sunny days. The age of patronage[4] had passed away. The age[5] of general curiosity and intelligence had not arrived. The number of readers is at present so great that a popular author may subsist in comfort and opulence on the profits of his works. In the reigns of William the Third, of Anne, and of George the First, even such men as Congreve and Addison would scarcely have been able

---

1. Voy. plus loin, page 384 : " *He tore his dinner like a famished wolf, with the veins swelling on his forehead, and the perspiration running down his cheeks.* "

2. Le *Literary Club*, dont faisaient partie, outre Johnson, Burke et Goldsmith.

3. *Came up to London*, arriva à Londres ; littéralement, *monta*, parce qu'en Angleterre on dit que l'on *monte* quand on va de province à Londres, et que l'on *descend* quand on va de Londres en province.

4. *Patronage*, la protection, les protecteurs.

5. *Age*, époque.

to live like gentlemen by the mere sale of their writings. But the deficiency of the natural demand for literature was, at the close of the seventeenth and at the beginning of the eighteenth century, more than made up [1] by artificial encouragement, by a vast system of bounties and premiums. There was, perhaps, never a time at which the rewards of literay merit were so splendid, at which men who could write well found such easy admittance into the most distinguished society, and to the highest honours of the state. The chiefs of both the great parties into which the kingdom was divided patronised literature with emulous munificence . . . .

At the time when Johnson commenced his literary career, a writer had little to hope from the patronage of powerful individuals. The patronage of the public did not yet furnish the means of comfortable subsistence. The prices paid by booksellers to authors were so low that a man of considerable talents and unremitting industry could do little more than provide for the day which was passing over him. The lean kine had eaten up the fat kine. The thin and withered ears had devoured the good ears [2]. The season of rich harvests was over, and the period of famine had begun. All that is squalid and miserable might now be summed up in the word Poet. That word denoted a creature dressed like a scarecrow, familiar with compters and spunging-houses [3].

---

1. *Made up*, compensé.
2. Allusion aux deux rêves de Pharaon interprétés par Joseph : " *Pharaoh dreamed; and, behold, he stood by the river. And, behold, there came up out of the river seven well favoured kine and fatfleshed; and they fed in a meadow. And, behold, seven other kine came up after them out of the river, ill favoured and leanfleshed,... and... did eat up the seven well favoured and fat kine. So Pharaoh awoke. And he slept and dreamed the second time : and, behold, seven ears of corn came up upon one stalk, rank and good. And, behold, seven thin ears and blasted with the east wind sprung up after them. And the seven thin ears devoured the seven rank and full ears.* " GENESIS, xli.

3. *Compters and spunging-houses*, orthographe ancienne de *counters and sponging-houses*. Le nom de *counter* s'appliquait particulièrement à trois prisons de Londres pour débiteurs insolvables. On appelait *sponging-house* la maison du *bailiff* (sorte d'huissier) où le débiteur insolvable passait vingt-quatre heures avant d'être envoyé en prison, pour lui laisser le temps de faire appel à ses amis. Quant à l'origine du mot *sponging-house*, on l'attribue à l'exploitation dont étaient victimes les malheureux débiteurs qui payaient un prix exorbitant pour leur nourri-

Even the poorest pitied him; and they well might pity him. For if their condition was equally abject, their aspirings were not equally high, nor their sense of insult equally acute. To lodge in a garret up four pair of stairs [1], to dine in a cellar among footmen out of place [2], to translate ten hours a day for the wages of a ditcher, to be hunted by bailiffs from one haunt of beggary and pestilence to another, to sleep on a bulk in June and amidst the ashes of a glass-house in December, to die in an hospital and to be buried in a parish vault, was the fate of more than one writer who, if he had lived thirty years earlier, would have been admitted to the sittings of the Kitcat or the Scriblerus club, would have sat in Parliament, and would have been entrusted with embassies to the High Allies; who, if he had lived in our time, would have found encouragement scarcely less munificent in Albemarle Street or in Paternoster Row [3].

As every climate has its peculiar diseases; so every walk of life [4] has its peculiar temptations. The literary character, assuredly, has always had its share of faults, vanity, jealousy, morbid sensibility. To these faults, were now superadded the faults which are commonly found in men whose livelihood is precarious, and whose principles are exposed to the trial of severe distress. All the vices of the gambler and of the beggar were blended with those of the author. The prizes [5] in the wretched lottery of book-making were scarcely less ruinous than

ture pendant le séjour forcé dans cette maison où leur argent se trouvait absorbé comme de l'eau par une éponge.

1. *Up four pair of stairs*, au quatrième. *Pair of stairs* s'emploie souvent dans le sens de *flight of stairs*, escalier conduisant d'un étage à l'autre. Bien que venant du français *paire*, le sens de *pair* n'a pas toujours été, en anglais, limité à celui de *couple*; il a longtemps été synonyme de *set* (nombre d'objets formant un tout); ainsi on a dit, *a pair of cards*, un paquet de cartes; *a pair of beads*, un chapelet (*bead*, grain de chapelet). — *Pair* ne prend pas forcément la marque du pluriel.

2. *Out of place*, sans place.

3. La maison de John Murray, le célèbre éditeur, se trouve dans *Albemarle street*. Dans *Paternoster Row* sont réunies les librairies en gros qui servent d'intermédiaires entre les éditeurs et les librairies de détail. Le nom de cette rue viendrait de ce qu'à l'origine il s'y vendait surtout des livres de prières.

4. *Walk of life*, carrière.

5. *Prizes*, numéros gagnants.

the blanks[1]. If good fortune came, it came in such a manner that it was almost certain to be abused. After months of starvation and despair, a full third night[2] or a well-received dedication filled the pocket of the lean, ragged, unwashed poet with guineas. He hastened to enjoy those luxuries with the images of which his mind had been haunted while he was sleeping amidst the cinders and eating potatoes at the Irish ordinary in Shoe Lane. A week of taverns soon qualified him for another year of night-cellars. Such was the life of Savage, of Boyse, and of a crowd of others. Sometimes blazing in gold-laced hats and waistcoats; sometimes lying in bed because their coats had gone to pieces, or wearing paper cravats because their linen was in pawn; sometimes drinking Champagne and Tokay, sometimes standing at the window of an eating-house, to snuff up the scent of what they could not afford to taste; they knew luxury; they knew beggary; but they never knew comfort. These men were irreclaimable. They looked on a regular and frugal life with the same aversion which an old gipsy or a Mohawk hunter feels for a stationary abode, and for the restraints and securities of civilised communities. They were as untameable, as much wedded to their desolate freedom, as the wild ass. They could no more be broken in to the offices of social man than the unicorn could be trained to serve and abide by the crib[3]. It was well if they did not, like beasts of a still fiercer race, tear the hands which ministered to their necessities. To assist them was impossible; and the most benevolent of mankind at length became weary of giving relief which was dissipated with the wildest profusion as soon as it

---

1. *Blanks*, numéros perdants.
2. *Third night*, troisième représentation : « Les droits d'auteurs, tels que nous les entendons aujourd'hui au théâtre, étaient chose entièrement inconnue alors. Tout le profit qu'un écrivain retirait d'une pièce jouée, c'était le produit de la troisième représentation. » A. BELJAME, *Le public et les hommes de lettres*, page 114.

3. Allusion biblique : " *Who hath sent out the wild ass free?... Whose house I have made the wilderness, and the barren land his dwellings. He scorneth the multitude of the city... Will the unicorn be willing to serve thee, or abide by thy crib?* " JOB, XXXIX. — Dans la traduction corrigée, publiée il y a quelques années, *unicorn* a été remplacé par *wild ox...*

had been received. If a sum was bestowed on the wretched adventurer, such as, properly husbanded, might have
supplied him for six months, it was instantly spent in
strange freaks of sensuality, and, before forty-eight
hours had elapsed, the poet was again pestering all his
acquaintance for twopence to get a plate of shin of beef
at a subterraneous cook-shop. If his friends gave him
an asylum in their houses, those houses were forthwith
turned into bagnios and taverns. All order was destroyed;
all business was suspended. The most good-natured
host began to repent of his eagerness to serve a man of
genius in distress when he heard his guest roaring for
fresh punch at five o'clock in the morning[1]. . . . . . .

Into calamities and difficulties such as these Johnson
plunged in his twenty-eighth year. From that time till
he was three or four and fifty[2], we have little information respecting him: little, we mean, compared with the
full and accurate information which we possess respecting his proceedings and habits towards the close of his
life. He emerged at length from cock-lofts[3] and six-
penny ordinaries into the society of the polished and the
opulent. His fame was established. A pension sufficient
for his wants had been conferred on him; and he came
forth to astonish a generation with which he had almost
as little in common as with Frenchmen or Spaniards.

In his early years he had occasionally seen the great;
but he had seen them as a beggar[4]. He now came
among them as a companion. The demand[5] for amusement and instruction had, during the course of twenty
years, been gradually increasing. The price of literary
labour had risen ; and those rising[6] men of letters with
whom Johnson was henceforth to associate were for the

1. Ces détails sont, en grande partie, empruntés à la *Vie de Savage* par Johnson.

2. *Three or four and fifty* = *fifty-three or fifty-four*, façon de compter encore usitée pour l'indication de l'âge.

3. *Cock-lofts*, greniers, mansardes.

4. *As a beggar*, en qualité de men-diant.

5. *Demand*, demande, dans le sens où l'on dit *l'offre et la demande* en économie politique.

6. *Rising*, en train de devenir cé-lèbres.

most part persons widely different from those who had walked about with him all night in the streets for want of a lodging . . . .

Johnson came among them the solitary specimen of a past age [1], the last survivor of the genuine race of Grub Street hacks ; the last of that generation of authors whose abject misery and whose dissolute manners had furnished inexhaustible matter to the satirical genius of Pope. From nature, he had received an uncouth figure, a diseased constitution, and an irritable temper. The manner in which the earlier years of his manhood had been passed had given to his demeanour, and even to his moral character, some peculiarities appalling to the civilised beings who were the companions of his old age. The perverse irregularity of his hours, the slovenliness of his person, his fits of strenuous exertion, interrupted by long intervals of sluggishness, his strange abstinence, and his equally strange voracity, his active benevolence, contrasted with the constant rudeness and the occasional ferocity of his manners in society, made him, in the opinion of those with whom he lived during the last twenty years of his life, a complete original. An original he was, undoubtedly, in some respects. But if we possessed full information concerning those who shared his early [2] hardships, we should probably find that what we call his singularities of manner were, for the most part, failings which he had in common with the class to which he belonged. He ate as it was natural that a man should eat, who, during a great part of his life, had passed the morning in doubt whether he should have food for the afternoon. The habits of his early life had accustomed him to bear privation with fortitude, but not to taste pleasure with moderation. He could fast ; but when he did not fast, he tore his dinner like a famished wolf, with the veins swelling on his forehead, and the perspiration running down his cheeks. He scarcely ever took wine.

1. *Age*, époque. | 2. *Early*, de sa jeunesse.

But when he drank it, he drank it greedily and in large
tumblers.   These were, in fact, mitigated symptoms of
that same moral disease which raged with such deadly
malignity in his friends Savage and Boyse.   The rough-
ness and violence which he showed in society were to
be expected from a man whose temper, not naturally
gentle, had been long tried by the bitterest calamities,
by the want of meat, of fire, and of clothes, by the im-
portunity of creditors, by the insolence of booksellers, by
the derision of fools, by the insincerity of patrons, by
that bread which is the bitterest of all food, by those
stairs which are the most toilsome of all paths [1], by that
deferred hope which makes the heart sick.   Through all
these things the ill-dressed, coarse, ungainly pedant had
struggled manfully up to eminence and command.   It
was natural that, though his heart was undoubtedly generous and humane, his demeanour in society should be
harsh and despotic.   For severe distress he had sympathy, and not only sympathy, but munificent relief.
But for the suffering which a harsh world inflicts upon a
delicate mind he had no pity ; for it was a kind of suffering
which he could scarcely conceive.   He would carry home
on his shoulders a sick and starving girl from the streets.
He turned his house into a place of refuge for a crowd of
wretched old creatures who could find no other asylum ;
nor could all their peevishness and ingratitude weary out
his benevolence.   But the pangs of wounded vanity
seemed to him ridiculous ; and he scarcely felt sufficient
compassion even for the pangs of wounded affection.   He
had seen and felt so much of [2] sharp misery, that he was
not affected by paltry vexations ; and he seemed to think
that every body ought to be as much hardened to those
vexations as himself.   He was angry with Boswell for

1. Allusion à ce passage de la *Divine Comédie* de Dante :

Tu proverai si come sa di sale
Lo pane altrui e com'è duro calle
Lo scendere et il salir per l'altrui scale.
(Paradis, Chant xvii.)

Traduction de Mme Tastu : « Tu
apprendras ce que contient de sel le
pain d'autrui et quel dur sentier c'est
à monter et à descendre que l'escalier de l'étranger. »

2. *Of*, en fait de.

complaining of a headache, with Mrs. Thrale for grumbling about the dust on the road, or the smell of the kitchen. These were, in his phrase[1], " foppish lamentations, " which people ought to be ashamed to utter in a world so full of sin and sorrow. Goldsmith crying because the Good-natured Man[2] had failed, inspired him with no pity. Though his own health was not good, he detested and despised valetudinarians. Pecuniary losses, unless they reduced the loser absolutely to beggary, moved him very little. People whose hearts had been softened by prosperity might weep, he said, for such events; but all that could be expected of a plain man was not to laugh. He was not much moved even by the spectacle of Lady Tavistock dying of a broken heart[3] for the loss of her lord[4]. Such grief he considered as a luxury reserved for the idle and the wealthy. A washerwoman, left a widow with nine small children, would not have sobbed herself to death[5].

A person who troubled himself so little about small or sentimental grievances was not likely to be very attentive to the feelings of others in the ordinary intercourse of society. He could not understand how a sarcasm or a reprimand could make any man really unhappy. " My dear doctor[6], " said he to Goldsmith, " what harm does it do to a man to call him Holofernes? " Politeness has been well defined as benevolence in small things. Johnson was impolite, not because he wanted benevolence, but because small things appeared smaller to him than to people who had never known what it was to live for fourpence halfpenny a day.

The characteristic peculiarity of his intellect was

---

1. *In his phrase*, suivant son expression.

2. Comédie de Goldsmith jouée pour la première fois en 1768.

3. *Of a broken heart* (d'un cœur brisé), de chagrin.

4. *Her lord*. Traduisez : son mari.

5. *Would not have sobbed herself to death* (mot à mot : ne se serait pas sanglotée à mort), ne serait pas morte à force de sangloter.

6. Au cours d'un voyage en Italie, Goldsmith s'était fait décerner, à Padoue, un diplôme qui lui permit, à son retour en Angleterre, d'exercer la médecine et de prendre le titre de docteur. Johnson avait le titre de docteur en droit.

the union of great powers with low prejudices. If we judged of him by the best parts of his mind, we should place him almost as high as he was placed by the idolatry of Boswell; if by the worst parts of his mind, we should place him even below Boswell himself. Where he was not under the influence of some strange scruple, or some domineering passion, which prevented him from boldly and fairly investigating a subject, he was a wary and acute reasoner, a little too much inclined to scepticism, and a little too fond of paradox. No man was less likely to be imposed upon by fallacies in argument or by exaggerated statements of fact. But if, while he was beating down sophisms and exposing false testimony, some childish prejudices, such as would excite laughter in a well managed nursery, came across him[1], he was smitten as if by enchantment. His mind dwindled away under the spell from gigantic elevation to dwarfish littleness. Those who had lately been admiring its amplitude and its force were now as much astonished at its strange narrowness and feebleness as the fisherman in the Arabian tale, when he saw the Genie, whose stature had overshadowed the whole seacoast, and whose might seemed equal to a contest with armies, contract himself to the dimensions of his small prison, and lie there the helpless slave of the charm of Solomon[2].

Johnson was in the habit of sifting with extreme severity the evidence[3] for all stories which were merely odd. But when they were not only odd but miraculous, his severity relaxed. He began to be credulous precisely at the point where the most credulous people begin to be sceptical. It is curious to observe, both in his writings and in his conversation, the contrast between the disdainful manner in which he rejects unauthenticated anecdotes, even when they are consistent with

---

1. *Came across him*, se trouvait sur son chemin.

2. Voy. l'*Histoire du l'écheur* dans les *Mille et une Nuits*.

3. *Evidence*, témoignages.

the general laws of nature, and the respectful manner
in which he mentions the wildest stories relating to the
invisible world. A man who told him of a water-spout
or a meteoric stone generally had the lie direct[1] given
him[2] for his pains. A man who told him of a prediction or a dream wonderfully accomplished was sure of
a courteous hearing[3]. " Johnson ", observed Hogarth,
" like King David, says in his haste that all men are
liars "[4]. " His incredulity ", says Mrs. Thrale, " amounted almost to disease ". She tells us how he browbeat
a gentleman, who gave him an account of a hurricane
in the West Indies, and a poor quaker who related some
strange circumstance about the red-hot balls fired at the
siege of Gibraltar[5]. " It is not so. It cannot be true.
Don't tell that story again. You cannot think how poor
a figure you make in telling it ". He once said, half
jestingly we suppose, that for six months he refused to
credit the fact of the earthquake at Lisbon[6], and that he
still believed the extent of the calamity to be greatly
exaggerated. Yet he related with a grave face how old
Mr. Cave of St. John's Gate saw a ghost, and how this
ghost was something of a shadowy being. He went
himself on a ghost-hunt[7] to Cock Lane, and was angry
with John Wesley for not following up another scent of
the same kind with proper spirit[8] and perseverance.

. . . .

The judgments which Johnson passed on books were,
in his own time, regarded with superstitious veneration,
and, in our time, are generally treated with indiscrim-
inate contempt. They are the judgments of a strong
but enslaved understanding. The mind of the critic
was hedged round by an uninterrupted fence of prejudices and superstitions. Within his narrow limits, he

---

1. *The lie direct*, un démenti for-
mel, brutal.
2. *Had... given him* (avait... donné
à lui), recevait.
3. *Of a courteous hearing* (d'une
audition courtoise), d'être écouté avec
courtoisie.
4. " *I said in my haste, All men are
liars.* " Psaume 116.
5. En 1779.
6. En 1755.
7. *On a ghost-hunt*, à la chasse au
fantôme.
8. *Spirit*, ardeur.

displayed a vigour and an activity which ought to have enabled him to clear [1] the barrier that confined him.

How it chanced that a man who reasoned on his premises so ably, should assume his premises so foolishly, is one of the great mysteries of human nature. The same inconsistency may by observed in the schoolmen [2] of the middle ages. Those writers show so much acuteness and force of mind in arguing on their wretched data [3], that a modern reader is perpetually at a loss to comprehend how such minds came by [4] such data. Not a flaw in the superstructure of the theory which they are rearing escapes their vigilance. Yet they are blind to the obvious unsoundness of the foundation. It is the same with some eminent lawyers. Their legal arguments are intellectual prodigies, abounding with the happiest analogies and the most refined distinctions. The principles of their arbitrary science being once admitted, the statute-book and the reports being once assumed as the foundations of reasoning, these men must be allowed to be perfect masters of logic. But if a question arises as to the postulates on which their whole system rests, if they are called upon to vindicate the fundamental maxims of that system which they have passed their lives in studying, these very men often talk the language of savages or of children. Those who have listened to a man of this class in his own court [5], and who have witnessed the skill with which he analyses and digests a vast mass of evidence [6], or reconciles a crowd of precedents which at first sight seem contradictory, scarcely know him again when, a few hours later, they hear him speaking on the other side of Westminster Hall [7] in his capacity of legislator. They

1. *Clear*, franchir.
2. *Schoolmen*, scolastiques, nom donné aux théologiens du moyen âge.
3. *Data*, données; pluriel latin de *datum*, donné, chose donnée.
4. *Came by* (se sont procuré), ont trouvé.
5. *Court*, cour (tribunal).

6. *Evidence*, preuves, témoignages.
7. Jusqu'à ces dernières années le palais de justice (*Law Courts*) était contigu aux Chambres du Parlement (*Houses of Parliament*) dont seule une vaste salle, *Westminster Hall*, le séparait. Le nouveau palais de justice (*New Law Courts*) est situé dans le Strand.

can scarcely believe that the paltry quirks which are
faintly heard through a storm of coughing, and which do
not impose on the plainest country gentleman, can proceed from the same sharp and vigorous intellect which
had excited their admiration under the same roof, and
on the same day.

Johnson decided literary questions like a lawyer, not
like a legislator. He never examined foundations where
a point was already ruled [1]. His whole code of criticism rested on pure assumption [2], for which he sometimes quoted a precedent or an authority, but rarely
troubled himself to give a reason drawn from the nature
of things. He took it for granted that the kind of poetry
which flourished in his own time, which he had been
accustomed to hear praised from his childhood, and
which he had himself written with success, was the best
kind of poetry. In his biographical work [3] he has repeatedly laid it down as an undeniable proposition that
during the latter part of the seventeenth century, and
the earlier part of the eighteenth, English poetry had
been in a constant progress of improvement. Waller,
Denham, Dryden, and Pope, had been, according to
him, the great reformers. He judged of all works of
the imagination by the standard established among his
own contemporaries. Though he allowed Homer to
have been a greater man than Virgil, he seems to have
thought the Æneid a greater poem than the Iliad.
Indeed he well might have thought so; for he preferred
Pope's Iliad to Homer's. . . . .

He was undoubtedly an excellent judge of compositions fashioned on his own principles. But when a
deeper philosophy was required, when he undertook to
pronounce judgment on the works of those great minds
which " yield homage only to eternal laws ", his failure
was ignominious. . . . .

Some of Johnson's whims on literary subjects can be

1. *Ruled* (terme de droit), décidé. | priori, sans preuves.
2. *Assumption*, principes admis à | 3. *The Lives of the English Poets.*

compared only to that strange nervous feeling which made him uneasy if he had not touched every post between the Mitre tavern[1] and his own lodgings. His preference of Latin epitaphs to English epitaphs is an instance. An English epitaph, he said, would disgrace Smollett. He declared that he would not pollute the walls of Westminster Abbey with an English epitaph on Goldsmith. What reason there can be for celebrating a British writer in Latin, which there was not for covering the Roman arches of triumph with Greek inscriptions, or for commemorating the deeds of the heroes of Thermopylæ in Egyptian hieroglyphics, we are utterly unable to imagine.

On men and manners, at least on the men and manners of a particular place and a particular age, Johnson had certainly looked with a most observant and discriminating eye. His remarks on the education of children, on marriage, on the economy of families, on the rules of society, are always striking, and generally sound. In his writings, indeed, the knowledge of life which he possessed in an eminent degree is very imperfectly exhibited. Like those unfortunate chiefs of the middle ages who were suffocated by their own chainmail and cloth of gold, his maxims perish under that load of words which was designed for their defence and their ornament. But it is clear from the remains of his conversation, that he had more of that homely wisdom which nothing but experience and observation can give than any writer since the time of Swift. If he had been content to write as he talked, he might have left books on the practical art of living superior to the Directions to Servants[2].

Yet even his remarks on society, like his remarks on literature, indicate a mind at least as remarkable for

1. Dans *Mitre Court*, près de *Fetter lane;* dans cette taverne Johnson, Boswell et Goldsmith se réunissaient fréquemment.

2. *Directions to Servants*, conseils aux domestiques. C'est peut-être, après les *Voyages de Gulliver*, le plus populaire des ouvrages de Swift. Tout saturé de l'ironie et de l'humour particuliers à l'auteur, cet opuscule est en même temps une étude de mœurs terriblement réaliste.

narrowness as for strength. He was no master of the
great science of human nature. He had studied, not
the genus man, but the species Londoner. Nobody was
ever so thoroughly conversant with all the forms of life
and all the shades of moral and intellectual character
which were to be seen from Islington to the Thames,
and from Hyde-Park corner to Mile-end green. But his
philosophy stopped at the first turnpike-gate[1]. Of the
rural life of England he knew nothing; and he took it
for granted that every body who lived in the country
was either stupid or miserable. " Country gentlemen ", said he, " must be unhappy; for they have not
enough to keep their lives in motion "; as if all those
peculiar habits and associations which made Fleet Street
and Charing Cross the finest views in the world to himself had been essential parts of human nature. Of
remote countries and past times he talked with wild and
ignorant presumption. " The Athenians of the age of
Demosthenes ", he said to Mrs. Thrale, " were a people
of brutes, a barbarous people ". In conversation with
Sir Adam Ferguson he used similar language. " The
boasted Athenians ", he said, " were barbarians. The
mass of every people must be barbarous where there is
no printing ". The fact was this : he saw that a Londoner who could not read was a very stupid and brutal
fellow : he saw that great refinement of taste and activity of intellect were rarely found in a Londoner who had
not read much; and, because it was by means of books
that people acquired almost all their knowledge in the
society with which he was acquainted, he concluded, in
defiance of[2] the strongest and clearest evidence[3], that
the human mind can be cultivated by means of books
alone. An Athenian citizen might possess very few
volumes; and the largest library to which he had access

---

1. Les *turnpike-gates* ou *turnpikes*
sont des barrières disposées de distance en distance sur les routes, et
où l'on perçoit un péage destiné à
l'entretien de la route.

2. *In defiance of*, en dépit de.

3. *Evidence*, preuves, témoignages.

might be much less valuable than Johnson's bookcase in
Bolt Court.   But the Athenian might pass every morning in conversation with Socrates, and might hear
Pericles speak four or five times every month.   He saw
the plays of Sophocles and Aristophanes : he walked
amidst the friezes of Phidias and the paintings of Zeuxis :
he knew by heart the choruses of Æschylus : he heard
the rhapsodist[1] at the corner of the street reciting the
shield of Achilles[2] or the Death of Argus, he was a
legislator, conversant with high questions of alliance,
revenue, and war : he was a soldier, trained under a
liberal and generous discipline : he was a judge, compelled every day to weigh the effect of opposite arguments.   These things were in themselves an education,
an education eminently fitted, not, indeed, to form exact
or profound thinkers, but to give quickness to the perceptions, delicacy to the taste, fluency to the expression,
and politeness to the manners.   All this was overlooked.
An Athenian who did not improve his mind by reading
was, in Johnson's opinion, much[3] such a person as a
Cockney[4] who made his mark[5], much such a person as
black Frank[6] before he went to school, and far inferior
to a parish clerk[7] or a printer's devil[8].

Johnson's friends have allowed that he carried to a
ridiculous extreme his unjust contempt for foreigners.
He pronounced the French to be a very silly people,
much behind us, stupid, ignorant creatures.   And this
judgment he formed after having been at Paris about a
month, during which he would not talk French, for fear
of giving the natives an advantage over him in conver-

1. *Rhapsodist*, rapsode, déclama-
teur ambulant qui allait de ville en
ville récitant les vers des poètes.
2. *The shield of Achilles*, le bou-
clier d'Achille, dont la description
occupe une partie du dix-huitième
chant de l'Iliade. Achille est le personnage principal du poème d'Ho-
mère.
3. *Much* (beaucoup), à peu près.
4. *Cockney*, sobriquet donné aux
Londoniens de la Cité.

5. *Who made his mark* (qui faisait
sa marque), c'est-à-dire qui, ne sachant pas écrire, traçait une croix en
guise de signature.
6. *Black Frank*, c'est-à-dire *the
negro Frank*. Voy. page 36.
7. *Parish clerk*, clerc de paroisse,
celui qui lit les répons, qui prend
soin de l'église et qui remplit souvent
les fonctions de fossoyeur.
8. *Printer's devil;* dans une imprimerie, apprenti qui fait les courses.

sation. He pronounced them, also, to be an indelicate people, because a French footman touched the sugar with his fingers. . . . .

Johnson's visit to the Hebrides[1] introduced him to a state of society completely new to him; and a salutary suspicion of his own deficiencies seems on that occasion to have crossed his mind for the first time. He confessed, in the last paragraph of his Journey, that his thoughts on national manners were the thoughts of one who had seen but little, of one who had passed his time almost wholly in cities. This feeling, however, soon passed away. It is remarkable that to the last he entertained a fixed contempt for all those modes of life and those studies which tend to emancipate the mind from the prejudices of a particular age or a particular nation. Of foreign travel and of history he spoke with the fierce and boisterous contempt of ignorance. "What does a man learn by travelling? Is Beauclerk the better for travelling? What did Lord Charlemont learn in his travels except that there was a snake in one of the pyramids of Egypt?" History was, in his opinion, to use the fine expression of Lord Plunkett, and old almanack : historians could, as he conceived, claim no higher dignity than that of almanack-makers; and his favourite historians were those who, like Lord Hailes, aspired to no higher dignity. He always spoke with contempt of Robertson. Hume he would not even read[2]. He affronted one of his friends for talking to him about Catiline's conspiracy, and declared that he never desired to hear of the Punic war[3] again as long as he lived.

Assuredly one fact which does not directly affect our own interests, considered in itself, is no better worth knowing than another fact. The fact that there is a snake

---

1. C'est en 1773 que Johnson fit, aux îles Hébrides, un voyage dont il publia le récit sous le titre de *A Journey to the Western Islands of Scotland.*

2. *Hume etc… read,* inversion pour *He would not even read Hume.*

3. *The Punic war (punic,* punique, carthaginoise), la guerre punique; il serait plus exact de dire *les guerres puniques,* car il y eut trois grandes guerres entre Rome et Carthage.

in a pyramid, or the fact that Hannibal crossed the Alps,
are in themselves as unprofitable to us as the fact that
there is a green blind in a particular house in Threadneedle Street, or the fact that a Mr. Smith[1] comes into
the city every morning on the top of one the Blackwall
stages[2]. But it is certain that those who will not crack
the shell of history will never get at the kernel. Johnson,
with hasty arrogance, pronounced the kernel worthless,
because he saw no value in the shell. The real use of
travelling to distant countries and of studying the annals
of past times is to preserve men from the contraction of
mind which those can hardly escape whose whole communion is with one generation and one neighbourhood,
who arrive at conclusions by means of an induction not
sufficiently copious, and who therefore constantly con-
found exceptions with rules, and accidents with essential
properties. . . . .

Johnson, as Mr. Burke most justly observed, appears
far greater in Boswell's books than in his own. His conversation appear to have been quite equal to his writings
in matter, and far superior to them in manner. When
he talked, he clothed his wit and his sense in forcible
and natural expressions. As soon as he took his pen in
his hand to write for the public, his style became systematically vicious. All his books are written in a learned[3]
language, in a language which nobody hears from his
mother or his nurse, in a language in which nobody ever
quarrels, or drives bargains, or makes love, in a language in which nobody ever thinks. It is clear that
Johnson himself did not think in the dialect in which he
wrote. The expressions which came first to his tongue
were simple, energetic, and picturesque. When he wrote
for publication, he did his sentences out of English into[4]
Johnsonese[5]. His letters from the Hebrides to Mrs. Thrale

---

1. Macaulay choisit ce nom parce
que c'est un des plus répandus en
Angleterre.

2. *Stages*, diligences.

3. *Learned*, savant.

4. *Did... out of... into*, traduisait...
de... en.

5. *Johnsonese*, mot fabriqué par
Macaulay pour désigner la langue de
Johnson,

are the original of that work of which the Journey to the Hebrides is the translation; and it is amusing to compare the two versions. "When we were taken up stairs," says he in one of his letters, "a dirty fellow bounced out of the bed on which one of us was to lie." This incident is recorded in the Journey as follows: "Out of one of the beds on which we were to repose started up, at our entrance, a man black as a Cyclops from the forge." Sometimes Johnson translated aloud. "The Rehearsal[1]," he said, very unjustly, "has not wit enough to keep it sweet[2];" then, after a pause, "it has not vitality enough to preserve it from putrefaction."

Byron[3].

Of the deep and painful interest which this book excites no abstract can give a just notion. So sad and dark a story is scarcely to be found in any work of fiction; and we are little disposed to envy the moralist who can read it without being softened.

The pretty fable by which the Duchess of Orleans illustrated the character of her son the Regent[4] might, with little change, be applied to Byron. All the fairies, save one, had been bidden to his cradle. All the gossips[5] had been profuse of their gifts. One had bestowed nobility, another genius, a third beauty. The malignant elf who had been uninvited came last, and, unable to reverse what her sisters had done for their favourite, had mixed up a curse with every blessing. In the rank of Lord Byron, in his understanding, in his character, in his very person, there was a strange union of opposite extremes. He was born to[6] all that men covet and admire.

---

1. *The Rehearsal*, la Répétition, comédie du duc de Buckingham (1671), dans laquelle, sous le nom de *Bayes*, il tourne en ridicule le célèbre poète Dryden.
2. *Sweet*, saine.
3. Extrait de l'*Essai sur Byron*.
4. *The Regent*, Philippe duc d'Orléans, qui fut régent pendant la minorité de Louis XV.
5. *Gossips*, commères, dans le sens de *marraines*.
6. *He was born to*, il avait, en venant au monde, trouvé.

But in every one of those eminent advantages which he
possessed over others was mingled something of misery
and debasement. He was sprung from a house, ancient
indeed and noble, but degraded and impoverished by a
series of crimes and follies [1] which had attained a scandalous publicity. The kinsman [2] whom he succeeded had
died poor, and, but for [3] merciful judges, would have
died upon the gallows. The young peer had great intellectual powers; yet there was an unsound part in his
mind. He had naturally a generous and feeling heart :
but his temper was wayward and irritable. He had a
head which statuaries loved to copy, and a foot the deformity of which the beggars in the streets mimicked.
Distinguished at once by the strength and by the weakness of his intellect, affectionate yet perverse, a poor lord,
and a handsome cripple, he required, if ever man required, the firmest and the most judicious training. But
capriciously as nature had dealt with him, the parent [4]
to whom the office of forming his charcter was intrusted
was more capricious still. She passed from paroxysms
of rage to paroxysms of tenderness. At one time she
stifled him with her caresses : at another time she in-
sulted his deformity. He came [5] into the world; and
the world treated him as his mother had treated him,
sometimes with fondness, sometimes with cruelty, never
with justice. It indulged [6] him without descrimination,
and punished him without discrimination. He was truly
a spoiled child, not merely the spoiled child of his parent,
but the spoiled child of nature, the spoiled child of fortune,
the spoiled child of fame, the spoiled child of society. His
first poems [7] were received with a contempt which, feeble

1. Un de ses ancêtres, William
Byron, fut condamné à mort à la
suite d'un duel où il tua son adver-
saire. Il ne fut pas exécuté, mais il
termina sa vie, à moitié fou, dans une
grande solitude. Un de ses neveux,
John Byron, marié deux fois, ruina
ses deux femmes, et fit mourir de
chagrin la première, qu'il avait
épousée après divorce.

2. Le William Byron dont nous
venons de parler.

3. *But for*, sans.

4. *Parent* (le père ou la mère) ici :
la mère.

5. *He came*, il fit son entrée.

6. *Indulged*, gâta.

7. *Hours of Idleness* (1807).

as they were, they did not absolutely deserve. The poem [1] which he published on his return from his travels was, on the other hand, extolled far above its merit. At twenty-four he found himself on the highest pinnacle of literary fame, with Scott, Wordsworth, Southey, and a crowd of other distinguished writers beneath his feet. There is scarcely an instance in history of so sudden a rise to so dizzy an eminence.

Every thing that could stimulate, and every thing that could gratify the strongest propensities of our nature, the gaze of a hundred drawing-rooms, the acclamations of the whole nation, the applause of applauded men, the love of lovely women, all this world and all the glory of it [2], were at once offered to a youth to whom nature had given violent passions, and whom education had never taught to control [3] them. He lived as many men live who have no similar excuse to plead for their faults. But his countrymen and his countrywomen would love him and admire him. They were resolved to see in his excesses only the flash and outbreak of that same fiery mind which glowed in his poetry. He attacked religion; yet in religious circles his name was mentioned with fondness; and in many religious publications his works were censured with singular tenderness. He lampooned the Prince Regent [4]; yet he could not alienate the Tories [5]. Every thing, it seemed, was to be forgiven to youth, rank, and genius.

Then came the reaction. Society, capricious in its indignation as it had been capricious in its fondness, flew into a rage with its froward and petted darling. He had been worshipped with an irrational idolatry. He was persecuted with an irrational fury. Much has been writ-

---

1. *Childe Harold* (1812).

2. Allusion biblique : " *The devil taketh him (Jesus) up into an exceeding high mountain, and sheweth him all the Kingdoms of the world, and the glory of them* ". ST MATTHEW, IV.

3. *Control*, gouverner.

4. *The Prince Regent*. — En 1811 le roi Georges III étant tombé en démence, son fils fut chargé de la régence, et, en 1820, il succéda à son père sous le nom de Georges IV.

5. *Tories*, surnom des conservateurs; le surnom des libéraux est *whigs*.

ten about those unhappy domestic occurrences which decided the fate of his life. Yet nothing is, nothing ever was, positively known to the public, but this, that he quarrelled with his lady[1], and that she refused to live with him. There have been hints in abundance, and shrugs and shakings of the head, and " Well, well, we know, " and " We could an if we would, " and " If we list to speak, " and " There be that might an they list"[2]. But we are not aware that there is before the world, substantiated by credible, or even by tangible evidence[3], a single fact indicating that Lord Byron was more to blame than any other man who is on bad terms with his wife. The professional men[4] whom Lady Byron consulted were undoubtedly of opinion that she ought not to live with her husband. But it is to be remembered that they formed that opinion without hearing both sides. We do not say, we do not mean to insinuate, that Lady Byron was in any respect[5] to blame. We think that those who condemn her on the evidence which is now before the public are as rash as those who condemn her husband. We will not pronounce any judgment, we cannot, even in our own minds, form any judgment, on a transaction which is so imperfectly known to us. It would have been well if, at the time of the separation, all those who knew as little about the matter then as we know about it now had shown that forbearance which, under such circumstances, is but common justice.

We know no spectacle so ridiculous as the British public in one of its periodical fits of morality. In general, elopements, divorces, and family quarrels, pass with little notice. We read the scandal, talk about it for a day, and forget it. But once in six or seven years our virtue becomes outrageous. We cannot suffer the laws of reli-

---

1. *His lady*, sa femme.
2. Ces expressions se trouvent dans Shakespeare (*Macbeth*, 1, iv, 176). *An* *if* et *an* = if; — *list* = would; — *there be* = there are [people].

3. *Evidence*, témoignages.
4. *Professional men* (professionnels), hommes de loi.
5. *In any respect*, sous quelque rapport que ce soit.

gion and decency to be violated. We must make a stand
against vice. We must teach libertines that the English
people appreciate the importance of domestic ties. Accordingly some unfortunate man, in no respect[1] more
depraved than hundreds whose offences have been treated with lenity, is singled out as an expiatory sacrifice. If
he has children, they are to be[2] taken from him. If he has
a profession, he is to be driven from it. He is cut[3] by the
higher orders, and hissed by the lower. He is, in truth, a
sort of whipping-boy[4], by whose vicarious agonies all the
other transgressors of the same class are, it is supposed,
sufficiently chastised. We reflect very complacently on
our own severity, and compare with great pride the high
standard of morals established in England with the Parisian laxity. At length our anger is satiated. Our victim
is ruined and heart-broken. And our virtue goes quietly
to sleep for seven years more.

It is clear that those vices which destroy domestic happiness ought to be as much as possible repressed. It is
equally clear that they cannot be repressed by penal legislation. It is therefore right and desirable that public
opinion should be directed against them. But it should
be directed against them uniformly, steadily, and tem-
perately, not by sudden fits and starts. There should be
one weight and one measure. Decimation is always an
objectionable mode of punishment. It is the resource of
judges too indolent and hasty to investigate facts and to
discriminate nicely between shades of guilt. It is an
irrational practice, even when adopted by military tribu-
nals. When adopted by the tribunal of public opinion,
it is infinitely more irrational. It is good that a certain
portion of disgrace should constantly attend on certain
bad actions. But it is not good that the offenders should
merely have to stand[5] the risks of a lottery of infamy,

1. *In no respect*, sous aucun rapport.
2. *They are to be*, il faut qu'ils
soient.
3. *Cut*, abandonné, renié.

4. *Whipping-boy*, enfant autrefois
attaché à la personne d'un jeune
prince et qui recevait les corrections
méritées par celui-ci.
5. *Stand* (être exposés à), courir.

that ninety-nine out of every hundred should escape, and that the hundredth, perhaps the most innocent of the hundred, should pay for all. . . . .
. . . . The public, without knowing any thing whatever about the transactions[1] in his family, flew into a violent passion[2] with him, and proceeded to invent stories which might justify its anger. Ten or twenty different accounts of the separation, inconsistent with each other, with themselves, and with common sense, circulated at the same time. What evidence there might be for any one of these, the virtuous people who repeated them neither knew nor cared. For in fact these stories were not the causes, but the effects of the public indignation. They resembled those loathsome slanders which abject libellers were in the habit of publishing about Bonaparte; such as that he poisoned a girl with arsenic when he was at the military school, that he hired a grenadier to shoot Dessaix at Marengo. There was a time when anecdotes like these obtained some credence from persons who, hating the French emperor without knowing why, were eager to believe any thing which might justify their hatred. Lord Byron fared in the same way[3]. His countrymen were in a bad humour with him. His writings and his character had lost the charm of novelty. He had been guilty of the offence which, of all offences, is punished most severely; he had been overpraised; he had excited too warm an interest; and the public, with its usual justice, chastised him for its own folly. . . . .

The obloquy which Byron had to endure was such as might well have shaken a more constant mind. The newspapers were filled with lampoons. The theatres shook with execrations. He was excluded from circles where he had lately been the observed of all observers[4].

1. *The transactions*, ce qui s'était passé.
2. *Passion*, colère.
3. *Fared in the same way*, eut le même destin, fut traité de la même façon. Ici *to fare* = avoir tel et tel sort.
4. *The observed of all observers*, le flatté de tous les flatteurs (sens vieilli).

All those creeping things [1] that riot in the decay of nobler natures hastened to their repast; and they were right; they did [2] after their kind. It is not every day that the savage envy of aspiring [3] dunces is gratified by the agonies of such a spirit, and the degradation of such a name.

The unhappy man left his country for ever. The howl of contumely followed him across the sea, up the Rhine, over the Alps; it gradually waxed fainter; it died away; those who had raised it began to ask each other, what, after all, was the matter about which they had been so clamorous, and wished to invite back the criminal whom they had just chased from them. His poetry became more popular than it had ever been; and his complaints were read with tears by thousands and tens of thousands who had never seen his face.

He had fixed his home on the shores of the Adriatic, in the most picturesque and interesting of cities [4], beneath the brightest of skies, and by the brightest of seas. Censoriousness was not the vice of the neighbours whom he had chosen. From the public opinion of the country of his adoption, he had nothing to dread. With the public opinion of the country of his birth, he was at open war. He plunged into wild and desperate excesses, ennobled by no generous or tender sentiment. From Venice he sent forth volume after volume, full of eloquence, of wit, of pathos [5], of ribaldry, and of bitter disdain. His health sank under the effects of his intemperance. His hair turned grey. His food ceased to nourish him. A hectic fever withered him up. It seemed that his body and mind were about to perish together. . . . .

. . . .

A nation [6], once the first among the nations, preeminent in knowledge, preeminent in military glory, the cradle of philosophy, of eloquence, and of the fine arts,

1. *Things*, êtres.
2. *Did*, agissaient.
3. *Aspiring*, ambitieux.

4. Venise.
5. *Pathos*, pathétique, sentiment.
6. La Grèce.

had been for ages bowed down under a cruel yoke[1]. All the vices which oppression generates, the abject vices which it generates in those who submit to it, the ferocious vices which it generates in those who struggle against it, had deformed the character of that miserable race. The valour which had won the great battle of human civilisation, which had saved Europe, which had subjugated Asia, lingered[2] only among pirates and robbers. The ingenuity[3], once so conspicuously displayed in every department of physical and moral science, had been depraved into a timid and servile cunning. On a sudden this degraded people had risen on their oppressors. Discountenanced or betrayed by the surrounding potentates, they had found in themselves something of that which might well supply the place of all foreign assistance, something of the energy of their fathers.

As a man of letters, Lord Byron could not but be interested in the event[4] of this contest. His political opinions, though, like all his opinions, unsettled, leaned strongly towards the side of liberty. He had assisted the Italian insurgents[5] with his purse, and, if their struggle against the Austrian government had been prolonged, would probably have assisted them with his sword. But to Greece he was attached by peculiar ties. He had when young[6] resided in that country. Much of his most splendid popular poetry had been inspired by its scenery and by its history. Sick[7] of inaction, degraded in his own eyes by his private vices and by his literary failures[8], pining for untried excitement and honourable distinction, he carried his exhausted body and his wounded spirit to the Grecian camp.

His conduct in his new situation showed so much vigour and good sense as to justify us in believing[9] that,

---

1. Le joug de la Turquie.
2. *Lingered* (s'attardait, restait), se rencontrait encore.
3. *Ingenuity*, ingéniosité.
4. *Event*, résultat.
5. En 1821.
6. *When young* = when he was young.
7. *Sick*, dégoûté, écœuré.
8. Allusion au journal mort-né le *Liberal* que Byron fonda de concert avec un de ses amis, et qui n'eut que quatre numéros.
9. *To justify us in believing* (pour

if his life had been prolonged, he might have distinguished himself as a soldier and a politician. But pleasure
and sorrow had done the work of seventy years upon his
delicate frame. The hand of death was upon him : he
knew it; and the only wish which he uttered was that he
might die sword in hand.

This was denied to him. Anxiety, exertion, exposure,
and those fatal stimulants which had become indispensable to him, soon stretched him on a sick bed, in a
strange[1] land, amidst strange faces, without one human
being that he loved near him. There, at thirty-six, the
most celebrated Englishman of the nineteenth century
closed his brilliant and miserable career.

We cannot even now retrace those events without feeling something of what was felt by the nation, when it
was first known that the grave had closed over so much
sorrow and so much glory; something of what was felt by
those who saw the hearse, with its long train of coaches,
turn slowly northward, leaving behind it that cemetery[2]
which had been consecrated by the dust of so many great
poets, but of which the doors were closed against all that
remained of Byron. We well remember that on that
day, rigid moralists could not refrain from weeping for
one so young, so illustrious, so unhappy, gifted with such
rare gifts, and tried by such strong temptations. It is
unnecessary to make any reflections. The history carries its moral with it. Our age has indeed been fruitful
of warnings to the eminent, and of consolations to the
obscure. Two men have died within our recollection,
who, at a time of life[3] at which many poeple have hardly
completed their education, had raised themselves, each
in his own department[4], to the height of glory. One of
them died at Longwood; the other at Missolonghi. . .

Never had any writer so vast a command of the whole

nous justifier en croyant, pour nous justifier quand nous croyons), pour justifier notre ferme opinion.

1. *Strange*, étrangère.
2. C'est-à-dire l'abbaye de West- minster (*Westminster Abbey*), où sont enterrés la plupart des grands hommes de l'Angleterre.
3. *A time of life*, un âge.
4. *Department*, branche.

eloquence of scorn, misanthropy and despair. That Marah was never dry. No art could sweeten, no draughts[1] could exhaust, its perennial waters of bitterness. Never was there such variety in monotony as that of Byron. From maniac[2] laughter to piercing lamentation, there was not a single note of human anguish of which he was not master. Year after year, and month after month, he continued to repeat that to be wretched is the destiny of all; that to be eminently wretched is the destiny of the eminent; that all the desires by which we are cursed lead alike to misery; if they are not gratified, to the misery of disappointment; if they are gratified, to the misery of satiety. His heroes are men who have arrived by different roads at the same goal of despair, who are sick[3] of life, who are at war with society, who are supported in their anguish only by an unconquerable pride resembling that of Prometheus on the rock or of Satan in the burning marl[4], who can master their agonies by the force of their will, and who, to the last, defy the whole power of earth and heaven. He always described himself as a man of the same kind with his favourite creations, as a man whose heart had been withered, whose capacity for happiness was gone and could not be restored, but whose invincible spirit dared the worst that could befall him here or hereafter.

How much of this morbid feeling sprang from an original disease of the mind, how much from real misfortune, how much from the nervousness of dissipation, how much was fanciful, how much was merely affected, it is impossible for us, and would probably have been impossible for the most intimate friends of Lord Byron, to decide. Whether there ever existed, or can ever exist, a person answering to the description which he gave of himself,

---

1. *Draught* (du verbe *to draw*, tirer, puiser) signifie : ce que l'on puise, ce que l'on boit d'un seul coup.
2. *Maniac*, de fou.
3. *Sick*, dégoûtés.
4. Allusion à ce passage de Milton :

On dry land
He lights, if it were land that ever burn'd
With solid, as the lake with liquid, fire.
. . . . To support uneasy steps
Over the burning marle, etc...

(Paradise Lost, 1.)

may be doubted : but that he was not such a person is beyond all doubt. It is ridiculous to imagine that a man whose mind was really imbued with scorn of his fellow-creatures would have published three or four books every year in order to tell them so; or that a man who could say with truth that he neither sought sympathy nor needed it would have admitted all Europe to hear his farewell to his wife, and his blessings on his child. In the second canto of Childe Harold, he tells us that he is insensible to fame and obloquy :

> "Ill may such contest now the spirit move,
> Which heeds nor keen reproof nor partial praise."

Yet we know on the best evidence [1] that, a day or two before he published these lines, he was greatly, indeed childishly, elated by the compliments paid to his maiden speech [2] in the House of Lords.

We are far, however, from thinking that his sadness was altogether feigned. He was naturally a man of great sensibility; he had been ill educated; his feelings had been early exposed to sharp trials; he had been crossed in his boyish love [3]; he had been mortified by the failure of his first literary efforts [4]; he was straitened in pecuniary circumstances [5]; he was unfortunate in his domestic relations; the public treated him with cruel injustice; his health and spirits suffered from his dissipated habits of life; he was, on the whole, an unhappy man. He early discovered that, by parading his unhappiness before the multitude, he produced an immense sensation. The world gave him every encouragement to talk about his mental sufferings. The interest which his first confessions excited induced him to affect much that

1. *Evidence*, témoignage.
2. *Maiden speech*, premier discours, discours de début.
3. A seize ans, Byron devint amoureux d'une de ses cousines qui, loin de le prendre au sérieux, ne tarda pas à en épouser un autre.

4. Les *Hours of Idleness*, qui parurent en 1807 et furent fort mal traitées par l'*Edinburgh Review*.
5. *He was straitened in pecuniary circumstances* (il était gêné dans sa situation pécuniaire), il avait des embarras d'argent.

he did not feel; and the affectation probably reacted on his feelings. How far the character in which he exhibited himself was genuine, and how far theatrical, it would probably have puzzled himself to say.

———

Caractère des Puritains [1].

We would speak first [2] of the Puritans, the most remarkable body of men, perhaps, which the world has ever produced. The odious and ridiculous parts of their character lie on the surface. He that runs may read them; nor have there been wanting [3] attentive and malicious observers to point them out. For many years after the Restoration [4], they were the theme of unmeasured invective and derision. They were exposed to the utmost licentiousness of the press and of the stage, at the time when the press and the stage were most licentious [5]. They were not men of letters; they were, as a body, unpopular; they could not defend themselves; and the public would not take them under its protection. They were therefore abandoned, without reserve, to the tender mercies of the satirists and dramatists. The ostentatious simplicity of their dress, their sour aspect, their nasal twang, their stiff posture, their long graces, their Hebrew names [6], the Scriptural phrases which they introduced on every occasion, their contempt of human learning, their detestation of polite amusements, were indeed

1. Extrait de l'*Essai sur Milton.*

2. Dans cette partie de son *Essai*, Macaulay étudie la situation et le caractère des partis à l'époque de la guerre civile.

3. *Nor have these been wanting* = and *these have* not *been wanting*, et il n'a pas manqué de. — Au commencement d'une proposition, *nor* équivaut souvent à *and... not.*

4. *The Restoration*, la Restauration de 1660.

5. Voy. plus loin le morceau intitulé *la Corruption et les Puritains.*

6. Les Puritains, attachant plus d'importance à l'Ancien Testament qu'au Nouveau, donnaient de préférence à leurs enfants des noms tirés de l'Ancien, tels que Ebenezer, Hephzibah. Ils allaient même jusqu'à transformer des phrases entières de la Bible en noms propres; par exemple, ces deux noms cités par Macaulay dans son *Essai sur Bunyan* : serjeant *Bind-their-Kings in chains* et captain *Hew-Agay-in-pieces-before-the-Lord.*

fair game for the laughers. But it is not from the laughers alone that the philosophy of history is to be learnt. And he who approaches this subject should carefully guard against the influence of that potent ridicule which has already misled so many excellent writers. .   .   .   .

... Those who roused the people to resistance, who directed their measures through a long series of eventful years, who formed, out of the most unpromising materials, the finest army that Europe had ever seen, who trampled down King, Church, and Aristocracy, who, in the short intervals of domestic sedition and rebellion, made the name of England terrible to every nation on the face of the earth. were no vulgar fanatics. Most of their absurdities were mere external badges, like the signs of freemasonry, or the dresses of friars. We regret that these badges were not more attractive. We regret that a body to whose courage and talents mankind has owed inestimable obligations, had not the lofty elegance which distinguished some of the adherents of Charles the First, or the easy good-breeding for which the court of Charles the Second was celebrated. But, if we must make our choice, we shall, like Bassanio in the play, turn from the specious caskets which contain only the Death's head and the Fool's head, and fix on the plain leaden chest which conceals the treasure.

The Puritans were men whose minds had derived a peculiar character from the daily contemplation of superior beings and eternal interests. Not content with acknowledging, in general terms, an overruling Providence, they habitually ascribed every event to the will of the Great Being, for whose power nothing was too vast, for whose inspection nothing was too minute. To know him, to serve him, to enjoy him, was with them the great end of existence. They rejected with contempt the ceremonious homage which other sects substituted for the pure worship of the soul. Instead of catching occasional glimpses of the Deity through an obscuring veil, they aspired to gaze full on his intolerable brightness, and to commune with him face to face. Hence originated their contempt for terrestrial distinctions. The difference between the greatest and the meanest of mankind seemed to vanish, when compared with the boundless interval which separated the whole race from Him on whom their own eyes were constantly fixed. They recognised no title to superiority but his favour; and, confident of that favour, they despised all the accomplishments and all the dignities of the world. If they were unacquainted with the works of philosophers and poets, they were deeply read in the oracles of God. If their names were not found in the registers of heralds, they were recorded in the Book of Life[1]. If their steps were not accompanied by a splendid train of menials, legions of ministering angels had charge over them. Their palaces were houses not made with hands; their diadems crowns of glory which should never fade away. On the rich and the eloquent, on nobles and priests, they looked down with contempt: for they esteemed themselves rich in a more precious treasure, and eloquent in a more sublime language, nobles by the right of an earlier creation, and priests by the imposition of a mightier hand[2]. The very meanest of them was a being to whose fate a mysterious and terrible importance belonged, on whose slightest action the spirits of light and darkness looked with anxious interest, who had been destined, before heaven and earth were created, to enjoy a felicity which should continue when heaven and earth should have passed away. Events which short-sighted politicians ascribed to earthly causes, had been ordained on his account. For his sake empires had risen, and flourished, and decayed. For his sake the Almighty had proclaimed his will by the pen of the Evangelist, and the harp of the prophet. He had been wrested by no common deliverer from the grasp of no common foe. He had been ransom-

1. *The Book of Life*, le Livre de Vie. En théologie, le décret de Dieu touchant les élus.

2. Allusion à l'expression *imposi-tion of hands* (ou *laying on of hands*), imposition des mains, rite par lequel l'évêque confère les ordres.

ed by the sweat of no vulgar agony, by the blood of no earthly sacrifice. It was for him that the sun had been darkened, that the rocks had been rent, that the dead had risen, that all nature had shuddered at the sufferings of her expiring God.

Thus the Puritan was made up of two different men, the one all self-abasement[1], penitence, gratitude, passion; the other proud, calm, inflexible, sagacious. He prostrated himself in the dust before his Maker : but he set his foot on the neck of his king. In his devotional retirement, he prayed with convulsions, and groans, and tears. He was half-maddened by glorious or terrible illusions. He heard the lyres of angels or the tempting whispers of fiends. He caught a gleam of the Beatific Vision[2], or woke screaming from dreams of everlasting fire. Like Vane, he thought himself intrusted with the sceptre of the millennial year. Like Fleetwood, he cried in the bitterness of his soul that God had hid his face from him. But when he took his seat in the council, or girt on his sword for war, these tempestuous workings of the soul had left no perceptible trace behind them. People who saw nothing of the godly but their uncouth visages, and heard nothing from them but their groans and their whining hymns, might laugh at them. But those had little reason to laugh who encountered them in the hall of debate or in the field of battle. These fanatics brought to civil and military affairs a coolness of judgment and an immutability of purpose which some writers have thought inconsistent with their religious zeal, but which were in fact the necessary effects of it. The intensity of their feelings on one subject made them tranquil on every other. One overpowering sentiment had subjected to itself pity and hatred, ambition and fear. Death had lost its terrors and pleasure its charms. They had their smiles and their tears, their raptures and their

<hr>

1. *Self-abasement* (abaissement de soi-même), humilité.
2. *The Beatific Vision*, la Vision Béatifique; en théologie, vision directe de Dieu dont jouissent au ciel les anges et les saints.

sorrows, but not for the things of this world. Enthusiasm had made them Stoics, had cleared their minds from every vulgar passion and prejudice, and raised them above the influence of danger and of corruption. It sometimes might lead them to pursue unwise ends, but never to choose unwise means. They went through the world, like Sir Artegal's iron man Talus [1] with his flail, crushing and trampling down oppressors, mingling with human beings, but having neither part nor lot [2] in human infirmities, insensible to fatigue, to pleasure, and to pain, not to be pierced by any weapon, not to be withstood by any barrier.

______

Cromwell [3].

The death of Charles [4] and the strong measures which led to it raised Cromwell to a height of power fatal to the infant [5] Commonwealth. No men occupy so splendid a place in history as those who have founded monarchies on the ruins of republican institutions. Their glory, if not of the purest, is assuredly of the most seductive and dazzling kind. In nations broken to the curb, in nations long accustomed to be transferred from one tyrant to another, a man without eminent qualities may easily gain supreme power. The defection of a troop of guards, a conspiracy of eunuchs, a popular tumult, might place an indolent senator or a brutal soldier on the throne of the Roman world. Similar revolutions have often occurred in the despotic states of Asia. But a community which has heard the voice of truth and experienced the pleasures of liberty, in which the merits of statesmen and of systems are freely canvassed, in which

1. *Sir Artegal* et *Talus*, personnages du poème de Spenser *The Faery Queen;* ils symbolisent : le premier, la justice; le second, le pouvoir exécutif.

2. *Neither part nor lot.* — *Part* et *lot* sont synonymes. Il y a donc là un pléonasme, assez fréquent dans les locutions proverbiales. Celle-ci est tirée de la Bible (*Acts*, viii, 21).

3. Extrait de l'*Essai sur Hallam's Constitutional History.*

4. Charles Ier, exécuté en 1649.

5. *Infant*, jeune.

obedience is paid, not to persons, but to laws, in which magistrates are regarded, not as the lords, but as the servants of the public, in which the excitement of a party is a necessary of life, in which political warfare is reduced to a system of tactics; such a community is not easily reduced to servitude. Beasts of burden may easily be managed by a new master. But will the wild ass submit to the bonds? Will the unicorn serve and abide by the crib[1]? Will leviathan hold out his nostrils to the hook[2]? The mythological conqueror of the East[3], whose enchantments reduced wild beasts to the tameness of domestic cattle, and who harnessed lions and tigers to his chariot, is but an imperfect type of those extraordinary minds which have thrown a spell on the fierce spirits of nations unaccustomed to control, and have compelled raging factions to obey their reins and swell their triumph. The enterprise, be it good or bad, is one which requires a truly great man. It demands courage, activity, energy, wisdom, firmness, conspicuous virtues, or vices so splendid and alluring as to resemble virtues.

Those who have succeeded in this arduous undertaking form a very small and a very remarkable class. Parents of tyranny, heirs of freedom, kings among citizens, citizens among kings, they unite in themselves the characteristics of the system which springs from them, and those of the system from which they have sprung. Their reigns shine with a double light, the last and dearest rays of departing freedom mingled with the first and brightest glories of empire in its dawn. The high qualities of such a prince lend to despotism itself a charm drawn from the liberty under which they were formed, and which they have destroyed. He resembles an European who settles within the Tropics, and carries thither the strength and the energetic habits acquired in regions

1. Voy. note 3, page 39.
2. *" Canst thou draw out leviathan with an hook?... Canst thou put an hook into his nose?... Will he make, many supplications unto thee?"* Job, XLI. — On suppose que le *leviathan* de Job était le crocodile.
3. Bacchus.

more propitious to the constitution. He differs as widely from princes nursed in the purple of imperial cradles, as the companions of Gama from their dwarfish and imbecile progeny, which, born in a climate unfavourable to its growth and beauty, degenerates more and more, at every descent, from the qualities of the original conquerors.

In this class three men stand preeminent, Cæsar, Cromwell, and Bonaparte. The highest place in this remarkable triumvirate belongs undoubtedly to Cæsar. He united the talents of Bonaparte to those of Cromwell; and he possessed also, what neither Cromwell nor Bonaparte possessed, learning, taste, wit, eloquence, the sentiments and the manners of an accomplished gentleman.

. . . .

Mr. Hallam truly says that, though it is impossible to rank Cromwell with Napoleon as a general, yet "his exploits were as much above the level of his contemporaries and more the effects of an original uneducated capacity." Bonaparte was trained in the best military schools; the army which he led to Italy was one of the finest that ever existed. Cromwell passed his youth and the prime of his manhood in a civil situation. He never looked on war till he was more than forty years old. He had first to form himself, and then to form his troops. Out of[1] raw levies he created an army, the bravest and the best disciplined, the most orderly in peace, and the most terrible in war, that Europe had seen. He called this body into existence. He led it to conquest. He never fought a battle without gaining it. He never gained a battle without annihilating the force opposed to him. Yet his victories were not the highest glory of his military system. The respect which his troops paid to property their attachment to the laws and religion of their country, their submission to the civil power, their temperance, their intelligence, their industry, are without parallel. It was after the Restoration[2] that the spirit which their great

1. *Out of,* avec. | 2. De 1660.

leader had infused into them was most signally displayed.
At the command of the established government, an established government which had no means of enforcing
obedience, fifty thousand soldiers, whose backs no enemy
had ever seen, either in domestic or in continental war,
laid down their arms, and retired into the mass of the
people, thenceforward to be distinguished only by superior diligence, sobriety, and regularity in the pursuits of
peace, from the other members of the community which
they had saved.

In the general spirit and character of his administration, we think Cromwell far superior to Napoleon.   " In
civil government," says Mr. Hallam, "there can be no
adequate parallel between one who had sucked only the
dregs of a besotted fanaticism, and one to whom the
stores of reason and philosophy were open." These expressions, it seems to us, convey the highest eulogium
on our great countryman. Reason and philosophy did
not teach the conqueror of Europe to command his passions, or to pursue, as a first object, the happiness of his
people. They did not prevent him from risking his fame
and his power in a frantic contest against the principles of
human nature and the laws of the physical world, against
the rage of the winter and the liberty of the sea. They did
not exempt him from the influence of that most pernicious
of superstitions, a presumptuous fatalism. They did not
preserve him from the inebriation of prosperity, or res-
train him from indecent querulousness in adversity. On
the other hand, the fanaticism of Cromwell never urged
him on impracticable undertakings, or confused his perception of the public good. Our countryman, inferior to
Bonaparte in invention, was far superior to him in wisdom. The French Emperor is among conquerors what
Voltaire is among writers, a miraculous child. His
splendid genius was frequently clouded by fits of humour
as absurdly perverse as those of the pet of the nursery, who
quarrels with [1] his food, and dashes his playthings to pie-

1. *Quarrels with*, se plaint de.

ces. Cromwell was emphatically[1] a man. He possessed, in an eminent degree, that masculine and fullgrown[2] robustness of mind, that equally diffused intellectual health, which, if our national partiality does not mislead us, has peculiarly characterised the great men of England. Never was any ruler so conspicuously born for sovereignty. The cup which has intoxicated almost all others, sobered him[3]. His spirit, restless from[4] its own buoyancy in a lower sphere, reposed in majestic placidity as soon as it had reached the level congenial to it. He had nothing in common with that large class of men who distinguish themselves in subordinate posts, and whose incapacity becomes obvious as soon as the public voice summons them to take the lead. Rapidly as[5] his fortunes grew, his mind expanded more rapidly still. Insignificant as a private citizen, he was a great general; he was a still greater prince. Napoleon had a theatrical manner, in which the coarseness of a revolutionary guardroom was blended with the ceremony of the old Court of Versailles. Cromwell, by the confession even of his enemies, exhibited in his demeanour the simple and natural nobleness of a man neither ashamed of his origin nor vain of his elevation, of a man who had found his proper place in society, and who felt secure that he was competent to fill it. Easy, even to familiarity, where his own dignity was concerned, he was punctilious only for his country. His own character he left to take care of itself; he left it to be defended by his victories in war, and his reforms in peace. But he was a jealous and implacable guardian of the public honour. He suffered a crazy Quaker to insult him in the gallery of Whitehall, and revenged himself only by liberating him and giving him a dinner. But he was prepared to risk the chances of war to avenge the blood of a private Englishman.

---

1. *Emphatically*, dans toute la force du terme.

2. *Full-grown* (pleinement développée), mûre.

3. *Sobered him*, lui donna du sang-froid.

4. *From*, à cause de.

5. *Rapidly as* (rapidement comme), si rapidement que.

His administration was glorious, but with no vulgar glory. It was not one of those periods of overstrained and convulsive exertion which necessarily produce debility and languor. Its energy was natural, healthful, temperate. He placed England at the head of the Protestant interest[1], and in the first rank of Christian powers. He taught every nation to value her friendship and to dread her enmity. But he did not squander her resources in a vain attempt to invest her with that supremacy which no power, in the modern system of Europe, can safely affect, or can long retain.

This noble and sober wisdom had its reward. If he did not carry the banners of the Commonwealth in triumph to distant capitals, if he did not adorn Whitehall with the spoils of the Stadthouse and the Louvre, if he did not portion out Flanders and Germany into principalities for his kinsmen and his generals, he did not, on the other hand[2], see his country overrun by the armies of nations which his ambition had provoked. He did not drag out the last years of his life an exile and a prisoner, in an unhealthy climate and under an ungenerous gaoler, raging with the impotent desire of vengeance, and brooding over visions of departed glory. He went down to his grave in the fulness of power and fame; and he left to his son[3] an authority which any man of ordinary firmness and prudence would have retained.

Bunyan's Pilgrim's Progress [4].

That wonderful book, while it obtains admiration from the most fastidious[5] critics, is loved by those who are too simple to admire it. . . . .

1. *Interest*, parti.
2. *On the other hand*, d'autre part.
3. Richard Cromwell, qui renonça au pouvoir au bout de six mois.
4. Extrait de l'*Essai sur Bunyan's Pilgrim's Progress*. — *The Pilgrim's Progress* (le Voyage du Pèlerin), récit allégorique, est l'œuvre capitale de Bunyan.
5. *Fastidious*, difficiles, délicats.

In the wildest parts of Scotland the Pilgrim's Progress is the delight of the peasantry. In every nursery the Pilgrim's Progress is a greater favourite than Jack the Giant-killer[1]. Every reader knows the straight and narrow path[2] as well as he knows a road in which he has gone backward and forward a hundred times. This is the highest miracle of genius, that things which are not should be as though[3] they were, that the imaginations of one mind should become the personal recollections of another. And this miracle the tinker[4] has wrought . . . .

Bunyan is almost the only writer who ever gave to the abstract the interest of the concrete. In the works of many celebrated authors, men are mere personifications. We have not a jealous man, but jealousy, not a traitor, put perfidy, not a patriot, but patriotism. The mind of Bunyan, on the contrary, was so imaginative that personifications, when he dealt with them, became men. A dialogue between two qualities, in his dream[5], has more dramatic effect than a dialogue between two human beings in most plays. In this respect the genius of Bunyan bore a great resemblance to that of a man who had very little else in common with him, Percy Bysshe Shelley. The strong imagination of Shelley made him an idolater in his own despite[6]. Out of the most indefinite terms of a hard, cold, dark, metaphysical system, he made a gorgeous Pantheon, full of beautiful, majestic, and life-like forms. He turned atheism itself into a mythology, rich with visions as glorious as the gods that live in the marble of Phidias, or the virgin saints that smile on us from the canvass of Murillo. The Spirit of Beauty, the Principle of Good, the Principle of Evil, when he treated of

---

1. *Jack the Giant-Killer*, Jean le tueur de géants, héros d'un de ces vieux contes d'enfants que les Anglais appellent *nursery tales*.

2. Que Bunyan décrit dans son livre.

3. *Should be as though*, soient comme si.

4. Bunyan était chaudronnier.

5. *His dream*, le *Pilgrim's Progress*, qu'il donne comme le récit d'un rêve qu'il a fait.

6. *In his own despite*, malgré lui.

them, ceased to be abstractions. They took shape and colour. They were no longer mere words; but " intelligible forms ", " fair humanities ", objects of love, of adoration, or of fear. As there can be no stronger sign of a mind destitute of the poetical faculty than that tendency which was so common among the writers of the French school to turn images into abstractions, Venus, for example, into Love, Minerva into Wisdom, Mars into War, and Bacchus into Festivity, so there can be no stronger sign of a mind truly poetical than a disposition to reverse this abstracting process, and to make individuals out of[1] generalities. Some of the metaphysical and ethical theories of Shelley were certainly most absurd and pernicious. But we doubt whether any modern poet has possessed in an equal degree some of the highest qualities of the great ancient masters. The words bard and inspiration, which seem so cold and affected when applied to other modern writers, have a perfect propriety when applied to him. He was not an author, but a bard. His poetry seems not to have been an art, but an inspiration. Had he lived to the full age of man[2], he might not improbably have given to the world some great work of the very highest rank in design and execution . . . .

Grace Abounding[3] is indeed one of the most remarkable pieces of autobiography[4] in the world. It is a full and open confession of the fancies which passed through the mind of an illiterate man, whose affections were warm, whose nerves were irritable, whose imagination was ungovernable, and who was under the influence of the strongest religious excitement. In whatever age Bunyan had lived, the history of his feelings would, in all probability, have been very curious. But the time

1. *Out of*, avec.

2. Shelley mourut à trente ans.

3. *Grace Abounding* est, après *The Pilgrim's Progress*, l'œuvre la plus importante de Bunyan.

4. *Pieces of autobiography*, auto-biographies. Il y a, en anglais, un grand nombre d'expressions où un terme abstrait ou général devient concret ou particulier par l'adjonction du mot *piece*, pièce, article : *a piece of furniture*, un meuble; *a piece of injustice*, *a piece of generosity*, etc.

in which his lot was cast[1] was the time of a great
stirring of the human mind[2]. A tremendous burst of
public feeling, produced by the tyranny of the hierarchy,
menaced the old ecclesiastical institutions with destruction. To the gloomy regularity of one intolerant Church
had succeeded the license of innumerable sects, drunk
with the sweet and heady must of their new liberty.
Fanaticism, engendered by persecution, and destined
to engender persecution in turn, spread rapidly through
society. Even the strongest and most commanding
minds were not proof against this strange taint. . . .

The history of Bunyan is the history of a most excitable mind in an age of excitement. By most of his
biographers he has been treated with gross injustice.
They have understood in a popular sense all those
strong terms of self-condemnation which he employed
in a theological sense. They have, therefore, represented him as an abandoned wretch, reclaimed[3] by
means almost miraculous; or, to use their favourite
metaphor, "as a brand plucked from the burning"[4].
Mr. Ivimey calls him the depraved Bunyan and the
wicked tinker of Elstow. Surely Mr. Ivimey ought to
have been too familiar with the bitter accusations which
the most pious people are in the habit of bringing
against themselves, to understand literally all the
strong expressions which are to be found in the Grace
Abounding. . . . .

Those horrible internal conflicts which Bunyan has
described with so much power of language prove, not
that he was a worse man than his neighbours, but that
his mind was constantly occupied by religious consider-
ations, that his fervour exceeded his knowledge, and
that his imagination exercised despotic power over his
body and mind. He heard voices from heaven. He

1. *His lot was cast* (son sort fut
jeté), il lui fut donné de vivre, son
destin le fit vivre.

2. C'est-à-dire l'époque de la diffu-
sion et du règne des idées puritaines.

3. *Reclaimed*, sauvé, converti.

4. Allusion biblique : "*Is not this
a brand plucked out of the fire?*"
ZECHARIA, III, 2.

saw strange visions of distant hills, pleasant and sunny
as his own Delectable Mountains[1]. From those abodes
he was shut out, and placed in a dark and horrible wilderness, where he wandered through ice and snow,
striving to make his way into the happy region of light.
At one time he was seized with an inclination to work
miracles. At another time he thought himself actually[2]
possessed by the devil. He could distinguish the blas-
phemous whispers. He felt his infernal enemy pulling
at his clothes behind him. He spurned with his feet
and struck with his hands at the destroyer. Sometimes
he was tempted to sell his part in the salvation of mankind. Sometimes a violent impulse urged him to start
up from his food[3], to fall on his knees, and to break
forth into prayer. At length he fancied that he had
committed the unpardonable sin[4]. His agony con-
vulsed his robust frame. He was, he says, as if his
breast bone would split; and this he took for a sign that
he was destined to burst asunder like Judas. The agitation of his nerves made all his movements trem-
ulous; and this trembling, he supposed, was a visible
mark of his reprobation, like that which had been set on
Cain[5]. At one time, indeed, an encouraging voice
seemed to rush in at the window, like the noise of wind,
but very pleasant, and commanded, as he says, a great
calm in his soul. At another time, a word of comfort
"was spoke loud unto him; it showed a great word;
it seemed to be writ[6] in great letters". But these
intervals of ease were short. His state, during two
years and a half, was generally the most horrible that
the human mind can imagine. "I walked", says he,

1. Dans *The Pilgrim's Progress.*
2. *Actually*, réellement.
3. *To start up from his food* (à se
lever brusquement de sa nourriture),
à interrompre brusquement son repas.
4. *The unpardonable sin* désigne,
dans la langue religieuse, le péché de
blasphème contre le Saint-Esprit.
C'est une allusion à ce passage du
Nouveau Testament : " *All manner
of sin and blasphemy shall be forgiven
unto men : but the blasphemy against
the Holy Ghost shall not be forgiven
unto men.* " St Matthew, xii, 31.
5. Après le meurtre d'Abel : " *And
the Lord set a mark upon Cain, lest
any finding him should kill him.* "
Genesis, iv.
6. *Spoke, unto, writ,* formes anciennes de *spoken, to, written.*

with his own peculiar eloquence, " to a neighbouring town; and sat down upon a settle in the street, and fell into a very deep pause[1] about the most fearful state my sin had brought me to; and, after long musing, I lifted up my head; but methought I saw as if the sun that shineth[2] in the heavens did grudge to give me light; and as if the very stones in the street, and tiles upon the houses, did band themselves against me. Methought that they all combined together to banish me out of the world. I was abhorred of them, and unfit to dwell among them, because I had sinned against the Saviour. Oh, how happy now was every creature over I[3]! for they stood fast, and kept their station. But I was gone[4] and lost ". Scarcely any madhouse could produce an instance of delusion so strong, or of misery so acute.

It was through this valley of the Shadow of Death[5], overhung by darkness, peopled with devils, resounding with blasphemy and lamentation, and passing amidst quagmires, snares, and pitfalls, close by the very mouth of hell, that Bunyan journeyed to that bright and fruitful land of Beulah, in which he sojourned during the latter period of his pilgrimage. The only trace which his cruel sufferings and temptations seem to have left behind them was an affectionate compassion for those who were still in the state in which he had once been.

William Pitt[6].

Pitt was undoubtedly a great man. But his was not a complete and well-proportioned greatness. The public

---

1. *Pause* est pris ici dans le sens de *rêverie*.

2. *Shineth* = shines. — Autrefois les verbes prenaient, à la troisième personne du singulier de l'indicatif, la terminaison -*eth*. Les verbes *to do* et *to have* faisaient *doth* et *hath*.

3. *Over I*, tournure familière pour *over me*, plus que moi.

4. *Gone* a ici le même sens que *lost*.

5. Décrite dans *The Pilgrim's Progress*.

6. Extrait de l'Essai sur *The Earl of Chatham*.

life of Hampden or of Somers resembles a regular drama, which can be criticized as a whole, and every scene of which is to be viewed in connection with the main action. The public life of Pitt, on the other hand[1], is a rude though striking piece, a piece abounding in incongruities, a piece without any unity of plan, but redeemed by some noble passages, the effect of which is increased by the tameness or extravagance of what precedes and of what follows. His opinions were unfixed. His conduct at some of the most important conjunctures of his life was evidently determined by pride and resentment. He had one fault, which of all human faults is most rarely found in company with true greatness. He was extremely affected. He was an almost solitary instance of a man of real genius, and of a brave, lofty, and commanding spirit, without simplicity of character. He was an actor in the Closet, an actor at Council, an actor in Parliament; and even in private society he could not lay aside his theatrical tones and attitudes. We know that one of the most distinguished of his partisans often complained that he could never obtain admittance to Lord Chatham's room till every thing was ready for the representation, till the dresses and properties[2] were all correctly disposed, till the light was thrown with Rembrandtlike[3] effect on the head of the illustrious performer, till the flannels[4] had been arranged with the air of a Grecian drapery, and the crutch placed as gracefully as that of Belisarius or Lear.

Yet, with all his faults and affectations, Pitt had, in a very extraordinary degree, many of the elements of greatness. He had splendid talents, strong passions, quick sensibility, and vehement enthusiasm for the grand and the beautiful. There was something about him which ennobled tergiversation itself. He often went

1. *On the other hand*, d'autre part.
2. *Properties* (terme de théâtre), accessoires.
3. *Rembrandt-like* (semblable à R.), à la Rembrandt.
4. Pitt était goutteux.

wrong, very wrong. But, to quote the language of Wordsworth,

> " He still retained
> 'Mid [1] such abasement, what he had received
> From nature, an intense and glowing mind " [2].

... In our time, the audience [3] of a member of Parliament is the nation. The three or four hundred persons who may be present while a speech is delivered may be pleased or disgusted by the voice and action of the orator; but, in the reports which are read the next day by hundreds of thousands, the difference between the noblest and the meanest figure [4], between the richest and the shrillest tones, between the most graceful and the most uncouth gesture, altogether vanishes. A hundred years ago, scarcely any report of what passed within the walls of the House of Commons was suffered to get abroad. In those times, therefore, the impression which a speaker might make on the persons who actually [5] heard him was every thing. His fame out of doors [6] depended entirely on the report of those who were within the doors. In the Parliaments of that time, therefore, as in the ancient commonwealths, those qualifications which enhance the immediate effect of a speech, were far mor important ingredients in the composition of an orator than at present. All those qualifications Pitt possessed in the highest degree. On the stage, he would have been the finest Brutus or Coriolanus ever seen. Those who saw him in his decay, when his health was broken, when his mind was untuned [7], when he had been removed from that stormy assembly [8] of which he thoroughly knew the temper, and over which he possessed unbounded influence, to a small, a torpid, and an unfriendly audience [9], say

1. *'Mid*, abréviation poétique pour *amid*, au milieu de.

2. Ces vers se trouvent dans l'*Excursion*. (Liv. II.)

3. *Audience*, auditoire.

4. *Figure*, tournure, aspect.

5. *Actually*, réellement, de leurs propres oreilles.

6. *Out of doors*, au dehors, à l'extérieur.

7. *Untuned*, confus, trouble.

8. La Chambre des Communes.

9. La Chambre des Lords.

that his speaking was then, for the most part, a low, monotonous muttering, audible only to those who sat close to him, that when violently excited, he sometimes raised his voice for a few minutes, but that it soon sank again into an unintelligible murmur. Such was the Earl of Chatham; but such was not William Pitt[1]. His figure[2], when he first appeared in Parliament, was strikingly graceful and commanding, his features high and noble, his eye full of fire. His voice, even when it sank to a whisper, was heard to the remotest benches; and when he strained it to its full extent, the sound rose like the swell of the organ of a great cathedral, shook the house with its peal, and was heard through lobbies and down staircases, to the Court of Requests[2] and the precincts of Westminster Hall. He cultivated all these eminent advantages with the most assiduous care. His action[3] is described by a very malignant observer as equal to that of Garrick. His play of countenance was wonderful : he frequently disconcerted a hostile orator by a single glance of indignation or scorn. Every tone, from the impassioned cry to the thrilling aside[4] was perfectly at his command. It is by no means improbable that the pains which he took to improve his great personal advantages had, in some respects, a prejudicial operation, and tended to nourish in him that passion for theatrical effect which, as we have already remarked, was one of the most conspicuous blemishes in his character.

But it was not solely or principally to outward accomplishments that Pitt owed the vast influence which, during nearly thirty years, he exercised over the House of Commons. He was undoubtedly a great orator; and, from the descriptions of his contemporaries, and the fragments of his speeches which still remain, it is not difficult to discover the nature and extent of his oratorical powers.

1. C'est en 1766 que *William Pitt* devint *Earl of Chatham.* .

2. *The Court of Requests*, la Cour des Requêtes, ancien tribunal qui s'occupait des suppliques adressées au souverain.

3. *Action*, action, jeu.

4. *Aside*, aparté.

He was no speaker of set speeches. His few prepared discourses were complete failures. The elaborate panegyric which he pronounced on General Wolfe was considered as the very worst of all his performances. " No man, " says a critic who had often heard him, " ever knew so little what he was going to say ". Indeed his facility amounted to a vice. He was not the master, but the slave of his own speech. So little self-command had he when once he felt the impulse, that he did not like to take part in a debate when his mind was full of an important secret of state. " I must sit still, " he once said on such an occasion; " for, when once I am up, every thing that is in my mind comes out. "

Yet he was not a great debater. That he should not have[1] been so when first he entered the House of Commons is not strange. Scarcely any person has ever become so without long practice, and many failures. It was by slow degrees, as Burke said, that the late Mr. Fox became the most brilliant and powerful debater that ever lived. Mr. Fox himself attributed his own success to the resolution which he formed when very young, of speaking, well or ill, at least once every night[2]. " During five whole sessions, " he used to say, " I spoke every night but one; and I regret only that I did not speak on that night too. " It would be difficult to name any eminent debater who has not made himself a master of his art at the expense of his audience[3].

But as this art is one which even the ablest men have seldom acquired without long practice, so it is one which men of respectable abilities, with assiduous and intrepid practice, seldom fail to acquire. It is singular that in such an art, Pitt, a man of splendid talents, of great fluency, of great boldness, a man whose whole life was passed in parliamentary conflict, a man who, during sev-

1. *That he should not have*, qu'il n'ait pas.
2. *Every night*, chaque soir. c'est-à-dire à chaque séance, les séances de la Chambre des Communes ayant lieu le soir.
3. *Audience*, auditoire.

eral years, was the leading minister of the Crown in the House of Commons, should never have attained to high excellence. He spoke without premeditation; but his speech followed the course of his own thoughts and not the course of the previous discussion. He could, indeed, treasure up in his memory some detached expression of a hostile orator, and make it the text for lively ridicule or solemn reprehension. Some of the most celebrated bursts of his eloquence were called forth by an unguarded word, a laugh, or a cheer. But this was the only sort of reply in which he appears to have excelled. He was perhaps the only great English orator who did not think it any advantage to have the last word, and who generally spoke by choice[1] before[2] his most formidable opponents. His merit was almost entirely rhetorical. He did not succeed either in exposition or in refutation; but his speeches abounded with lively illustrations, striking apophthegms, well told anecdotes, happy allusions, passionate appeals. His invective and sarcasm were terrific. Perhaps no English orator was ever so much feared.

But that which gave most effect to his declamation was the air of sincerity, of vehement feeling, of moral elevation, which belonged to all that the said. His style was not always in the purest taste. Several contemporary judges pronounced it too florid. Walpole, in the midst of the rapturous eulogy which he pronounces on one of Pitt's greatest orations, owns that some of the metaphors were too forced. Some of Pitt's quotations and classical stories are too trite for a clever schoolboy. But these were niceties for which the audience cared little. The enthusiasm of the orator infected all who heard him; his ardour and his noble bearing put fire into the most frigid conceit, and gave dignity to the most puerile allusion.

1. *By choice* (par choix), volontairement.

2. *Before*, avant.

DEUXIÈME PARTIE

QUESTIONS LITTÉRAIRES

L'Éducation des Femmes au seizième et au dix-septième siècles[1].

Anne, the mother of Francis Bacon, was distinguished both as a linguist and as a theologian. She corresponded in Greek, and translated a series of sermons on fate and free-will from the Tuscan. . . . .

Lady Bacon[2] was doubtless a lady of highly cultivated mind after the fashion of her age. But we must not suffer ourselves to be deluded into the belief that she and her sisters were more accomplished women than many who are now living. On this subject there is, we think, much misapprehension[3]. We have often heard men who wish, as almost all men of sense wish, that women should be highly educated, speak with rapture of the English ladies of the sixteenth century, and lament that they can find no modern damsel resembling those fair pupils of Ascham and Aylmer who compared, over their embroidery[4], the styles of Isocrates and Lysias, and who, while the horns were sounding and the dogs in full cry[5], sat in the lonely oriel, with eyes rivetted to that immortal page[6] which tells how meekly

---

1. Extrait de l'*Essai sur Bacon*.
2. *Lady Bacon*. — Devant un nom propre *Lady* est l'indication d'un titre de noblesse ; la mère de Bacon s'appelait *Lady Bacon*, parce que son mari était *Sir* Nicholas Bacon. — *Sir* se met devant le prénom des barons ou des baronets. Voy. note 1, page 89.
3. *Misapprehension*, idées fausses.
4. *Over their embroidery* (au-dessus de leur broderie), tout en brodant.
5. Allusion à un passage très connu du *Schoolmaster* d'Ascham. Il raconte qu'il surprit un jour son élève, Lady Jane Grey, en train de lire le *Phédon* de Platon, tandis que ses parents se mettaient en route pour la chasse.
6. Le *Phédon*, où sont racontés les derniers moments de Socrate.

and bravely the first great martyr of intellectual liberty took the cup from[1] his weeping gaoler. But surely these complaints have very little foundation. We would by no means disparage the ladies of the sixteenth century or their pursuits. But we conceive that those who extol them at the expense of the women of our time forget one very obvious and very important circumstance. In the time of Henry the Eighth and Edward the Sixth, a person who did not read Greek and Latin could read nothing, or next to[2] nothing. The Italian was the only modern language which possessed any thing that could be called a literature. All the valuable books then extant in all the vernacular dialects of Europe would hardly have filled a single shelf. England did not yet possess Shakspeare's plays and the Fairy Queen[3], nor France Montaigne's Essays, nor Spain Don Quixote. In looking round a well-furnished library, how many English or French books can, we find which were extant when Lady Jane Grey and Queen Elizabeth received their education? Chaucer, Gower, Froissart, Comines, Rabelais, nearly complete the list. It was therefore absolutely necessary that a woman should be uneducated or classically educated. Indeed, without a knowledge of one of the ancient languages no person could then have any clear notion of what was passing in the political, the literary, or the religious world. The Latin was in the sixteenth century all and more than all that the French was in the eighteenth. It was the language of courts as well as of the schools. It was the language of diplomacy; it was the language of theological and political controversy. Being a fixed language, while the living languages were in a state of fluctuation, and being universally known to the learned and the polite, it was employed by almost every writer who aspired to a wide and durable reputation. A person who was ignorant of it was shut out from all

1. *From*, des mains de.
2. *Next to*, presque.

3. *The Fairy Queen*, la Reine des Fées, poème de Spenser.

acquaintance, not merely with Cicero and Virgil, not merely with heavy treatises on canon-law and school-divinity, but with the most interesting memoirs, state papers, and pamphlets of his own time. . . . .

This is no longer the case. All political and religious controversy is now conducted in the modern languages. The ancient tongues are used only in comments on the ancient writers. The great productions of Athenian and Roman genius are indeed still what they were. But though their positive value is unchanged, their relative value, when compared with the whole mass of mental wealth possessed by mankind, has been constantly falling. They were the intellectual all of our ancestors. They are but a part of our treasures. Over[1] what tragedy could Lady Jane Grey have wept, over what comedy could she have smiled, if the ancient dramatists had not been in her library? A modern reader can make shift without[2] OEdipus and Medea, while he possesses Othello and Hamlet. If he knows nothing of Pyrgopolynices and Thraso, he is familiar with Bobadil, and Bessus, and Pistol, and Parolles. If he cannot enjoy the delicious irony of Plato, he may find some compensation in that of Pascal. If he is shut out from Nephelococcygia he may take refuge in Lilliput. We are guilty, we hope, of no irreverence towards those great nations to which the human race owes art, science, taste, civil and intellectual freedom, when we say, that the stock bequeathed by them to us has been so carefully improved that the accumulated interest now exceeds the principal. We believe that the books which have been written in the languages of western Europe, during the last two hundred and fifty years, — translations from the ancient languages of course included, — are of greater value than all the books which at the beginning of that period were extant in the world. With the modern languages of Europe

1. *Over*, à la lecture de.

2. *Make shift without* (faire expédient sans) se passer de.

English women are at least as well acquainted as English men. When, therefore, we compare the acquirements of Lady Jane Grey with those of an accomplished young woman of our own time, we have no hesitation in awarding the superiority to the latter.

L'Histoire [1].

HISTORY, at least in its state of ideal perfection, is a compound of poetry and philosophy. It impresses general truths on the mind by a vivid representation of particular characters and incidents. But, in fact, the two hostile elements of which it consists have never been known to form a perfect amalgamation; and, at length, in our own time, they have been completely and professedly separated. Good histories, in the proper sense of the word, we have not. But we have good historical romances, and good historical essays. . . .

To make the past present, to bring the distant near, to place us in the society of a great man or on the eminence which overlooks the field of a mighty battle, to invest with the reality of human flesh and blood beings whom we are too much inclined to consider as personified qualities in an allegory, to call up our ancestors before us with all their peculiarities of language, manners, and garb, to show us over [2] their houses, to seat us at their tables, to rummage their old-fashioned wardrobes, to explain the uses of their ponderous furniture, these parts of the duty, which properly belongs to the historian, have been appropriated by the historical novelist. On the other hand [3], to extract the philosophy of history, to direct our judgment of events and men, to trace the connection of causes and effects, and to

1. Extrait de l'Essai sur *Hallam's Constitutional History.*
2. *To show us over* (nous guider partout dans), nous faire visiter de fond en comble.
3. *On the other hand*, d'autre part.

draw from the occurrences of former times general lessons of moral and political wisdom, has become the business of a distinct class of writers.

Of the two kinds of composition into which history has been thus divided, the one may be compared to a map, the other to a painted landscape. The picture, though it places the country before us, does not enable us to ascertain with accuracy the dimensions, the distances, and the angles. The map is not a work of imitative art. It presents no scene to the imagination; but it gives us exact information as to the bearings[1] of the various points, and is a more useful companion to the traveller or the general than the painted landscape could be, though it were the grandest that ever Rosa[2] peopled with outlaws, or the sweetest over which Claude[3] ever poured the mellow effulgence of a setting sun.

It is remarkable that the practice of separating the two ingredients of which history is composed has become prevalent on the Continent as well as in this country. Italy has already produced a historical novel, of high merit and of still higher promise[4]. In France, the practice has been carried to a length[5] somewhat whimsical. M. Sismondi publishes a grave and stately history of the Merovingian Kings, very valuable, and a little tedious. He then sends forth as a companion[6] to it a novel, in which he attempts to give a lively representation of characters and manners. This course, as it seems to us, has all the disadvantages of a division of labour, and none of its advantages. We understand the expediency of keeping the functions of cook and

1. *Bearings*, situation.

2. *Rosa*, Salvator Rosa, peintre italien du dix-septième siècle.

3. *Claude*, c'est-à-dire Claude Gelée, plus connu sous le nom de *Lorrain*, peintre français du dix-septième siècle.

4. Macaulay semble faire allusion au roman de Manzoni *I Promess Sposi* (les Fiancés) qui parut en 1825-1827.

5. *To a length* (à une longueur), à un point.

6. Les Anglais emploient volontiers le mot *companion* pour désigner un livre qui sert de complément à un autre.

coachman distinct. The dinner will be better dressed, and the horses better managed. But where the two situations are united, as in the Maître Jacques of Molière, we do not see that the matter is much mended by the solemn form with which the pluralist passes from one of his employments to the other.

We manage these things better in England. Sir[1] Walter Scott gives us a novel; Mr. Hallam a critical and argumentative history. Both are occupied with the same matter. But the former looks at it with the eye of a sculptor. His intention is to give an express and lively image of its external form. The latter is an anatomist. His task is to dissect the subject to[2] its inmost recesses, and to lay bare before us all the springs of motion and all the causes of decay.

Poésie et Civilisation[3].

It is by his poetry that Milton is best known; and it is of his poetry that we wish first to speak. By the general suffrage of the civilised world, his place has been assigned among the greatest masters of the art[4]. His detractors, however, though outvoted[5], have not been silenced. There are many critics, and some of great name, who contrive in the same breath to extol the poems and to decry the poet. The works they acknowledge, considered in themselves, may be classed among the noblest productions of the human mind. But they will not allow the author to rank with those great men who, born in the infancy of civilisation, supplied, by

1. *Sir* ne doit pas se traduire ici par *monsieur*. Il faut le conserver tel quel en français. Il s'emploie devant le *prénom* (suivi ou non du nom de famille) de ceux qui ont le titre de *baronet*. On dira donc *Sir Walter Scott* ou *Sir Walter*; mais à aucun prix *Sir Scott*.

2. *To*, jusqu'à.

3. Extrait de l'Essai sur *Milton*.

4. *The art* (sous-entendu : *of poetry*). — Traduisez : *cet art*. Si c'était l'art en général il ne faudrait pas *the*.

5. *Outvoted*, mis en minorité. — *To vote*, voter; *to outvote*, voter en plus grand nombre que, apporter un plus grand nombre de suffrages que,

their own powers[1], the want of instruction, and, though destitute of models themselves, bequeathed to posterity models which defy imitation. Milton, it is said, inherited what his predecessors created; he lived in an enlightened age; he received a finished education; and we must therefore, if we would form a just estimate of his powers, make large deductions in consideration of these advantages.

We venture to say, on the contrary, paradoxical as the remark may appear, that no poet has ever had to struggle with more unfavourable circumstances than Milton. He doubted, as he has himself owned, whether he had not been born "an age too late". For this notion Johnson has thought fit to make him the butt of much clumsy ridicule. The poet, we believe, understood the nature of his art better than the critic. He knew that his poetical genius derived no advantage from the civilisation which surrounded him, or from the learning which he had acquired; and he looked back with something like regret to the ruder age of simple words and vivid impressions.

We think that, as civilisation advances, poetry almost necessarily declines. Therefore, though we fervently admire those great works of imagination which have appeared in dark ages, we do not admire them the more because they have appeared in dark ages. On the contrary, we hold that the most wonderful and splendid proof of genius is a great poem produced in a civilised age. We cannot understand why those who believe in that most orthodox article of literary faith, that the earliest poets are generally the best, should wonder at the rule as if it were the exception. Surely the uniformity of the phænomenon indicates a corresponding uniformity in the cause.

The fact is, that common observers reason from the progress of the experimental sciences to[2] that of the

1. *Powers*, capacités.
2. *Reason from... to*, tirent 'du progrès... un argument en faveur de.

imitative arts. The improvement of the former is gradual and slow. Ages are spent in collecting[1] materials, ages more[2] in separating and combining them. Even when a system has been formed, there is still something to add, to alter, or to reject. Every generation enjoys the use of a vast hoard bequeathed to it by antiquity, and transmits that hoard, augmented by fresh acquisitions, to future ages. In these pursuits[3], therefore, the first speculators[4] lie under great disadvantages[5], and, even when they fail, are entitled to praise. Their pupils with far inferior intellectual powers, speedily surpass them in actual[6] attainments. Any intelligent man may now, by resolutely applying himself for a few years to mathematics, learn more than the great Newton knew after half a century of study and meditation.

But it is not thus with[7] music, with painting, or with sculpture. Still less is it thus with poetry. The progress of refinement rarely supplies these arts with better objects of imitation. It may indeed improve the instruments which are necessary to the mechanical operations of the musician, the sculptor, and the painter. But language, the machine of the poet, is best fitted for his purpose in its rudest state. Nations, like individuals, first perceive, and then abstract. They advance from particular images to general terms. Hence the vocabulary of an enlightened society is philosophical, that of a half-civilised people is poetical.

This change in the language of men is partly the cause and partly the effect of a corresponding change in the nature of their intellectual operations, of a change by which science gains and poetry loses. Generalisation is necessary to the advancement of knowledge; but part-

---

1. *In collecting*, à amasser.
2. *Ages more* (des siècles en plus), d'autres siècles.
3. *Pursuits*, recherches, études.
4. *Speculators*, penseurs, philosophes, savants.

5. *Lie under great disadvantages*, sont dans une situation très désavantageuse.
6. *Actual*, réels.
7. *It is not thus with*, il n'en est pas ainsi de.

icularity is indispensable to the creations of the imagination. In proportion as men know more and think more, they look less at individuals and more at classes. They therefore make better theories and worse poems. They give us vague phrases instead of images, and personified qualities instead of men. They may be better able to analyse human nature than their predecessors. But analysis is not the business of the poet. His office is to portray, not to dissect. He may believe in a moral sense, like Shaftesbury; he may refer all human actions to self-interest, like Helvetius, or he may never think about the matter at all. His creed on such subjects will no more influence his poetry, properly so called [1], than the notions which a painter may have conceived respecting the lacrymal glands, or the circulation of the blood, will affect the tears of his Niobe, or the blushes of his Aurora. If Shakespeare had written a book on the motives of human actions, it is by no means certain that it would have been a good one. It is extremely improbable that it would have contained half so much able reasoning on the subject as is to be found in the Fable of the Bees [2]. But could Mandeville have created an Iago? Well as he knew how [3] to resolve characters into [4] their elements, would he have been able to combine those elements in such a manner as to make up a man, a real, living, individual man?

Perhaps no person can be a poet, or can even enjoy poetry, without a certain unsoundness of mind, if any thing which gives so much pleasure ought to be called unsoundness. By poetry we mean not [5] all writing in verse, nor even all good writing in verse. Our definition excludes many metrical compositions which, on other grounds [6], deserve the highest praise. By poetry

----

1. *Properly so called*, proprement dite.

2. De Mandeville.

3. *Well as he knew how*, si bien qu'il sût.

4. *Resolve... into*, réduire, ramener... à.

5. *We mean not.* — Dans le style soutenu, certains verbes peuvent conjuguer sans *do* à la forme négative.

6. *On other grounds*, sous d'autres rapports.

we mean the art of employing words in such a manner as to produce an illusion on the imagination, the art of doing by means of words what the painter does by means of colours. Thus the greatest of poets has described it, in lines universally admired for the vigour and felicity of their diction[1], and still more valuable on account of the just notion which they convey of the art in which he excelled :

> " As[2] imagination bodies forth[3]
> The forms of things unknown[4] the poet's pen
> Turns them[5] to shapes[6], and gives to airy nothing
> A local habitation and a name[7]. "

These are the fruits of the " fine frenzy "[8] which he ascribes to the poet — a fine frenzy doubtless, but still a frenzy. Truth, indeed, is essential to poetry; but it is the truth of madness. The reasonings are just; but the premises are false. After the first suppositions have been made, every thing ought to be consistent; but those first suppositions require a degree of credulity which almost amounts to a partial and temporary derangement of the intellect. Hence[9] of all people children are the most imaginative. They abandon themselves without reserve to every illusion. Every image which is strongly presented to their mental eye[10] produces on them the effect of reality. No man, whatever his sensibility may be, is ever affected by Hamlet or Lear, as a little girl is affected by the story of poor Red Riding-hood. She knows that it is all false, that wolves cannot speak, that there are no wolves in England[11]. Yet in spite of her knowledge she believes :

1. *Dicton*, style.
2. *As*, de même que.
3. *Bodies forth*, donne un corps à.
4. *Things unknown ;* inversion poétique pour *unknown things.*
4. *Them*, ces choses inconnues.
6. *Shapes*, être réels.
7. Shakespeare, *Midsummer Night's Dream*, V, 1, 14-17.

8. The poet's eye, in a fine frenzy rolling,
Both glance from heaven to earth,
[from earth to heaven.
(Id., *Id.*, V, 1, 12.)

9. *Hence* (de là), aussi.
10. *Their mental eye.* — Voy. plus loin : *the eye of the mind.*
11. Il y a trois ou quatre siècles, les

she weeps; she trembles; she dares not go into a dark room lest she should feel the teeth of the monster at her throat. Such is the despotism of the imagination over uncultivated minds.

In a rude state of society men are children with a greater variety of ideas. It is therefore in such a state of society that we may expect to find the poetical temperament in its highest perfection. In an enlightened age there will be much intelligence, much science, much philosophy, abundance of just classification and subtle analysis, abundance of wit and eloquence, abundance of verses, and even of good ones; but little poetry. Men will judge and compare; but they will not create. They will talk about the old poets, and comment on them, and to a certain degree enjoy them. But they will scarcely be able to conceive the effect which poetry produced on their ruder ancestors, the agony[1], the ecstasy, the plenitude of belief. The Greek Rhapsodist[2], according to Plato, could scarce recite Homer without falling into convulsions. The Mohawk hardly feels the scalping knife while he shouts his death-song. The power which the ancient bards of Wales and Germany exercised over their auditors seems to modern readers almost miraculous. Such feelings are very rare in a civilised community[3], and most rare among those who participate most in its improvements. They linger longest among the peasantry.

Poetry produces an illusion on the eye of the mind, as a magic lantern produces an illusion on the eye of the body. And, as the magic lantern acts best in a dark room, poetry effects its purpose most completely in a dark age. As[4] the light of knowledge breaks in[5] upon its exhibitions[6], as the outlines of certainty become more and more definite, and the shades of probability more

---

loups ont été exterminés en Angleterre.

1. *Agony*, angoisses.
2. Voy. note 1, page 50.
3. *Community*, société.

4. *As*, à mesure que
5. *Breaks in* (entre en brisant, fait irruption dans); traduisez : vient éclairer.
6. *Its exhibitions*, les tableaux qu'elle déroule à nos yeux.

and more distinct, the hues and lineaments of the phantoms which the poet calls up grow fainter and fainter. We cannot unite the incompatible advantages of reality and deception, the clear discernment of truth and the exquisite enjoyment of fiction.

He who, in an enlightened and literary society, aspires to be a great poet, must first become a little child. He must take to pieces the whole web of his mind. He must unlearn much of that knowledge which has perhaps constituted hitherto his chief title to superiority. His very talents will be a hindrance to him. His difficulties will be proportioned to his proficiency in the pursuits which are fashionable among his contemporaries; and that proficiency will in general be proportioned to the vigour and activity of his mind. And it is well if[1], after all his sacrifices and exertions, his works do not resemble a lisping man or a modern ruin. We have seen in our own time great talents, intense labour, and long meditation, employed in this struggle against the spirit of the age, and employed, we will not say absolutely in vain, but with dubious success and feeble applause.

If these reasonings be just, no poet has ever triumphed over greater difficulties than Milton. He received a learned education : he was a profound and elegant classical scholar[2] : he had studied all the mysteries of Rabbinical literature[3] : he was intimately acquainted with every language of modern Europe from which either pleasure or information was then to be derived. He was perhaps the only great poet of later times[4] who has been distinguished by the excellence of his Latin verse.

1. *It is well if* (c'est bien si), heureux si.
2. *Classical scholar* (qui est versé dans les études classiques), lettré.
3. *Rabbinical literature*, la littérature rabbinique, c'est à-dire les ouvrages d'exégèse écrits par les rabbins depuis l'ère chrétienne.
4. *Later times* (les derniers temps), les temps modernes.

De la Correction en Poésie[1].

Wherein[2] especially does the poetry of our times differ from that of the last century? Ninety-nine persons out of a hundred would answer that the poetry of the last century was correct, but cold and mechanical, and that the poetry of our time, though wild and irregular, presented[3] far more vivid images, and excited the passions far more strongly than that of Parnell, of Addison, or of Pope. In the same manner we constantly hear it said, that the poets of the age[4] of Elizabeth had far more genius, but far less correctness, than those of the age of Anne. It seems to be taken for granted, that there is some incompatibility, some antithesis between correctness and creative power. We rather suspect that this notion arises merely from an abuse of words, and that it has been the parent[5] of many of the fallacies which perplex the science of criticism.

What is meant by correctness in poetry? If by correctness be[6] meant the conforming to rules which have their foundation in truth and in the principles of human nature, then correctness in only another name for excellence. If by correctness be meant the conforming to rules purely arbitrary, correctness may be another name for dulness and absurdity . . . .

Troilus and Cressida is perhaps of all the plays of Shakspeare that which is commonly considered as the most incorrect. Yet is seems to us infinitely more correct in the sound sense of the term, than what are called the most correct plays of the most correct dramatists. Compare it, for example, with the Iphigénie of Racine. We are sure that the Greeks of Shakspeare bear a far greater resemblance than the Greeks of Racine to the real

1. Extrait de l'Essai sur *Byron*.
2. *Wherein* = in what.
3. *Presented*. présente. En anglais c'est l'emploi du conditionnel *would answer* qui explique cet emploi de l'imparfait.
4. *Age*, siècle.
5. *Parent*, mère.
6. *Be*, subjonctif fréquemment employé après *if* et *whether* dans le style soutenu.

Greeks who besieged Troy; and for this reason, that the Greeks of Shakspeare are human beings, and the Greeks of Racine mere names, mere words printed in capitals at the head of paragraphs of declamation. Racine, it is true, would have shuddered at the thought of making a warrior at the siege of Troy quote Aristotle[1]. But of what use is it to avoid a single anachronism, when the whole play is one[2] anachronism, the sentiments and phrases of Versailles in the camp of Aulis? . . . . . .

... In what sense, then, is the word correctness used by those who say that Pope was the most correct of English Poets, and that next to Pope came the late Mr. Gifford? What is the nature and value of that correctness, the praise of which is denied to Macbeth, to Lear, and to Othello[3], and given to Hoole's translations and to all the Seatonian prize-poems? We can discover no eternal rule, no rule founded in reason and in the nature of things, which Shakspeare does not observe much more strictly than Pope. But if by correctness be meant the conforming to a narrow legislation which[4], while lenient to the *mala in se*[5], multiplies, whithout a shadow of a reason, the *mala prohibita*[6], if by correctness be meant a strict attention to certain ceremonious observances, which are no more essential to poetry than etiquette to good government, or than the washings[7] of a Pharisee to devotion, then, assuredly, Pope may be a more correct poet than Shakspeare. . . . .

It would be amusing to make a digest of the irrational laws which bad critics have framed for the government of poets. First in celebrity and in absurdity stand the dramatic unities of place and time. No human being has ever been able to find any thing that could, even by courtesy, be called an argument for these unities, except

---

1. *Hector.* — ... " Young men, whom Aristotle thought unfit to hear moral philosophy ". *Troilus and Cressida*, II, II, 166.

2. *One*, un vaste.

3. Trois des principaux drames de Shakespeare.

4. *While*, sous-entendu : *it is*.

5. *Mala in se*, (latin), choses mauvaises en soi.

6. *Mala prohibita*, choses mauvaises [parce qu'elles sont] défendues.

7. *Washings*, ablutions.

that they have been deduced from the general practice of the Greeks. It requires no very profound examination to discover that the Greek dramas, often admirable as compositions, are, as exhibitions[1] of human character and human life, far inferior to the English plays of the age of Elizabeth. Every scholar knows that the dramatic part of the Athenian tragedies was at first subordinate to the lyrical part. It would, therefore, have been little less than a miracle if the laws of the Athenian stage had been found to suit plays in which there was no chorus. All the greatest masterpieces of the dramatic art have been composed in direct violation of the unities, and could never have been composed if the unities had not been violated. It is clear, for example, that such a character as that of Hamlet could never have been developed within the limits to which Alfieri confined himself. Yet such was the reverence of literary men during the last century for these unities that Johnson who, much to his honour, took the opposite side, was, as he says, " frightened at his own temerity ", and " afraid to stand against the authorities which might be produced against him[2] ".

. . . .

The correctness which the last century prized so much resembles the correctness of those pictures of the garden of Eden which we see in old Bibles. We have an exact square, enclosed by the rivers Pison, Gihon, Hiddekel, and Euphrates[3], each with a convenient bridge in the centre, rectangular beds of flowers, a long canal, neatly bricked and railed in[4], the tree of knowledge, clipped like one of the limes behind the Tuileries, standing in the centre of the grand alley, the snake twined round it, the man on the right hand, the woman on the left, and the beasts drawn up in an exact circle round them. In

---

1. *Exhibitions*, peintures.

2. Voici les propres termes de Johnson :" *When I speak thus slightly of dramatic rules, I cannot but recollect how much wit and learning may be produced against me; before* such *authorities I am afraid to stand.*" (*Preface to Shakespeare.*)

3. Le Phison, le Gihon, le Chidékel et le Phrat sont les quatre fleuves du Paradis Terrestre.

4. *Railed in*, entouré de grilles.

one sense the picture is correct enough. That is to say, the squares are correct; the circles are correct; the man and the woman are in a most correct line with the tree; and the snake forms a most correct spiral.

But if there were[1] a painter so gifted that he could place on the canvas that glorious paradise, seen by the interior eye of him[2] whose outward sight had failed with[3] long watching and labouring for liberty and truth, if there were a painter who could set before us the mazes of the sapphire brook[4], the lake with its fringe of myrtles, the flowery meadows, the grottoes overhung by vines, the forests shining with Hesperian fruit and with the plumage of gorgeous birds, the massy shade of that nuptial bower which showered down roses on the sleeping lovers, what should we think of a connoisseur who should tell us that this painting, though finer than the absurd picture in the old Bible, was not so correct? Surely we should answer, It is both finer and more correct; and it is finer because it is more correct. It is not made up of correctly drawn diagrams; but it is a correct painting, a worthy representation of that which it is intended to represent.

It is not in the fine arts alone that this false correctness is prized by narrow-minded men, by men who cannot distinguish means from ends, or what is accidental from what his essential. M. Jourdain[5] admired correctness in fencing. " You had no business to hit me then. You must never thrust in quart till you have thrust in tierce[6] ". M. Tomès[7] liked correctness in

---

1. *Were*. pour *was*, subjonctif fréquemment employé après *if* dans le style soutenu.

2. Milton qui, devenu aveugle, composa son *Paradis perdu*.

3. *With*, à la suite de.

4. Dans ces passages, Macaulay fait allusion à une page splendide du quatrième livre du *Paradis perdu*.

5. Le *Bourgeois Gentilhomme* de Molière.

6. M. Jourdain explique à sa servante Nicole comment on fait des armes, et lui met un fleuret entre les mains.

M. JOURDAIN.

Là, pousse-moi un peu pour voir.

NICOLE.

Eh bien! quoi? (*N. pousse plusieurs bottes à M. Jourdain.*)

M. JOURDAIN.

Tout beau! Holà! ho! Doucement! Diantre soit la coquine!

NICOLE.

Vous me dites de pousser.

M. JOURDAIN.

Oui, mais tu me pousses en tierce avant que de pousser en quarte, et tu n'as pas la patience que je pare. (Acte III, sc. III.)

7. Médecin, personnage de la comédie de Molière *l'Amour médecin*.

medical practice. "I stand up for Artemius[1]. That he killed his patient is plain enough. But still he acted quite according to rule. A man dead is a man dead; and there is an end of the matter. But if rules are to be broken, there is no saying[2] what consequences may follow". We have heard of an old German officer who was a great admirer of correctness in military operations. He used to revile Bonaparte for spoiling the science of war, which had been carried to such exquisite perfection by Marshal Daun. "In my youth we used to march and countermarch all the summer without gaining or losing a square league, and then we went into winter quarters. And now comes an ignorant, hot-headed young man, who flies about from Boulogne to Ulm, and from Ulm to the middle of Moravia, and fights battles in December. The whole system of his tactics is monstrously incorrect". The world is of opinion, in spite of critics like these, that the end of fencing is to hit, that the end of medicine is to cure, that the end of war is to conquer, and that those means are the most correct which best accomplish the ends.

And has poetry no end, no eternal and immutable principles? . . . .

Since its first great masterpieces were produced, every thing that is changeable in this world has been changed. Civilisation has been gained, lost, gained again. Religions, and languages, and forms of government, and usages of private life, and modes of thinking, all have undergone a succession of revolutions. Every thing has passed away but the great features of nature, and the heart of man, and the miracles of that art of which it is the office to reflect back the heart of man and the features of nature. Those two strange old poems[3], the wonder of ninety generations, still retain all their freshness. They still command the veneration of

1. « Quel parti prenez-vous dans la querelle des deux médecins Théophraste et Artémius? — Moi, je suis pour Artémius. — Et moi aussi. » (Acte II, sc. III.)

2. *There is no saying*, il est impossible de dire.

3. L'*Iliade* et l'*Odyssée*.

minds enriched by the literature of many nations and ages. They are still, even in wretched translations, the delight of schoolboys. Having survived ten thousand capricious fashions, having seen successive codes of criticism become obsolete, they still remain to us, immortal with the immortality of truth, the same when perused[1] in the study of an English scholar, as when they were first chanted at the banquets of the Ionian princes.

Poetry is, as was said[2] more than two thousand years ago, imitation. It is an art analogous in many respects[3] to the art of painting, sculpture, and acting[4]. The imitations of the painter, the sculptor, and the actor, are, indeed, within certain limits, more perfect than those of the poet. The machinery[5] which the poet employs consists merely of words; and words cannot, even when employed by such an artist as Homer or Dante, present to the mind images of visible objects quite so lively and exact as those which we carry away from looking on[6] the works of the brush and the chisel. But, on the other hand, the range of poetry is infinitely wider than that of any other imitative art, or than that of all the other imitative arts together. The sculptor can imitate only form; the painter only form and colour; the actor, until the poet supplies him with words, only form, colour, and motion. Poetry holds the outer world in common with the other arts. The heart of man is the province of poetry, and of poetry alone. The painter, the sculptor, and the actor can exhibit no more of human passion and character than that small portion which overflows into the gesture and the face, always an imperfect, often a deceitful, sign of

1. *When perused* = when *they are* perused.

2. *As was said*, comme on l'a dit. *On*, c'est Aristote au début de sa Poétique.

3. *In many respects*, sous bien des rapports.

4. *Acting* (l'action de jouer la co-médie). Traduisez *the art of painting, sculpture, and acting*, l'art du peintre, du sculpteur et de l'acteur.

5. *Machinery*, instruments, matériaux.

6. *From looking on*, après avoir regardé, quand nous venons de regarder.

that which is within. The deeper and more complex parts of human nature can be exhibited by means of words alone. Thus the objects of the imitation of poetry are the whole external and the whole internal universe, the face of nature, the vicissitudes of fortune, man as he is in himself, man as he appears in society, all things which really exist, all things of which we can form an image in our minds by combining together parts of things which really exist. The domain of this imperial art is commensurate with the imaginative faculty.

An art essentially imitative ought not surely to be subjected to rules which tend to make its imitations less perfect than they otherwise would be; and those who obey such rules ought to be called, not correct, but incorrect artists.

Portraits et Caricatures [1].

There is, in one respect [2], a remarkable analogy between the faces and the minds of men. No two faces are [3] alike; and yet very few faces deviate very widely from the common standard [4]. Among the eighteen hundred thousand human beings [5] who inhabit London, there is not one who could be taken by his acquaintance for another; yet we may walk from Paddington to Mile End without seeing one person in whom any feature is so overcharged that we turn round to stare at it. An infinite number of varieties lies between limits which are not very far asunder. The specimens which pass those limits on either side, form a very small minority.

It is the same with the characters of men. Here, too, the variety passes all enumeration. But the cases in

1. Extrait de l'Essai sur *Madame d'Arblay*.
2. *In one respect*, sous un rapport.
3. *No two faces are*, il n'y a pas deux visages qui soient.

4. *Standard*, type.
5. C'était la population de Londres à l'époque (1843) où fut écrit cet *Essai*. Elle est aujourd'hui de plus de quatre millions.

which the deviation from the common standard is striking and grotesque, are very few. In one mind avarice
predominates; in another, pride; in a third, love of
pleasure; just as in one countenance the nose is the
most marked feature, while in others the chief expression lies in the brow, or in the lines of the mouth.
But there are very few countenances in which nose,
brow, and mouth do not contribute, though in unequal
degrees, to the general effect; and so there are very few
characters in which one overgrown propensity makes all
others utterly insignificant.

It is evident that a portrait painter, who was [1] able
only to represent faces and figures such as those which
we pay money to see at fairs, would not, however spirited [2] his execution might be, take rank among the
highest artists. He must always be placed below those
who have skill to seize peculiarities which do not amount
to deformity. The slighter those peculiarities [3], the
greater is the merit of the limner who can catch them
and transfer them to his canvass. To paint Daniel
Lambert or the living skeleton, the pig-faced lady or
the Siamese twins, so that nobody can mistake them,
is an exploit within the reach of a sign-painter. A third-
rate artist might give us the squint of Wilkes, and the
depressed nose and protuberant cheeks of Gibbon. It
would require a much higher degree of skill to paint two
such men as Mr. Canning and Sir Thomas Lawrence,
so that nobody who had ever seen them could for a moment hesitate to assign each picture to its original.
Here the mere caricaturist would be quite at fault. He
would find in neither face any thing on which he could
lay hold for the purpose of making a distinction. Two
ample bald foreheads, two regular profiles, two full faces
of the same oval form, would baffle his art; and he
would be reduced to the miserable shift of writing their
names at the foot of his picture. Yet there was a great

1. *Who was*, qui serait.
2. *Spirited*, vivante.
3. Sous-entendu : *are.*

difference; and a person who had seen them once would
no more have mistaken one of them for the other than
he would have mistaken Mr. Pitt for Mr. Fox. But the
difference lay in delicate lineaments and shades [1],
reserved for pencils of a rare order.

This distinction runs [2] through all the imitative arts.
Foote's mimicry was exquisitely ludicrous, but it was
all caricature. He could take off [3] only some strange
peculiarity, a stammer or a lisp, a Northumbrian burr [4]
or an Irish brogue [5], a stoop or a shuffle. "If a man",
said Johnson, " hops on one leg, Foote can hop on one
leg ". Garrick, on the other hand, could seize those
differences of manner and pronunciation, which, though
highly characteristic, are yet too slight to be described.
Foote, we have no doubt, could have made the Haymarket theatre [6] shake with laughter by imitating a
conversation between a Scotchman and a Somersetshireman. But Garrick could have imitated a conversation between two fashionable men, both models of the
best breeding, Lord Chesterfield, for example, and Lord
Albemarle, so that no person could doubt which was
which [7], although no person could say that, in any
point, either Lord Chesterfield or Lord Albemarle spoke
or moved otherwise than in conformity with the usages
of the best society.

The same distinction is found in the drama and in
fictitious narrative. Highest among those who have
exhibited human nature by means of dialogue, stands
Shakspeare. His variety is like the variety of nature,
endless iversity, scarcely any monstrosity. The characters of which he has given us an impression, as vivid
as that which we receive from the characters of our
own associates, are to be reckoned by scores. Yet in

1. *Shades*, nuances.

2. *Runs* (court, a cours), se re-
trouve.

3. *Take off*, imiter, singer.

4. *Northumbrian burr*, façon de
prononcer l'anglais particulière aux
habitants du comté de Northumberland.

5. *Irish brogue*, accent irlandais.

6. Dont Foote fut directeur de 1767
à 1776.

7. *Which was which*, lequel était C.
et lequel était A.

all these scores hardly one character is to be found which deviates widely from the common standard, and which we should call very eccentric if we met it in real life. The silly notion that every man has one ruling passion, and that this clue, once known, unravels all the mysteries of his conduct, finds no countenance in the plays of Shakspeare. There man appears as he is, made up of a crowd of passions, which contend for the mastery over him, and govern him in turn. What is Hamlet's ruling passion? Or Othello's? Or Harry the Fifth's? Or Wolsey's? Or Lear's? Or Shylock's? Or Benedick's? Or Macbeth's? Or that of Cassius? Or that of Falconbridge? But we might go on for ever. Take a single example, Shylock. Is he so eager for money as to be indifferent to revenge? Or so eager for revenge as to be indifferent to money? Or so bent on both together as to be indifferent to the honour of his nation and the law of Moses? All his propensities are mingled with each other, so that, in trying to apportion to each its proper part, we find the same difficulty which constantly meets us in real life. A superficial critic may say, that hatred is Shylock's ruling passion. But how many passions have amalgamated to form that hatred? It is partly the result of wounded pride : Antonio has called him dog. It is partly the result of covetousness : Antonio has hindered him of half a million; and, when Antonio is gone, there will be no limit to the gains of usury. It is partly the result of national and religious feeling : Antonio has spit on the Jewish gabardine; and the oath of revenge has been sworn by the Jewish Sabbath. We might go through all the characters which we have mentioned, and through fifty more in the same way; for it is the constant manner of Shakspeare to represent the human mind as lying, not under the absolute dominion of one despotic propensity, but under a mixed government, in which a hundred powers balance each other. Admirable as he was in all parts of his art, we most admire him for this, that while he has left us a greater number of striking portraits than all other dramatists put together, he has scarcely left us a single caricature.

A line[1] must be drawn, we conceive, between artists of this class, and those poets and novelists whose skill lies in the exhibiting[2] of what Ben Jonson called humours. The words of Ben are so much to the purpose that we will quote them :

> " When some one peculiar quality
> Doth so possess[3] a man, that it doth draw
> All his affects[4], his spirits, and his powers,
> In their confluxions[5] all to run one way[6],
> This may be truly said to be a humour[7]. "

There are undoubtedly persons, in whom humours such as Ben describes have attained a complete ascendency. . . . .

Seeing that such humours exist, we cannot deny that they are proper subjects for the imitations of art. But we conceive that the imitation of such humours, however skilful and amusing, is not an achievement of the highest order; and, as such humours are rare in real life, they ought, we conceive, to be sparingly introduced into works which profess to be pictures of real life. Nevertheless, a writer may show so much genius in the exhibition of these humours as to be fairly entitled to a distinguished and permanent rank among classics. The chief seats of all, however, the places on the dais[8] and under the canopy, are reserved for the few who have excelled in the difficult art of portraying characters in which no single feature is extravagantly overcharged.

1. *A line,* une ligne (de démarcation).

2. *Exhibiting*, peinture.

3. *Doth... possess* = does possess = possesses. De même *doth draw* = draws.

4. *Affects*, affections, dispositions.

5. *In their confluxions* (dans leurs unions), quand ils s'unissent, se mêlent.

6. *One way*, dans une seule et même direction.

7. Ce passage se trouve dans *Every Man Out of his Humour*, Introduction.

8. *Dais* s'emploie souvent dans le même sens que *canopy*. Ici *dais* désigne particulièrement l'estrade, et *canopy*, le ciel qui domine cette estrade.

TROISIÈME PARTIE

HISTOIRE, DROIT POLITIQUE, PHILOSOPHIE

L'Église et les Enthousiastes [1].

We will at present advert to one important part of the policy of the Church of Rome. She thoroughly understands, what no other church has ever understood, how to deal with enthusiasts. In some sects, particularly in infant [2] sects, enthusiasm is suffered to be rampant [3]. In other sects, particularly in sects long established and richly endowed, it is regarded with aversion. The Catholic Church neither submits to enthusiasm nor proscribes it, but uses it. She considers it as a great moving force which in itself, like the muscular power of a fine horse, is neither good nor evil, but which may be so directed as to [4] produce great good or great evil; and she assumes the direction to herself. It would be absurd to run down a horse like a wolf. It would be still more absurd to let him run wild, breaking fences, and trampling down passengers. The rational course is to subjugate his will without impairing his vigour, to teach him to obey the rein, and then to urge him to full speed. When once he knows his master, he is valuable in proportion to his strength and spirit. Just such [5] has been the system of the Church of Rome with regard to enthusiasts. She knows

---

1. Extrait de l'Essai sur *Ranke's History of the Popes.*

2. *Infant*, toutes jeunes, qui viennent de naître.

3. *Rampant*, terme de blason, « se dit, en général, de tous les animaux représentés debout et s'élevant comme le long d'une rampe. » LITTRÉ. — Au figuré, il a pris le sens de déchainé, sans frein.

4. *So... as to*, de façon à.

5. *Just such* (exactement tel), tel exactement.

that, when religious feelings have obtained the complete
empire of the mind, they impart a strange energy, that
they raise men above the dominion of pain and pleasure,
that obloquy becomes glory, that death itself is con-
templated only as the beginning of a higher and happier
life. She knows that a person in this state is no object
of contempt. He may be vulgar, ignorant, visionary,
extravagant; but he will do and suffer things which it is
for her interest that somebody should do and suffer, yet
from which calm and sober-minded men would shrink.
She accordingly enlists him in her service, assigns to
him some forlorn hope[1], in which intrepidity and impe-
tuosity are more wanted than judgment and self-command, and sends him forth with her benedictions and
her applause.

In England it not unfrequently happens that a tinker[2]
or coal-heaver hears a sermon or falls in with[3] a tract[4]
which alarms him about the state of his soul. If he be[5]
a man of excitable nerves and strong imagination, he
thinks himself given over to the Evil Power. He doubts
whether he has not committed the unpardonable sin[6].
He imputes every wild fancy that springs up in his
mind to the whisper of a fiend. His sleep is broken by
dreams of the great judgment-seat, the open books,
and the unquenchable fire[7]. If, in order to escape from
these vexing thoughts, he flies to amusement or to licentious indulgence[8], the delusive relief only makes his
misery darker and more hopeless. At length a turn

1. *Forlorn hope.* — Sens ordinaire :
troupe abandonnée (*hope*, qu'il ne
faut pas confondre avec *hope*, espoir,
vient de *hoop*, mot hollandais qui signifie *troupe*), détachement de soldats
désignés pour un service où la mort
est à peu près certaine. — Ici *forlorn
hope* est pris dans le sens de *mission
très périlleuse.*
2. Voy. le morceau intitulé *Bunyan.*
3. *Falls in with*, rencontre.
4. *A tract*, une brochure religieuse.
5. Voy. note 1, page 99.
6. Voy. note 4, page 77.

7. Allusions bibliques : " *And I
saw a great white throne, and him
that sat on it, from whose face the
earth and the heaven fled away...
And I saw the dead... stand before
God; and the books were opened,
... and the dead were judged out of
those things which were written in the
books, according to their works...* "
REVELATION (*Apocalypse* XX, 11, 12).
— " *He will burn up the chaff with
unquenchable fire.* " ST MATTHEW,
III, 12.
8. *Indulgence*, plaisirs.

takes place. He is reconciled to his offended Maker[1]. To borrow the fine imagery of one[2] who had himself been thus tried, he emerges from the Valley of the Shadow of Death[3], from the dark land of gins and snares, of quagmires and precipices, of evil spirits, and ravenous beasts. The sunshine is on his path. He ascends the Delectable Mountains[4], and catches from their summit a distant view of the shining city which is the end of his pilgrimage. Then arises in his mind a natural and surely not a censurable desire, to impart to others the thoughts of which his own heart is full, to warn the careless, to comfort those who are troubled in spirit. The impulse which urges him to devote his whole life to the teaching of religion is a strong passion in the guise of a duty. He exhorts his neighbours; and, if he be a man of strong parts[5], he often does so with great effect. He pleads as if he were pleading for his life, with tears, and pathetic gestures, and burning words; and he soon finds with delight, not perhaps wholly unmixed with the alloy of human infirmity, that his rude eloquence rouses and melts hearers who sleep very composedly while the rector[6] preaches on the apostolical succession. Zeal for God, love for his fellow-creatures, pleasure in the exercise of his newly-discovered powers, impel him to become a preacher. He has no quarrel with the establishment[7], no objection to its formularies, its government, or its vestments. He would gladly be admitted among its humblest ministers. But, admitted or rejected, he feels that his vocation is determined. His orders[8] have come down to him, not through a long and doubtful series of Arian and Papist bishops, but direct from on high[9]. His commission is the same that on the Mountain of Ascen-

---

1. *Maker*, Créateur.
2. Bunyan.
3. Voy. page 78.
4. Décrites dans *The Pilgrim's Progress*.
5. *Parts*, capacités.

6. *Rector*, pasteur.
7. *The establishment*, l'Eglise établie, l'Eglise officielle.
8. *Orders*, ordres, au sens religieux du mot.
9. *From on high* (d'en haut), du ciel.

sion was given to the Eleven[1]. Nor will he[2], for lack of human credentials, spare to deliver the glorious message with which he is charged by the true Head of the Church. For a man thus minded, there is within the pale of the establishment no place. He has been at no college[3] he cannot construe a Greek author or write a Latin theme[4]; and he is told that, if he remains in the communion of the Church, he must do so as a hearer, and that, if he is resolved to be a teacher, he must begin by being a schismatic. His choice is soon made. He harangues on Tower Hill or in Smithfield. A congregation[5] is formed. A license is obtained. A plain brick building, with a desk and benches, is run up, and named Ebenezer[6] or Bethel[7]. In a few weeks the Church has lost for ever a hundred families, not one of which entertained the least scruple about her articles[8], her liturgy, her government, or her ceremonies.

Far different is the policy of Rome. The ignorant enthusiast whom the Anglican Church makes an enemy, and, whatever the polite and learned may think, a most dangerous enemy, the Catholic Church makes a champion. She bids him nurse[9] his beard, covers him with a gown and hood of coarse dark stuff, ties a rope round his waist, and sends him forth to teach in her name.

---

1. "*He appeared unto the eleven as they sat at meat... And he said unto them, Go ye into all the world, and preach the gospel to every creature.*" St Mark, xvi, 14, 15.

2. *Nor will he* = and *he will* not.

3. *College.* — Les deux universités d'Oxford et de Cambridge sont composées chacune d'un certain nombre d'établissements appelés *colleges*. Ce nom ne s'applique pas, comme chez nous, aux établissements d'enseignement secondaire ; on les appelle *schools* ou *grammar-schools*.

4. *Theme*, dissertation.

5. *Congregation*, assemblée de fidèles.

6. *Ebenezer* (en hébreu : pierre de secours), par allusion à la pierre commémorative élevée par Samuel à la suite d'une victoire sur les Philistins. (1. Samuel, VII, 12.)

7. *Bethel* (en hébreu : maison de Dieu); allusion à la pierre de Béthel sur laquelle Jacob s'endormit et qu'il dressa ensuite en souvenir de la vision qu'il eut pendant son sommeil. (Genèse, xxviii.)

8. Les trente-neuf articles qui constituent le credo de l'Église anglicane, et dont voici le titre exact dans le *Prayer-Book : " Articles agreed upon by the Archbishops and Bishops of both provinces and the whole Clergy, in the Convocation holden at London in the year* 1562, *for the avoiding of Diversities of Opinion, and for the Establishing of Consent touching true Religion.*"

9. *Nurse* (nourrir, soigner), laisser pousser.

He costs her nothing. He takes not a ducat away from the revenues of her beneficed[1] clergy. He lives by the alms of those who respect his spiritual character, and are grateful for his instructions. He preaches, not exactly in the style of Massillon, but in a way which moves the passions of uneducated hearers ; and all his influence is employed to strengthen the Church of which he is a minister. To that Church he becomes as strongly attached as any of the cardinals whose scarlet carriages and liveries crowd the entrance of the palace on the Quirinal[2]. . . . .

Even for female agency[3] there is a place in her system. To devout women she assigns spiritual functions, dignities, and magistracies. In our country, if a noble lady is moved by more than ordinary zeal for the propagation of religion, the chance is that[4], though she may disapprove of no one doctrine[5] or ceremony of the Established Church, she will end by giving her name to a new schism. If a pious and benevolent woman enters the cells of a prison to pray with the most unhappy and degraded of her own sex, she does so without any authority from the Church. No line of action is traced out for her; and it is well if the Ordinary does not complain of her intrusion, and if the Bishop does not shake his head at such irregular benevolence.

L'Histoire d'Angleterre[6].

The history of England is emphatically[7] the history of progress. It is the history of a constant movement

---

1. *Beneficed*, possesseur de bénéfices.

2. *The palace on the Quirinal* (le palais [situé] sur le [mont] Quirinal), le palais du Quirinal, qui était, à l'époque où écrivait Macaulay, la résidence d'été des papes. Il est aujourd'hui habité par le roi d'Italie.

3. *Female agency*, activité féminine.

4. *The chance is that*, il y a des chances pour que.

5. *No one doctrine*, aucune doctrine en particulier.

6. Extrait de l'Essai sur *Sir James Mackintosh*.

7. *Emphatically*, dans toute la force du terme, par excellence.

of the public mind, of a constant change in the institutions of a great society. We see that society, at the beginning of the twelfth century, in a state more miserable than the state in which the most degraded nations of the East now are. We see it subjected to the tyranny of a handful of armed foreigners[1]. We see a strong distinction of caste separating the victorious Norman from the vanquished Saxon. We see the great body of the population in a state of personal slavery. We see the most debasing and cruel superstition exercising boundless dominion over the most elevated and benevolent minds. We see the multitude sunk in brutal ignorance, and the studious few engaged in acquiring what did not deserve the name of knowledge. In the course of seven centuries the wretched and degraded race have become the greatest and most highly civilised people that ever the world saw, have spread their dominion over every quarter of the globe, have scattered the seeds of mighty empires and republics over vast continents of which no dim intimation had ever reached Ptolemy or Strabo, have created a maritime power which would annihilate in a quarter of an hour the navies of Tyre, Athens, Carthage, Venice, and Genoa together, have carried the science of healing, the means of locomotion and correspondence, every mechanical art, every manufacture, every thing that promotes the convenience of life, to a perfection which our ancestors would have thought magical, have produced a literature which may boast of works not inferior to the noblest which Greece has bequeathed to us, have discovered the laws which regulate the motions of the heavenly bodies, have speculated with exquisite subtilty on the operations of the human mind, have been the acknowledged leaders of the human race in the career of political improvement. The history of England is the history of this great change in the moral, intellec-

___

1. Les Normands qui firent la conquête de l'Angleterre en 1066.

tual, and physical state of the inhabitants of our own island. There is much amusing and instructive episodical matter; but this is the main action. . . . .
. . . .

We said that the history of England is the history of progress; and, when we take a comprehensive view of it, it is so. But when examined in small separate portions, it may with more propriety be called a history of actions and re-actions. We have often thought that the motion of the public mind in our country resembles that of the sea when the tide is rising. Each successive wave rushes forward, breaks, and rolls back; but the great flood is steadly coming in [1]. A person who looked [2] on the waters only for a moment might fancy that they were retiring [3]. A person who looked on them only for five minutes might fancy that they were rushing capriciously to and fro. But when he keeps his eye on them for a quarter of an hour, and sees one seamark [4] disappear after another, it is impossible for him to doubt of the general direction in which the ocean is moved. Just such [5] has been the course of events in England. In the history of the national mind, which is, in truth, the history of the nation, we must carefully distinguish between that recoil which regularly follows every advance and a great general ebb. If we take short intervals, if we compare 1640 [6] and 1660 [7], 1680 [8] and 1685 [9], we find a retrogression. But if we take centuries, if, for example, we compare 1794 [10] with 1660 or

---

1. *Is... coming in*, monte.
2. *Looked*, regarderait.
3. *They were retiring*, elles se retirent.
4. *Sea-mark* désigne ordinairement tout objet élevé situé sur la côte et servant de guide aux marins. Ici Macaulay l'applique particulièrement aux objets qui se trouvent à découvert à marée basse.
5. *Just such* (exactement tel), tel exactement.
6. 1640 est l'année où se réunit le Long Parlement qui détrôna Charles Ier.

7. 1660, date de la Restauration de la monarchie en Angleterre.

8. 1680 fut une année de grande agitation politique.

9. En 1685 le trône se trouva occupé par Jacques II, dont les projets tyranniques provoquèrent la Révolution de 1688.

10. En 1794 l'*Habeas Corpus Act* fut suspendu. Cette loi ordonne que tout individu accusé de crime ne sera mis en prison qu'après avoir comparu devant un magistrat, qui décide s'il y a lieu ou non de poursuivre.

with 1685, we cannot doubt in which direction society
is proceeding.

———

Les Bienfaits et les Maux de la Liberté [1].

Many evils, no doubt, were produced by the civil war [2].
They were the price of our liberty. Has the acquisition
been worth the sacrifice? It is the nature of the Devil
of tyranny to tear and rend the body which he leaves.
Are the miseries of continued possession less horrible
than the struggles of the tremendous exorcism?

If it were possible that a people brought up under an
intolerant and arbitrary system could subvert that system without acts of cruelty and folly, half the objections
to despotic power would be removed. We should, in
that case, be compelled to acknowledge that it at least
produces no pernicious effects on the intellectual and
moral character of a nation. We deplore the outrages
which accompany revolutions. But the more violent
the outrages [3], the more assured we feel that a revolution was necessary. The violence of those outrages will
always be proportioned to the ferocity and ignorance of
the people ; and the ferocity and ignorance of the people
will be proportioned to the oppression and degradation
under which they have been accustomed to live. Thus
it was in our civil war. The heads of the church and
state reaped only that which they had sown. The government had prohibited free discussion : it had done its best
to keep the people unacquainted with [4] their duties and
their rights. The retribution was just and natural. If
our rulers suffered from popular ignorance, it was because
they had themselves taken away the key of knowledge.
If they were assailed with blind fury, it was because they
had exacted an equally blind submission.

1. Extrait de l'Essai sur *Milton*.
2. La guerre civile qui se termina
en 1649 par l'exécution de Charles Ier.
3. Sous-entendu : *are*.
4. *Unacquainted with* (non infor-
més de), dans l'ignorance de.

It is the character of such revolutions that we always
see the worst of them at first.   Till men have been some
time free, they know not [1] how to use their freedom.
The natives of wine countries are generally sober.   In
climates where wine is a rarity intemperance abounds.
A newly liberated people may be compared to a northern
army encamped on the Rhine or the Xeres.   It is said
that, when soldiers in such a situation first find themselves able to indulge without restraint in such a rare
and expensive luxury [2], nothing is to be seen but intoxi-
cation.   Soon, however, plenty, teaches discretion; and,
after wine has been for a few months their daily fare,
they become more temperate than they had ever been in
their own country.   In the same manner, the final and
permanent fruits of liberty are wisdom, moderation, and
mercy.   Its immediate effects are often atrocious crimes,
conflicting errors, scepticism on points the most clear,
dogmatism on points the most mysterious.   It is just at
this crisis that its enemies love to exhibit it.   They pull
down the scaffolding from the half-finished edifice : they
point to the flying dust, the falling brick, the comfortless
rooms, the frightful irregularity of the whole appearance;
and then ask in scorn where the promised splendour and
comfort is to be found.   If such miserable sophisms were
to prevail, there would never be a good house or a good
government in the world.

   Ariosto tells a pretty story of a fairy, who, by some
mysterious law of her nature, was condemned to appear
at certain seasons in the form of a foul and poisonous
snake.   Those who injured her during the period of her
disguise were for ever excluded from participation in the
blessings which she bestowed.   But to those who, in
spite of her loathsome aspect, pitied and protected her,
she afterwards revealed herself in the beautiful and ce-
lestial form which was natural to her, accompanied their

1. *They know not*, pour *they do not
know*, tournure ancienne usitée en
poésie, ou en prose dans le style soutenu.

2. *Luxury*. Le sens général est *luxe;*
il se dit aussi d'un mets délicieux et
coûteux ou rare.

steps, granted all their wishes, filled their houses with wealth, made them happy in love and victorious in war. Such a spirit is Liberty. At times she takes the form of a hateful reptile. She grovels, she hisses, the stings. But woe to those who in disgust shall venture to crush her! And happy are those who, having dared to receive her in her degraded and frightful shape, shall at length be rewarded by her in the time of her beauty and her glory!

There is only one cure for the evils which newly-acquired freedom produces; and that cure is freedom. When a prisoner first leaves his cell, he cannot bear the light of day: he is unable to discriminate colours, or recognise faces. But the remedy is, not to remand[1] him into his dungeon, but to accustom him to the rays of the sun. The blaze of truth and liberty may at first dazzle and bewilder nations which have become half blind in the house of bondage. But let them gaze on, and they will soon be able to bear it. In a few years men learn to reason. The extreme violence of opinions subsides. Hostile theories correct each other. The scattered elements of truth cease to contend, and begin to coalesce. And at length a system of justice and order is educed out of the chaos.

Many politicians of our time are in the habit of laying it down as a self-evident proposition, that no people ought to be free till they are fit to use their freedom. The maxim is worthy of the fool in the old story, who resolved not to go into the water till he had learnt to swim. If men are to wait for liberty till they become wise and good in slavery, they may indeed wait for ever.

1. *Remand* (terme de la langue du palais), renvoyer.

La Corruption et les Puritains [1].

It must, indeed, be acknowledged, in justice to the writers of whom we have spoken thus severely [2], that they were, to a great extent [3], the creatures of their age [4]. And if it be [5] asked why that age encouraged immorality which no other age would have tolerated, we have no hesitation in answering that this great depravation of the national taste was the effect of the prevalence of Puritanism under the Commonwealth [6].

To punish public outrages on morals and religion is unquestionably within the competence of rulers. But when a government, not content with requiring decency, requires sanctity, it oversteps the bounds which mark its proper functions. And it may be laid down as an universal rule that a government which attempts more than it ought will perform less. A lawgiver who, in order to protect distressed borrowers, limits the rate of interest, either makes it impossible for the objects of his care to borrow at all, or places them at the mercy of the worst class of usurers. A lawgiver who, from tenderness for labouring men, fixes the hours of their work and the amount of their wages, is certain to make them far more wretched than he found them. And so a government which, not content with repressing scandalous excesses, demands from its subjects fervent and austere piety, will soon discover that, while attempting to render an impossible service to the cause of virtue, it has in truth only promoted vice.

For what are the means by which a government can effect its ends? Two only, reward and punishment; powerful means, indeed, for influencing the exterior act,

---

1. Extrait de l'Essai sur *The Comic Dramatists of the Restoration*.

2. Les auteurs dramatiques de la fin du dix-septième siècle.

3. *To a great extent*, dans une grande mesure.

4. *Age*, siècle, temps.

5. Voy. note 1, page 99.

6. *The Commonwealth* (la République), nom donné au gouvernement de l'Angleterre de 1649 à 1660.

but altogether impotent for the purpose of touching the
heart. A public functionary who is told that he will be
promoted if he is a devout Catholic, and turned out of
his place if he is not, will probably go to mass every
morning, exclude meat from his table on Fridays, shrive
himself regularly, and perhaps let his superiors know
that he wears a hair shirt next his skin. Under a Puritan government, a person who is apprised that piety is
essential to thriving in the world will be strict in the
observance of the Sunday, or, as he will call it, Sabbath[1],
and will avoid a theatre as if it were plague-stricken.
Such a show of religion as this the hope of gain and the
fear of loss will produce, at a week's notice[2], in any abundance which a government may require. But under this
show, sensuality, ambition, avarice, and hatred retain
unimpaired power, and the seeming convert has only added to the vices of a man of the world all the still darker
vices which are engendered by the constant practice of
dissimulation. The truth cannot be long concealed. The
public discovers that the grave persons who are proposed
to it as patterns are more utterly destitute of moral principle and of moral sensibility than avowed libertines. It
sees that these Pharisees are farther removed from real
goodness than publicans[3] and harlots. And, as usual, it
rushes to the extreme opposite to that which it quits. It
considers a high religious profession[4] as a sure mark of
meanness and depravity. On the very first day on
which the restraint of fear is taken away, and on which
men can venture to say what they think, a frightful peal
of blasphemy and ribaldry proclaims that the short-

1. Cet emploi du mot *Sabbath* au lieu de *Sunday* est un exemple de la préférence marquée des Puritains pour les noms et pour l'esprit de l'Ancien Testament. — Voy. note 6, page 64.

2. *At a week's notice* (à huit jours d'avis), en huit jours de temps, au bout de huit jours.

3. Allusion biblique : "*And when the scribes and Pharisees saw him eat with publicams and sinners, they said unto his disciples, How is it that he eateth and drinketh with publicans and sinners?*" ST MARK, II, 16. — *Publicans* est pris ici au sens biblique de *publicains*, collecteurs des impôts. En anglais moderne il signifie *cabaretier*.

4. *A high religious profession*, la profession de grands sentiments religieux (*profession* au sens de : déclaration publique).

sighted policy which aimed at making a nation of saints has made a nation of scoffers.

It was thus in France about the beginning of the eighteenth century. Louis the Fourteenth in his old age became religious : he determined that his subjects should be religious too : he shrugged his shoulders and knitted his brows if he observed at his levee or near his dinner-table any gentleman who neglected the duties enjoined by the church, and rewarded piety with blue ribands[1], invitations to Marli, governments, pensions, and regiments. Forthwith Versailles became, in every thing but dress, a convent. The pulpits and confessionals were surrounded by swords and embroidery. The Marshals of France were much in prayer ; and there was hardly one among the Dukes and Peers who did not carry good little books in his pocket, fast during Lent, and communicate at Easter. Madame de Maintenon, who had a great share in the blessed work, boasted that devotion had become quite the fashion. A fashion indeed it was ; and like a fashion it passed away. No sooner had the old king been carried to St. Denis than the whole court unmasked. Every man hastened to indemnify himself, by the excess of licentiousness and impudence, for years of mortification. The same persons who, a few months before, with meek voices and demure looks, had consulted divines about the state of their souls, now surrounded the midnight table where, amidst the bounding of champagne corks, a drunken prince, hiccoughed out atheistical arguments and obscene jests. The early part of the reign of Louis the Fourteenth had been a time of license ; but the most dissolute men of that generation would have blushed at the orgies of the Regency.

It was the same with our fathers in the time of the Great Civil War[2]. We are by no means unmindful of the great debt which mankind owes to the Puritans of that time, the deliverers of England, the founders of the

1. Le ruban bleu de l'Ordre du Saint-Esprit, institué par Henri III.   2. 1642-1649.

American Commonwealths[1]. But in the day of their power, those men committed one great fault, which left deep and lasting traces in the national character and manners. They mistook the end and overrated the force of government. They determined, not merely to protect religion and public morals from insult, an object for which the civil sword, in discreet hands, may be beneficially employed, but to make the people committed to their rule truly devout. Yet, if they had only reflected on events which they had themselves witnessed and in which they had themselves borne a great part, they would have seen what was likely to be the result of their enterprise. They had lived under a government which, during a long course of years, did all that could be done, by lavish bounty and by rigorous punishment, to enforce conformity to the doctrine and discipline of the Church of England. No person suspected of hostility to that church had the smallest chance of obtaining favour at the court of Charles[2]. Avowed dissent was punished by imprisonment, by ignominious exposure[3], by cruel mutilations[4], and by ruinous fines. And the event had been that the Church had fallen; and had, in its fall, dragged down with it a monarchy which had stood six hundred years. The Puritan might have learned, if from nothing else, yet from his own recent victory, that governments which attempt things beyond their reach are likely not merely to fail, but to produce an effect directly the opposite of that which they contemplate as desirable.

All this was overlooked. The saints were to inherit the earth[5]. The theatres were closed. The fine arts were

---

1. En 1620, une petite troupe de Puritains anglais (exilés en Hollande sous le règne d'Elisabeth), s'embarquèrent pour le Nouveau Monde, où ils fondèrent la colonie de Massachusetts. Leur exemple fut bientôt suivi par une foule de leurs coreligionnaires.

2. Charles Ier.

3. Macaulay veut parler du pilori, poteau auquel on attachait certains condamnés sur la place publique où ils étaient exposés aux insultes de la populace. Le pilori fut aboli en France en 1789 et en Angleterre en 1837.

4. Une des plus fréquentes consistait à couper les oreilles du condamné.

5. Allusion biblique : " *What man is he that feareth the Lord?... His seed shall inherit the earth.* " Psalms, xxv.

placed under absurd restraints. Vices which had never before been even misdemeanours [1] were made capital felonies [2]. It was solemnly resolved by Parliament "that no person shall be employed but such as the House shall be satisfied of his real godliness." The pious assembly had a Bible lying on the table for reference [3]. If they had consulted it they might have learned that the wheat and the tares [4] grow together inseparably, and must either be spared together or rooted up together. To know whether a man was really godly was impossible. But it was easy to know whether he had a plain dress, lank hair, no starch in his linen, no gay furniture in his house; whether he talked through his nose, and showed the whites of his eyes; whether he named his children Assurance [5], Tribulation, and Maher-shalal-hash-baz; whether he avoided Spring Garden [6] when in town [7] and abstained from hunting and hawking when in the country; whether he expounded hard scriptures [8] to his troop of dragoons, and talked in a committee of ways and means [9] about seeking the Lord [10]. These were tests which could easily be applied. The misfortune was that they were tests which proved nothing. Such as they were, they were employed by the dominant party. And the consequence was that a crowd of impostors, in every walk of life [11], began to mimic and to caricature what were then regarded as the outward signs of sanctity. The nation was not duped. The

1. *Misdemeanours*, des délits.

2. *Capital felonies*, crimes punis de mort.

3. *For reference*, pour consulter.

4. Allusion biblique : "... *A man sowed good seed in his field ... His enemy came and sowed tares among the wheat... When the blade was sprung up, and brought forth fruit, then appeared the tares also... So the servants of the householder came and said... Will thou that we go and gather them up? But he said, Nay; lest while ye gather up the tares, ye root up also the wheat with them.*" ST MATTHEW, XIII.

5. *Assurance*, c'est-à-dire *Assurance of Salvation*, certitude du salut. Voy. note 5, page 64.

6. Sorte de jardin-restaurant, situé dans St-James's Park. C'était le rendez-vous de la société élégante du dix-septième siècle.

7. *In town*, en ville, c'est-à-dire à Londres.

8. *Hard scriptures*, des passages difficiles de l'Écriture.

9. *Committee of ways and means* (comité des voies et moyens), se dit de la Chambre des Communes réunie en comité général pour examiner la façon dont on pourra se procurer les sommes inscrites au budget.

10. Expression biblique.

11. *Walk of life*, rang, condition.

restraints of that gloomy time were such as would have been impatiently borne, if imposed by men who were universally believed to be saints. Those restraints became altogether insupportable when they were known to be kept up for the profit of hypocrites. It is quite certain that, even if the royal family had never returned, even if Richard Cromwell or Henry Cromwell [1] had been at the head of the administration, there would have been a great relaxation of manners. Before the Restoration [2] many signs indicated that a period of license was at hand. The Restoration crushed for a time the Puritan party, and placed supreme power in the hands of a libertine [3]. The political counter-revolution assisted the moral counter-revolution, and was in turn assisted by it. A period of wild and desperate [4] dissoluteness followed. Even in remote manor-houses and hamlets the change was in some degree felt; but in London the outbreak of debauchery was appalling; and in London the places most deeply infected were the Palace [5], the quarters inhabited by the aristocracy, and the Inns of Court [6]. It was on the support of these parts of the town that the play-houses depended. The character of the drama became conformed to the character of its patrons. The comic poet was the mouthpiece of the most deeply corrupted part of a corrupted society. And in the plays before us we find, distilled and condensed, the essential spirit of the fashionable world during the Anti-puritan reaction.

The Puritan had affected formality; the comic poet laughed at decorum. The Puritan had frowned at innocent diversions; the comic poet took under his patronage the most flagitious excesses. The Puritan had canted [7], the comic poet blasphemed. The Puritan had made an affair

---

1. Fils d'Olivier Cromwell.
2. 1660.
3. Charles II.
4. *Desperate*, effrénée.
5. C'est-à-dire *the Palace of Whitehall*.
6. *The Inns of Court.* — On donne ce nom à quatre sociétés (*the Inner Temple, the Middle Temple, Lincoln's Inn* et *Gray's Inn*) dont l'union forme la corporation des avocats, qui a le privilège de se recruter elle-même. — Le sens ordinaire du mot *inn* est *auberge;* mais il a eu longtemps le sens de : habitation. hôtel, collège.
7. *Canted*, affecté un langage pieux.

of gallantry felony without benefit of clergy [1]; the comic poet represented it as an honourable distinction. The Puritan spoke with disdain of the low standard of popular morality; his life was regulated by a far more rigid code; his virtue was sustained by motives unknown to men of the world. Unhappily it had been amply proved in many cases, and might well be suspected in many more, that these high pretensions were unfounded. Accordingly, the fashionable circles, and the comic poets who were the spokesmen of those circles, took up [2] the notion that all professions of piety and integrity were to be construed by the rule of contrary [3]; that it might well be doubted whether there was such a thing as virtue in the world; but that, at all events, a person who affected to be better than his neighbours was sure to be [4] a knave.

Machiavel [5].

We doubt whether any name in literary history be so generally odious as that of the man whose character and writings we now propose to consider. The terms in which he is commonly described would seem to import that he was the Tempter, the Evil Principle, the discoverer of ambition and revenge, the original inventor of perjury, and that, before the publication of his fatal Prince [6], there had never been a hypocrite, a tyrant, or a traitor, a simulated virtue, or a convenient crime. One writer gravely assures us that Maurice of Saxony learned all his fraudulent policy from that execrable volume.

. 1. *Benefit of clergy*, bénéfice de clergie, « privilège établi autrefois en faveur de certains criminels, dans le cas où ils possédaient les premiers éléments des lettres... En Angleterre, usage (aboli en 1827) suivant lequel un meurtrier, dans les cas graciables, est sauvé du dernier supplice, lorsqu'il peut lire quelques lignes de vieux caractères saxons. » LITTRÉ.

2. *Took up*, adoptèrent.

3. *By the rule of contrary* (par la règle du contraire), en en prenant le contre-pied.

4. *Was sure to be*, était certainement.

5. Extrait de l'Essai sur *Machiavel*.

6. L'ouvrage le plus important et le plus connu de Machiavel est intitulé *Il Principe*, le Prince.

Another remarks that since it was translated into Turkish, the Sultans have been more addicted than formerly to the custom of strangling their brothers. Lord Lyttelton charges the poor Florentine with the manifold treasons of the house of Guise, and with the massacre of St. Bartholomew. Several authors have hinted that the Gunpowder Plot [1] is to be primarily attributed to his doctrine, and seem to think that his effigy ought to be substituted for that of Guy Faux, in those processions by which the ingenuous youth of England annually commemorate the preservation of the Three Estates [2]. The Church of Rome has pronounced his works accursed things. Nor have our own countrymen been backward in testifying their opinion of his merits. Out of his surname [3] they have coined an epithet for a knave, and out of his Christian name a synonyme for the Devil [4].

It is indeed scarcely possible for any person, not well acquainted with the history and literature of Italy, to read without horror and amazement the celebrated treatise which has brought so much obloquy on the name of Machiavelli. Such a display of wickedness, naked yet not ashamed, such cool, judicious, scientific atrocity, seemed rather to belong to a fiend than to the most depraved of men. Principles which the most hardened ruffian would scarcely hint to his most trusted accomplice, or avow, without the disguise of some palliating sophism, even to his own mind, are professed without the slightest circumlocution, and assumed as the fundamental axioms of all political science.

It is not strange that ordinary readers should regard the author of such a book as the most depraved and

---

1. *The Gunpowder Plot*, le Complot des Poudres. Le 5 novembre 1605, un certain nombre de catholiques avaient, en plaçant des barils de poudre dans les caves du palais du Parlement, formé le projet de faire sauter le roi, la Chambre des Lords et la Chambre des Communes. On fut averti à temps du complot.

2. *The Three Estates*, c'est-à-dire le roi, les Lords et les Communes.

3. *Surname*, nom de famille.

4. *Old Nick* (le vieux Nicolas) est en effet un des termes dont on se sert pour désigner le diable, le mot *devil*, comme nombre d'autres termes de la langue religieuse, étant banni de la conversation des gens bien élevés. On l'appelle aussi *Old Scratch* ou *Old Harry*.

shameless of human beings.   Wise men, however, have always been inclined to look with great suspicion on the angels and dæmons of the multitude : and in the present instance, several circumstances have led even superficial observers to question the justice of the vulgar decision. It is notorious that Machiavelli was, through life, a zealous republican.   In the same year in which he composed his manual of Kingcraft, he suffered imprisonment and torture in the cause of public liberty.   It seems inconceivable that the martyr of freedom should have designedly acted as the apostle of tyranny.   Several eminent writers have, therefore, endeavoured to detect in this unfortunate performance[1] some concealed mean ing, more consistent with the character and conduct of the author than that which appears at the first glance.

One hypothesis is that Machiavelli intended to practise on the young Lorenzo de Medici a fraud similar to that which Sunderland is said to have employed against our James the Second, and that he urged his pupil to violent and perfidious measures, as the surest means of accelerating the moment of deliverance and revenge.   Another supposition which Lord Bacon seems to countenance, is that the treatise was merely a piece of grave irony, intended to warn nations against the arts of ambitious men.   It would be easy to show that neither of these solutions is consistent with many passages in The Prince itself.   But the most decisive refutation is that which is furnished by the other works of Machiavelli.   In all the writings which he gave to the public, and in all those which the research of editors has, in the course of three centuries, discovered, in his Comedies, designed for the entertainment of the multitude, in his Comments on Livy, intended for the perusal of the most enthusiastic patriots of Florence, in his History, inscribed to one of the most amiable and estimable of the Popes[2], in his

---

1. *Performance,* œuvre. | 2. Clément VII.

public dispatches, in his private memoranda, the same obliquity of moral principle for which The Prince is so severely censured is more or less discernible. We doubt whether it would be possible to find, in all the many volumes of his compositions, a single expression indicating that dissimulation and treachery had ever struck him as discreditable.

After this, it may seem ridiculous to say that we are acquainted with few writings which exhibit so much elevation of sentiment, so pure and warm a zeal for the public good, or so just a view of the duties and rights of citizens, as those of Machiavelli. Yet so it is. And even from The Prince itself we could select many passages in support of this remark. To a reader of our age and country his inconsistency is, at first, perfectly bewildering. The whole man seems to be an enigma, a grotesque assemblage of incongruous qualities, selfishness and generosity, cruelty and benevolence, craft and simplicity, abject villany and romantic heroism. One sentence is such as a veteran diplomatist would scarcely write in cipher for the direction of his most confidential spy; the next seems to be extracted from a theme[1] composed by an ardent schoolboy on the death of Leonidas. act of dexterous perfidy, and an act of patriotic self-devotion, call forth the same kind and the same degree of respectful admiration. The moral sensibility of the writer seems at once to be morbidly obtuse and morbidly acute. Two characters altogether dissimilar are united in him. They are not merely joined, but interwoven. They are the warp and the woof of his mind; and their combination, like that of the variegated threads in shot[2] silk, gives to the whole texture a glancing[3] and ever-changing appearance. The explanation might have been easy, if he had been a very weak or a very affected man. But he was evidently neither the one nor the other. His works prove, beyond all contradiction, that his under-

1. *Theme*, dissertation.
2. *Shot*, gorge-de-pigeon.

3. *Glancing*, chatoyant.

standing was strong, his taste pure, and his sense of the ridiculous exquisitely keen.

This is strange : and yet the strangest is behind[1]. There is no reason whatever to think, that those amongst whom he lived saw any thing shocking or incongruous in his writings.   Abundant proofs remain of the high estimation in which both his works and his person were held by the most respectable among his contemporaries. Clement the Seventh patronised the publication of those very books which the Council of Trent[2], in the following generation, pronounced unfit for the perusal of Christians.   Some members of the democratical party censured the Secretary[3] for dedicating The Prince to a patron who bore the unpopular name of Medici.   But to those immoral doctrines which have since called forth such severe reprehensions no exception[4] appears to have been taken.   The cry[5] against them was first raised beyond the Alps and seems to have been heard with amazement in Italy.   The earliest assailant, as far as we are aware, was a countryman of our own, Cardinal Pole. The author of the Anti-Machiavelli[6] was a French Protestant.

It is, therefore, in the state of moral feeling among the Italians of those times that we must seek for the real explanation of what seems most mysterious in the life and writings of this remarkable man. . . . .

In the Italian States, as in many natural bodies, untimely decrepitude was the penalty of precocious maturity. Their early greatness, and their early decline, are principally to be attributed to the same cause, the preponderance which the towns acquired in the political system.

In a community[7] of hunters or of shepherds, every man easily and necessarily becomes a soldier. His ordin-

---

1. *The strangest is behind* (le plus étrange est en arrière, à la suite), il nous reste à voir le plus étrange.

2. Le Concile de Trente qui fut tenu de 1545 à 1563, et qui lança l'anathème contre les protestants.

3. Machiavel fut sécrétaire de la République florentine.

4. *To take exception to...*, critiquer, blâmer.

5. *Cry*, clameur de réprobation.

6. Il y a un *Anti-Machiavel* dû à la plume du grand Frédéric.

7. *Community*, société.

ary avocations are perfectly compatible with all the duties of military service. However remote may be the expedition on which he is bound[1], he finds it easy to transport with him the stock from which he derives his subsistence. The whole people is an army; the whole year a march. Such was the state of society which facilitated the gigantic conquests of Attila and Tamerlane.

But a people which subsists by the cultivation of the earth is in a very different situation. The husbandman is bound to the soil on which he labours. A long campaign would be ruinous to him. Still his pursuits are such as give to his frame both the active and the passive strength necessary to a soldier. Nor[2] do they, at least in the infancy of agricultural science, demand his uninterrupted attention. At particular times of the year he is almost wholly unemployed, and can, without injury to himself, afford the time necessary fort a short expedition. Thus the legions of Rome were supplied during its earlier wars. The season during which the fields did not require the presence of the cultivators sufficed for a short inroad and a battle. These operations, too frequently interrupted to produce decisive results, yet served to keep up among the people a degree of discipline and courage which rendered them, not only secure, but formidable. The archers and billmen[3] of the middle ages, who, with provisions for forty days at their backs, left the fields for the camp, were troops of the same description.

But when commerce and manufactures begin to flourish a great change takes place. The sedentary habits of the desk and the loom render the exertions and hardships of war insupportable. The business of traders and artisans requires their constant presence and attention. In such a community there is little superfluous time; but there is generally much superfluous money. Some

---

1. Ne pas confondre *to be bound,* être lié, avec *to be bound,* être en partance, se mettre en route.
2. *Nor do they... demand* = and *they* do not demand.
3. *Billmen,* soldats armés de *bills.* On appelait ainsi une sorte de hallebarde.

members of the society are, therefore, hired to relieve the rest from a task inconsistent with their habits and engagements. . . . .

When war becomes the trade of a separate class, the least dangerous course left to a government is to form that class into a standing army. It is scarcely possible, that men can pass their lives in the service of one state, without feeling some interest in its greatness. Its victories are their victories. Its defeats are their defeats. The contract loses something of its mercantile character. The services of the soldier are considered as the effects of patriotic zeal, his pay as the tribute of national gratitude. To betray the power which employs him, to be even remiss in its service, are in his eyes the most atrocious and degrading of crimes.

When the princes and commonwealths of Italy began to use hired troops, their wisest course would have been to form separate military establishments. Unhappily this was not done. The mercenary warriors of the Peninsula, instead of being attached to the service of different powers, were regarded as the common property of all. The connection between the state and its defenders was reduced to the most simple and naked traffic. The adventurer brought his horse, his weapons, his strentgh, and his experience, into the market. Whether the King of Naples, or the Duke of Milan, the Pope or the Signory [1] of Florence, struck the bargain, was to him a matter of perfect indifference. He was for the highest wages and the longest term. When the campaign for which he had contracted was finished, there was neither law nor punctilio to prevent him from instantly turning his arms against his late masters. The soldier was altogether disjoined from the citizen and from the subject.

The natural consequences followed. Left to the conduct of men who neither loved those whom they defended,

---

1. *The Signory* (prononcez *si'niori*), la Seigneurie, nom donné autrefois au gouvernement de plusieurs répu- bliques italiennes. En anglais ce mot s'écrit souvent *Seigniory*.

nor hated those whom they opposed, who were often
bound by stronger ties to the army against which they
fought than to the state which they served, who lost by the
termination of the conflict, and gained by its prolonga-
tion, war completely changed its character. Every man
came into the field of battle impressed with the knowledge that, in a few days, he might be taking the pay of
the power against which he was then employed, and
fighting by the side of his enemies against his associates.
The strongest interests and the strongest feelings concur-
red to mitigate the hostility of those who had lately been
brethren in arms, and who might soon be brethren in
arms once more. Their common profession was a bond
of union not to be forgotten even when they were engaged in the service of contending parties. Hence it
was that[1] operations, languid and indecisive beyond[2]
any recorded in history, marches and counter-marches,
pillaging, expeditions and blockades, bloodless capitula-
tions and equally bloodless combats, make up the military history of Italy during the course of nearly two
centuries. Mighty armies fight from sunrise to sunset.
A great victory is won. Thousands of prisoners are
taken ; and hardly a life is lost. A pitched battle seems
to have been really less dangerous than an ordinary civil
tumult.

Courage was now no longer necessary even to the
military character. Men grew old in camps, and acquired
the highest renown by their warlike achievements, without
being once required to face serious danger. The political
consequences are too well known. The richest and most
enlightened part of the world was left undefended to the
assaults of every barbarous invader, to the brutality
of Switzerland, the insolence of France, and the fierce
rapacity of Arragon. The moral effects which followed
from this state of things were still more remarkable.

Among the rude nations which lay beyond the Alps,

1. *Hence it was that*, c'est pour | 2. *Beyond* (au delà de), plus que.
cela que. |

valour was absolutely indispensable. Without it none
could be eminent; few could be secure. Cowardice was,
therefore, naturally considered as the foulest reproach.
Among the polished Italians, enriched by commerce,
governed by law, and passionately attached to literature,
every thing was done by superiority of intelligence.
Their very wars, more pacific than the peace of their
neighbours, required rather civil than military qualifications. Hence, while courage was the point of honour in
other countries, ingenuity[1] became the point of honour
in Italy.

From these principles were deduced, by processes
strictly analogous, two opposite systems of fashionable
morality. Through the greater part of Europe, the vices
which peculiarly belong to timid dispositions, and which
are the natural defence of weakness, fraud, and, hypocrisy, have always been most disreputable. On the other
hand, the excesses of haughty and daring spirits have been
treated with indulgence, and even with respect. The
Italians regarded with corresponding lenity those crimes
which require self-command, and address, quick observation, fertile invention, and profound knowledge of
human nature. . . . .

So wide was the difference between the Italians and
their neighbours. A similar difference existed between
the Greeks of the second century before Christ, and their
masters the Romans. The conquerors, brave and re-
solute, faithful to their engagements, and strongly influenced by religious feelings, were, at the same time,
ignorant, arbitrary, and cruel. With[2] the vanquished
people were deposited all the art, the science, and the
literature of the Western world. In poetry, in philosophy, in painting, in architecture, in sculpture, they
had no rivals. Their manners were polished, their
perceptions acute, their invention ready; they were tole-
rant, affable, humane; but of courage and sincerity they

1. *Ingenuity*, l'ingéniosité, l'habi-   2. *With*, chez.
leté.

were almost utterly destitute. Every rude centurion consoled himself for his intellectual inferiority, by remarking that knowledge and taste seemed only to make men atheists, cowards, and slaves. The distinction long continued to be strongly marked, and furnished an admirable subject for the fierce sarcasms of Juvenal.

The citizen of an Italian commonwealth was the Greek of the time of Juvenal and the Greek of the time of Pericles, joined in one. Like the former, he was timid and pliable, artful and mean. But, like the latter, he had a country. Its independence and prosperity were dear to him. If his character were degraded by some base crimes, it was, on the other hand[1], ennobled by public spirit and by an honourable ambition. . .

Habits of dissimulation and falsehood, no doubt, mark a man of our age and country as utterly worthless and abandoned. But it by no means follows that a similar judgment would be just in the case of an Italian of the middle ages. On the contrary, we frequently find those which we are accustomed to consider as certain indications of a mind altogether depraved, in company with great and good qualities, with generosity, with benevolence, with disinterestedness. . . . .

In this respect no history suggests more important reflections than that of the Tuscan and Lombard commonwealths. The character of the Italian statesman seems, at first sight, a collection of contradictions, a phantom as monstrous as the portress of hell in Milton, half divinity, half snake, majestic and beautiful above, grovelling and poisonous below[2]. We see a man whose thoughts and words have no connection with each other, who never hesitates at an oath when he wishes to seduce, who never wants a pretext when he is inclined to betray. His cruelties spring, not from the heat of blood, or the insanity of uncontrolled power, but from deep and cool

1. *On the other hand*, d'autre part.
2. Woman to the waist, and fair,
But ending foul in many a scaly fold
Voluminous and vast, a serpent armed
With mortal sting.
(*Paradise Lost*, II.)

meditation.   His passions like well-trained troops, are impetuous by rule, and in their most headstrong fury never forget the discipline to which they have been accustomed.   His whole soul is occupied with vast and complicated schemes of ambition : yet his aspect and language exhibit nothing but philosophical moderation. Hatred and revenge eat into his heart : yet every look is a cordial smile, every gesture a familiar caress..   He never excites the suspicion of his adversaries by petty provocations.   His purpose is disclosed only when it is accomplished.   His face is unruffled, his speech is courteous, till vigilance is laid asleep, till a vital point is exposed, till a sure aim is taken ; and then he strikes for the first and last time.   Military courage, the boast of the sottish German, of the frivolous and prating Frenchman, of the romantic and arrogant Spaniard, he neither possesses nor values.   He shuns danger, not because he is insensible to shame, but because, in the society in which he lives, timidity has ceased to be shameful.   To do an injury openly is, in his estimation, as wicked as to do it secretly, and far less profitable.   With him the most honourable means are those which are the surest, the speediest, and the darkest.   He cannot comprehend how a man should scruple to deceive those whom he does not scruple to destroy,   He would think it madness to declare open hostilities against rivals whom he might stab in a friendly embrace, or poison in a consecrated wafer.

Yet this man, black with the vices which we consider as most loathsome, traitor, hypocrite, coward, assassin, was by no means destitute even of those virtues which we generally consider as indicating superior elevation of character.   In civil courage, in perseverance, in presence of mind, those barbarous warriors, who were foremost in the battle or the breach, were far his inferiors.   Even the dangers which he avoided with a caution almost pusillanimous never confused his perceptions, never paralysed his inventive faculties, never wrung out one secret from his smooth tongue, and his inscrutable brow. Though a dangerous enemy, and a still more dangerous accomplice, he could be a just and beneficent ruler. With so much unfairness in his policy, there was an extraordinary degree of fairness in his intellect. Indifferent to truth in the transactions of life, he was honestly devoted to truth in the researches of speculation[1]. Wanton cruelty was not in his nature. On the contrary, where no political object was at stake, his disposition was soft and humane. The susceptibility of his nerves and the activity of his imagination inclined him to sympathise with the feelings of others, and to delight in the charities[2] and courtesies of social life. Perpetually descending to actions which might seem to mark[3] a mind diseased through all its faculties, he had nevertheless an exquite sensibility, both for the natural and the moral sublime, for every graceful and every lofty conception. Habits of petty intrigue and dissimulation might have rendered him incapable of great general views, but that[4] the expanding effect of his philosophical studies counteracted the narrowing tendency. He had the keenest enjoyment of wit, eloquence, and poetry. The fine arts profited alike by the severity of his judgment, and by the liberality of his patronage. The portraits of some of the remarkable Italians of those times are perfectly in harmony with this description. Ample and majestic foreheads, brows strong and dark, but not frowning, eyes of which the calm full gaze, while it expresses nothing, seems to discern every thing, cheeks pale with thought and sedentary habits, lips formed with feminine delicacy, but compressed with more than masculine decision, mark out[5] men at once enterprising and timid, men equally skilled in[6] detecting the purpose

---

1. *Speculation*, la science, la philosophie.

2. *Charities* a ici le sens de : rapports fondés sur la charité, la sympathie, la bienveillance.

3. *To mark*, indiquer.

4. *But that* (si ce n'est que); *but that...*, etc... *counter-acted* = *if the expanding effect of his philosophical studies had not counteracted*.

5. *Mark out*, indiquent.

6. *Skilled in*, habiles à.

of others, and in concealing their own, men who must have been formidable enemies and unsafe allies, but men, at the same time, whose tempers were mild and equable, and who possessed an amplitude and subtlety of intellect which would have rendered them eminent either in active or in contemplative life, and fitted them either to govern or to instruct mankind.

Every age and every nation has certain characteristic vices, which prevail almost universally, which scarcely any person scruples to avow, and which even rigid moralists but faintly censure. Succeeding generations change the fashion of their morals, with the fashion of their hats and their coaches; take some other kind of wickedness under their patronage, and wonder at the depravity of their ancestors. Nor is this all [1]. Posterity, that high court of appeal which is never tired of eulogising its own justice and discernment, acts on such occasions like a Roman dictator after a general mutiny. Finding the delinquents too numerous to be all punished, it selects some of them at hazard, to bear the whole penalty of an offence in which they are not more deeply implicated than those who escape. Whether decimation [2] be [3] a convenient mode of military execution, we know not [4], but we solemnly protest against the introduction of such a principle into the philosophy of history.

In the present instance, the lot has fallen on Machiavelli, a man whose public conduct was upright and honourable, whose views of morality, where they differed from those of the persons around him, seemed to have differed for the better, and whose only fault was, that, having adopted some of the maxims then generally received, he arranged them more luminously, and expressed them more forcibly, than any other writer.

---

1. *Nor is this all* = and *this is* not *all.*
 2. Voyez page 57.
3. *Be*, subjonctif fréquemment employé après *whether* dans le style soutenu.
4. Voyez note 5, page 92.

L'Église et l'État[1].

Mr. Gladstone's whole theory[2] rests on this great fund-amental proposition, that the propagation of religious truth is one of the principal ends of government, as government. If Mr. Gladstone has not proved this proposition, his system vanishes at once.

We are desirous, before we enter on the discussion of this important question, to point out clearly a distinction which, though very obvious, seems to be overlooked by many excellent people. In their opinion, to say that the ends of government are temporal and not spiritual is tantamount to saying that the temporal welfare of man is of more importance than his spiritual welfare. But this is an entire mistake. The question is not whether spiritual interests be[3] or be not superior in importance to temporal interests; but whether the machinery which happens at any moment to be employed for the purpose of protecting certain temporal interests of a society be necessarily such a machinery as is fitted to promote the spiritual interests of that society. Without a division of labour the world could not go on. It is of very much more importance that men should have food than that they should have pianofortes. Yet it by no means follows that every pianoforte-maker ought to add the business of a baker to his own; for, if he did so, we should have both much worse music and much worse bread. It is of much more importance that the knowledge of religious truth should be wisely diffused than that the art of sculpture should flourish among us. Yet it by no means follows that the Royal Academy[4] ought to unite with its present

1. Extrait de l'Essai sur *Gladstone on Church and State*.

2. Exposée dans l'ouvrage à propos duquel Macaulay écrivit cet Essai, et qui a pour titre *The State in its Relations with the Church*, 1839.

3. Voyez note 6, page 96.

4. *The Royal Academy*, dont le titre complet est *The Royal Academy of Arts*, fut fondée en 1768. Il s'y fait, tous les ans, en mai, juin et juillet, une exposition d'œuvres de peintres et sculpteurs anglais contemporains; c'est quelque chose d'analogue à la fois à notre Salon et à notre école des Beaux-Arts. La Royal Academy est installée dans New Burlington House, Piccadilly.

functions those of the Society for promoting Christian
Knowledge, to distribute theological tracts, to send forth
missionaries, to turn out[1] Nollekens for being[2] a Catholic, Bacon for being a Methodist[3], and Flaxman for being
a Swedenborgian.   For the effect of such folly would be
that we should have the worst possible academy of
arts, and the worst possible society for the promotion of
Christian knowledge.   The community[4], it is plain,
would be thrown into universal confusion, if it were
supposed to be the duty of every association which is
formed for one good object to promote every other good
object.

As to some of the ends of civil government, all people
are agreed.   That it is designed to protect our persons
and our property, that it is designed to compel us to
satisfy our wants, not by rapine, but by industry, that
it is designed to compel us to decide our differences,
not by the strong hand[5], but by arbitration, that it is
designed to direct our whole force, as that of one man,
against any other society which may offer us injury[6],
these are propositions which will hardly be disputed.

Now these are matters in which man, without any
reference to any higher being, or to any future state, is
very deeply interested.   Every human being, be he[7]
idolater, Mahometan, Jew, Papist, Socinian, Deist, or
Atheist, naturally loves life, shrinks from pain, desires
comforts which can be enjoyed only in communities
where property is secure.   To be murdered, to be tortured, to be robbed, to be sold into slavery, to be exposed to the outrages of gangs of foreign banditti calling
themselves patriots, these are evidently evils from
which men of every religion, and men of no religion,
wish to be protected; and therefore it will hardly be
disputed that men of every religion, and of no religion,

---

1. *Turn out*, expulser.

2. *For being*, parce qu'il est.

3. Voyez note 2, page 20.

4. *Community*, société.

5. *By the strong hand*, par la force,
par la violence.

6. *Offer us injury* (nous offrir une
injure), essayer de nous nuire.

7. *Be he*, qu'il soit.

have thus far [1] a common interest in being [2] well governed.

But the hopes and fears of man are not limited to this short life, and to this visible world. He finds himself surrounded by the signs of a power and wisdom higher than his own; and, in all ages and nations, men of all orders of intellect, from Bacon and Newton, down to the rudest tribes of cannibals, have believed in the existence of some superior mind. Thus far the voice of mankind is almost unanimous. But whether there be one God, or many, what may be his natural and what his moral attributes, in what relation his creatures stand to him, whether he have [3] ever disclosed himself to us by any other revelation than that which is written in all the parts of the glorious and well-ordered world which he has made, whether his revelation be contained in any permanent record, how that record should be interpreted, and whether it have pleased him to appoint any unerring interpreter on earth, these are questions respecting which there exists the widest diversity of opinion, and respecting which a large part of our race has, ever since the dawn of regular history, been deplorably in error.

Now here are two great objects : one is the protection of the persons and estates of citizens from injury : the other is the propagation of religious truth. No two objects more entirely distinct can well be imagined. The former belongs wholly to the visible and tangible world in which we live; the latter belongs to that higher world which is beyond the reach of our senses. The former belongs to this life; the latter to that which is to come. Men who are perfectly agreed as to the importance of the former object, and as to the way of obtaining it, differ as widely as possible respecting the latter object. We must, therefore, pause before we admit that the persons, be they who they may [4], who are intrusted with power for the promotion of the former object, ought

---

1. *Thus far* (aussi loin), jusque-là.
2. *In being*, à être.
3. Voyez note 6, page 96.

4. *Be they who they may* (qu'elles soient qui elles pourront), quelles qu'elles puissent être.

always to use that power for the promotion of the latter object.

Mr. Gladstone conceives that the duties of governments are paternal; a doctrine which we shall not believe till he can show us some government which loves, its sujects as a father loves a child, and which is as superior in intelligence to its subjects as a father is to a child. He tells us in lofty though somewhat indistinct language, that "Government occupies in moral the place of τὸ πᾶν [1] in physical science." If government be indeed τὸ πᾶν in moral science, we do not understand why rulers should not assume all the functions which Plato assigned to them [2]. Why should they not take away the child from the mother, select the nurse, regulate the school, overlook the playground, fix the hours of labour and of recreation, prescribe what ballads shall be sung, what tunes shall be played, what books shall be read, what physic shall be swallowed? Why should not they choose our wives, limit our expenses, and stint us to a certain number of dishes of meat, of glasses of wine, and of cups of tea! Plato, whose hardihood in speculation [3] was perhaps more wonderful than any other peculiarity of his extraordinary mind, and who shrank from nothing to which his principles led, went this whole length [4]. Mr. Gladstone is not so intrepid. He contents himself with laying down this proposition, that, whatever be the body which in any community is employed to protect the persons and property of men, that body ought, also, in its corporate capacity, to profess a religion, to employ its power for the propagation of that religion, and to require conformity to that religion, as an indispensable qualification for all civil office. . . . .

It is the duty, Mr. Gladstone tells us, of the persons, be they who they may [5], who hold supreme power in the state, to employ that power in order to promote whatever

---

1. *To pán*, en grec : le tout.
2. Dans son ouvrage intitulé *la République*.
3. *Speculation*, la pensée.

4. *This whole length* (cette distance entière), jusque-là.

5. Voyez note 4, page 138.

they may deem to be theological truth. Now, surely, before he can call on us[1] to admit this proposition, he is bound to prove that these persons are likely to do more good than harm by so employing their power.   .   .

.   .   .   .

We do not admit that, if a government were, for all its temporal ends, as perfect as human frailty allows, such government would, therefore, be necessarily qualified to propagate true religion. For we see that the fitness of governments to propagate true religion is by no means proportioned to their fitness for the temporal ends of their institution. Looking at individuals, we see that the princes under whose rule nations have been most ably protected from foreign and domestic disturbance, and have made the most rapid advances in civilisation, have been by no means good teachers of divinity. Take, for example, the best French sovereign, Henry the Fourth, a king who restored order, terminated a terrible civil war, brought the finances into an excellent condition, made his country respected throughout Europe, and endeared himself to the great body of the people whom he ruled. Yet this man was twice a Huguenot, and twice a Papist. He was, as Davila hints, strongly suspected of having no religion at all in theory; and was certainly not much under religious restraints in his practice. Take the Czar Peter[2], the Empress Catherine[3], Frederick the Great. It will surely not be disputed that these sovereigns, with all their faults, were, if we consider them with reference merely to the temporal ends of government, above the average of merit. Considered as theological guides, Mr. Gladstone would probably put them below the most abject drivellers of the Spanish branch of the house of Bourbon[4]. Again, when we pass from individuals to systems, we by no means find that the aptitude of governments for propagating religious truth is proportioned to

<hr>

1. *Call on us*, nous demander.
2. Pierre le Grand (1682-1725).
3. Catherine II, impératrice de Russie (1729-1796).
4. Le premier Bourbon d'Espagne fut Philippe V, petit-fils de Louis XIV.

their aptitude for secular functions. Without being blind
admirers either of the French or of the American institutions, we think it clear that the persons and property
of citizens are better protected in France and in New
England than in almost any society that now exists, or
that has ever existed; very much better, certainly, than in
the Roman empire under the orthodox rule of Constantine and Theodosius. But neither the government of
France, nor that of New England, is so organized as to
be fit for the propagation of theological doctrines. Nor
do we think it improbable that the most serious religious
errors might prevail in a state which, considered merely
with reference to temporal objects, might approach far
nearer than any that has ever been known to the ἰδέα[1] of
what a state should be.

But we shall leave this abstract question, and look at
the world as we find it. Does, then, the way in which
governments generally obtain their power make it at all
probable that they will be more favourable to orthodoxy
than to heterodoxy? A nation of barbarians pours down
on a rich and unwarlike empire, enslaves the people,
portions out the land, and blends the institutions which
it finds in the cities with those which it has brought from
the woods. A handful of daring adventurers from a civilised nation wander to some savage country, and reduce
the aboriginal race to bondage. A successful general
turns his arms against the state which he serves. A
society, made brutal by oppression, rises madly on its
masters, sweeps away all old laws and usages, and,
when its first paroxysm of rage is over, sinks down pas-
sively under any form of polity which may spring out
of the chaos. A chief of a party, as at Florence, becomes
imperceptibly a sovereign, and the founder of a dynasty.
A captain of mercenaries as at Milan, seizes on a city,
and by the sword makes himself its ruler. An elective
senate, as at Venice, usurps permanent and hereditary

---

1. *Idéa,* mot grec, idée, idéal.

power. It is in events such as these that governments
have generally originated ; and we can see nothing
in such events to warrant us in believing[1] that the
governments thus called into existence will be peculiarly
well fitted to distinguish between religious truth and
heresy.

When, again, we look at the constitutions of governments which have become settled, we find no great security for the orthodoxy of rulers. One magistrate holds
power because his name was drawn out of a purse ;
another, because his father held it before him. There
are representative systems of all sorts, large constituent
bodies, small constituent bodies, universal suffrage, high
pecuniary qualifications[2]. We see that, for the temporal
ends of government, some of these constitutions are very
skilfully constructed, and that the very worst of them is
preferable to anarchy. We see some sort of connection
between the very worst of them and the temporal well-
being of society. But it passes our understanding to
comprehend what connection any one of them has with
theological truth. . . . .

If, indeed, the magistrate would content himself with
laying his opinions and reasons before the people, and
would leave the people, uncorrupted by hope or fear, to
judge for themselves, we should see little reason to
apprehend that his interference in favour of error would
be seriously prejudicial to the interests of truth. Nor
do we[3], as will hereafter be seen[4], object to his taking
this course, when it is compatible with the efficient dis-
charge of his more especial duties. But this will not
satisfy Mr. Gladstone. He would have the magistrate
resort to means which have a great tendency to make
malcontents, to make hypocrites, to make careless

---

1. *To warrant us in believing*, qui
nous autorise à croire.

2. *Pecuniary qualifications*, cens
électoral. — *Qualification* désigne
toute *qualité* qui donne certains droits
à qui la possède. *Pecuniary qualifi-*
cation, qualité de quiconque possède
telle fortune, ou paie tel impôt exigé
par la loi pour être électeur.

3. *Nor do we* = and we do not.

4. *As will hereafter be seen*, comme
on le verra plus loin.

nominal conformists [1], but no tendency whatever to produce honest and rational conviction. It seems to us quite clear that an inquirer who has no wish except to know the truth, is more likely to arrive at the truth than an inquirer who knows that, if he decides one way, he shall be rewarded, and that, if he decides the other way, he shall be punished. Now, Mr. Gladstone would have governments propagate their opinions by excluding all dissenters from all civil offices. That is to say, he would have governments propagate their opinions by a process which has no reference whatever to the truth or falsehood of those opinions, by arbitrarily uniting certain worldly advantages with one set of doctrines, and certain worldly inconveniences with another set. It is of the very nature of argument to serve the interests of truth; but if rewards and punishments serve the interests of truth, it is by mere accident. It is very much easier to find arguments for the divine authority of the Gospel than for the divine authority of the Koran [2]. But it is just as easy to bribe or rack a Jew into Mahometanism as into Christianity.

From racks, indeed, and from all penalties directed against the persons, the property, and the liberty of heretics, the humane spirit of Mr. Gladstone shrinks with horror. He only maintains that conformity to the religion of the state ought to be an indispensable qualification for office [3]; and he would, unless we have greatly misunderstood him, think it his duty, if he had the power, to revive the Test Act [4], to enforce it rigorously, and to extend it to important classes who were formerly exempt from its operation.

This is indeed a legitimate consequence of his principles. But why stop here? Why not roast dissenters at

<hr>

1. *Nominal conformists*, conformistes nominaux, c'est-à-dire qui ne sont conformistes que de nom. Les *conformists* sont ceux qui acceptent les doctrines de l'Eglise anglicane. Les autres s'appellent *non-conformists*.

2. *Koran*, Coran ou Koran, livre sacré des Musulmans.

3. *Office*, fonctions publiques.

4. *The Test Act*, la Loi du Test (*test*, critérium, pierre de touche), loi votée en 1673 et abrogée en 1828. Elle imposait, à tout candidat aux fonctions publiques, certains serments et déclarations contraires aux doctrines des catholiques et des dissidents, qui se trouvaient ainsi écartés.

slow fires? All the general reasonings on which this
theory rests evidently lead to sanguinary persecution. If
the propagation of religious truth be a principal end of
government, as government; if it be the duty of a government to employ for that end its constitutional power;
if the constitutional power of governments extends, as it
most unquestionably does, to the making of laws for the
burning of heretics; if burning be, as it most assuredly
is, in many cases, a most effectual mode of suppressing
opinions; why should we not burn? If the relation in
which government ought to stand to tho people be, as
Mr. Gladstone tells us, a paternal relation, we are irre-
sistibly led to the conclusion that persecution is justifiable. For the right of propagating opinions by punishment is one which belongs to parents as clearly as the
right to give instruction.   A boy is compelled to attend
family worship : he is forbidden to read irreligious books :
if he will not learn his catechism, he is sent to bed without his supper : if he plays truant at church-time a
task is set[1] him. If he should[2] display the precocity of
his talents by expressing impious opinions before his
brothers and sisters, we should not much blame his
father for cutting short the controversy with a horsewhip.
All the reasons which lead us to think that parents are
peculiarly fitted to conduct the education of their children, and that education is a principal end of the parent-
al relation, lead us also to think, that parents ought to
be allowed to use punishment, if necessary, for the
purpose of forcing children, who are incapable of judging
for themselves, to receive religious instruction and to
attend religious worship.   Why, then, is this prerogative
of punishment, so eminently paternal, to be withheld
from a paternal government? It seems to us, also, to be
the height of absurdity to employ civil disabilities for the
propagation of an opinion, and then to shrink from employing other punishments for the same purpose. For

1. *Set*, infligée. | 2. *If he should*, s'il lui arrivait de.

nothing can be clearer than that, if you punish at all, you ought to punish enough. The pain caused by punishment is pure unmixed evil, and never ought to be inflicted, except for the sake of some good. It is mere foolish cruelty to provide penalties which torment the criminal without preventing the crime. Now it is possible, by sanguinary persecution unrelentingly inflicted, to suppress opinions. In this way the Albigenses were put down. In this way the Lollards were put down. In this way the fair promise of the Reformation was blighted in Italy and Spain. But we may safely defy M. Gladstone to point out a single instance in which the system which he recommends has succeeded.

And why should he be so tender-hearted ? What reason can he give for hanging a murderer, and suffering a heresiarch to escape without even a pecuniary mulct ? Is the heresiarch a less pernicious member of society than the murderer? Is not the loss of one soul a greater evil than the extinction of many lives? And the number of murders committed by the most profligate bravo that ever let out his poniard to hire[1] in Italy, or by the most savage buccaneer that ever prowled on the Windward Station, is small indeed, when compared with the number of souls which have been caught in the snares of one dexterous heresiarch. If, then, the heresiarch causes infinitely greater evils than the murderer, why is he not as proper an object of penal legislation as the murderer? We can give a reason, a reason, short, simple, decisive, and consistent. We do not extenuate the evil which the heresiarch produces; but we say that it is not evil of that sort against which it is the end of government to guard. But how Mr. Gladstone, who considers the evil which the heresiarch produces as evil of the sort against which it is the end of government to guard, can escape from the obvious consequence of his doctrine, we do not understand. The world is full of parallel cases. An orange-

1. *Let out... to hire*, loua.

woman[1] stops up the pavement with her wheelbarrow, and a policeman takes her into custody. A miser who has amassed a million suffers an old friend and benefactor to die in a workhouse, and cannot be questioned before any tribunal for his baseness and ingratitude. Is this because legislators think the orange-woman's conduct worse than the miser's? Not at all. It is because the stopping up of the pathway is one of the evils against which it is the business of the public authorities to protect society, and heartlessness is not one of those evils. It would be the height of folly to say that the miser ought, indeed, to be punished, but that he ought to be punished less severely than the orange-woman. . . . . . .

We consider the primary end of government as a purely temporal end, the protection of the persons and property of men.

We think that government, like every other contrivance of human wisdom, from the highest to the lowest, is likely to answer its main end best when it is constructed with a single view to that end. M. Gladstone, who loves Plato, will not quarrel with us for illustrating our proposition, after Plato's fashion, from[2] the most familiar objects. Take cutlery, for example. A blade which is designed both to shave and to carve will certainly not shave so well as a razor, or carve so well as a carving-knife. An academy of painting, which should also be a bank, would, in all probability, exhibit very bad pictures and discount very bad bills. A gas company, which should also be an infant school society, would, we apprehend, light the streets ill, and teach the children ill. On this principle, we think that government should be organised solely with a view to its main end; and that no part of its efficiency for that end should be sacrificed in order to promote any other end however excellent[3].

But does it follow from hence that governments ought

---

1. *Orange-woman*, marchande d'oranges.
2. *From*, au moyen de.

3. *However excellent*, si excellente qu'elle soit.

never to pursue any end other than their main end?   In no wise. Though it is desirable that every institution should have a main end, and should be so formed as to be in the highest degree efficient for that main end; yet if, without any sacrifice of its efficiency for that end, it can pursue any other good end, it ought to do so. Thus, the end for which a hospital is built is the relief of the sick, not the beautifying of the street. To sacrifice the health of the sick to splendour of architectural effect, to place the building in a bad air only that it may present a more commanding front to a great public place, to make the wards hotter or cooler than they ought to be, in order that the columns and windows of the exterior may please the passers-by, would be monstrous. But if, without any sacrifice of the chief object, the hospital can be made an ornament to the metropolis, it would be absurd not to make it so.

In the same manner, if a government can, without any sacrifice of its main end, promote any other good work, it ought to do so.   The encouragement of the fine arts, for example, is by no means the main end of government; and it would be absurd, in constituting a government, to bestow a thought on the question, whether it would be a government likely to train Raphaels and Domenichinos. But it by no means follows that it is improper for a government to form a national gallery of pictures. The same may be said of patronage bestowed on learned men, of the publication of archives, of the collecting of libraries, menageries, plants, fossils, antiques, of journeys and voyages for purposes of geographical discovery or astronomical observation. It is not for these ends that government is constituted. But it may well happen that a government may have at its command resources which will enable it, without any injury to its main end, to pursue these collateral ends far more effectually than any individual or any voluntary association could do. If so, government ought to pursue these collateral ends.

It is still more evidently the duty of government to

promote, always in subordination to its main end, every
thing which is useful as a means for the attaining of that
main end The improvement of steam navigation, for
example, is by no means a primary object of goverment.
But as steam vessels are useful for the purpose of national defence, and for the purpose of facilitating intercourse between distant provinces, and of thereby con-
solidating the force of the empire, it may be the bounden
duty[1] of government to encourage ingenious men to
perfect an invention which so directly tends to make the
state more efficient for its great primary end.

Now, on both these grounds[2], the instruction of the
people may with propriety engage the care of the government. That the people should be well educated is in
itself a good thing ; and the state ought therefore to promote this object, if it can do so without any sacrifice of
its primary object. The education of the people, conducted on those principles of morality which are common
to all the forms of Christianity, is highly valuable as a
means of promoting the main object for which government exists, and is on this ground well deserving the
attention of rulers. We will not at present go into[3] the
general question of education ; but will confine our remarks
to the subject which is more immediately before us,
namely, the religious instruction of the people.

We may illustrate our view of the policy which governments ought to pursue with respect to religious instruction, by recurring to the analogy of a hospital. Religious
instruction is not the main end for which a hospital is
built ; and to introduce into a hospital any regulations
prejudicial to the health of the patients, on the plea of
promoting their spiritual improvement, to send a ranting
preacher to a man who has just been ordered by the physician to lie quiet and try to get a little sleep, to impose
a strict observance of Lent on a convalescent who has

---

1. *Bounden duty* (devoir obliga-
toire), devoir absolu.

2. *On... these grounds*, pour ces...
motifs.

3. *Go into* (entrer dans) aborder.

been advised to eat heartily of nourishing food, to direct, as the bigoted Pius the Fifth actually did, that no medical assistance should be given to any person who declined spiritual attendance, would be the most extravagant folly. Yet it by no means [1] follows that it would not be right to have a chaplain to attend the sick, and to pay such a chaplain out of [2] the hospital funds. Whether it will be proper to have such a chaplain at all, and of what religious persuasion such a chaplain ought to be, must depend on circumstances. There may be a town in which it would be impossible to set up a good hospital without the help of people of different opinions : and religious parties may run so high [3] that, though people of different opinions are willing to contribute for the relief of the sick, they will not concur in the choice of any one chaplain. The high Churchmen [4] insist that, if there is a paid chaplain, he shall be a high Churchman. The Evangelicals stickle for an Evangelical. Here it would evidently be absurd and cruel to let an useful and humane design, about which all are agreed, fall to the ground, because all cannot agree about something else. The governors must either appoint two chaplains, and pay them both; or they must appoint none; and every one of them must, in his individual capacity, do what he can for the purpose of providing the sick with such religious instruction and consolation as will, in his opinion, be most useful to them.

We should say the same of government. Government is not an institution for the propagation of religion, any more than St. George's Hospital [5] is an institution for the propagation of religion : and the most absurd and pernicious consequences would follow, if Government should pursue, as its primary end, that which can never be more

---

1. *By no means*, en aucune façon, nullement.

2. *Out of*, sur.

3. *Run so high* (couler si haut, comme un fleuve qui coule à pleins bords), être si violents.

4. *High Churchmen* (voyez note 5, page 30), et *Evangelicals* sont les noms de deux partis de l'Église anglicane. Ces derniers s'appellent aussi *Low Churchmen*.

5. Situé près de *Hyde Park Corner*.

than its secondary end, though intrinsically more important than its primary end. But a government which
considers the religious instruction of the people as a secondary end, and follows out that principle faithfully,
will, we think, be likely to do much good and little harm.

We will rapidly run over some of the consequences to
which this principle leads, and point out how it solves
some problems which, on Mr. Gladstone's hypothesis,
admit of no satisfactory solution.

All persecution directed against the persons or property
of men is, on our principle, obviously indefensible. For,
the protection of the persons and property of men being
the primary end of government, and religious instruction
only a secondary end, to secure the people from heresy
by making their lives, their limbs, or their estates in-
secure, would be to sacrifice the primary end to the
secondary end. It would be as absurd as it would be in
the governors of a hospital to direct that the wounds of
all Arian and Socinian patients should be dressed in such
a way as to make them fester. . . . .

Supposing the circumstances of a country to be such,
that the government may with propriety, on our principles, give religious instruction to a people ; we have next
to inquire, what religion shall be taught. . . . .

. . . . In our opinion,
that religious instruction which the ruler ought, in his
public capacity[1] to patronise, is the instruction from
which he, in his conscience, believes that the people will
learn most good with the smallest mixture of evil. And
thus it is not necessarily his own religion that he will select. He will, of course, believe that his own religion is
unmixedly good. But the question which he has to consider is, not how much good his religion contains, but
how much good the people will learn, if instruction is
given them in that religion. He may prefer the doctrines
and government of the Church of England to those of the

____

· **1.** *In his public capacity*, comme homme public.

Church of Scotland. But if he knows that a Scotch congregation[1] will listen with deep attention and respect while an Erskine or a Chalmers sets before them the fundamental doctrines of Christianity, and that a glimpse of a surplice or a single line of a liturgy would be the signal for hooting and riot, and would probably bring stools and brickbats about the ears[2] of the minister, he acts wisely if he conveys religious knowledge to the Scotch rather by means of that imperfect Church, as he may think it, from which they will learn much, than by means of that perfect Church from which they will learn nothing. The only end of teaching is, that men may learn; and it is idle to talk of the duty of teaching truth in ways which only cause men to cling more firmly to falsehood.

Incapacités civiles des Juifs[3].

It is because men are not in the habit of considering what the end of government is, that Catholic disabilities and Jewish disabilities[4] have been suffered to exist so long. We hear of essentially Protestant governments and essentially Christian governments, words which mean just as much as essentially Protestant cookery, or essentially Christian horsemanship. Government exists for the purpose of keeping the peace, for the purpose of compelling us to settle our disputes by arbitration instead of settling them by blows, for the purpose of compelling us to supply our wants by industry, instead of supplying them by rapine. This is the only operation for which the machinery of government is peculiarly adapted, the only operation which wise governments ever propose to themselves as

1. *Congregation*, assemblée de fidèles, fidèles assemblés dans une église.

2. *About the ears* (autour des oreilles), sur la tête.

3. Extrait de l'Essai sur les *Civil Disabilities of the Jews.*

4. Les Catholiques et les Juifs ont, en Angleterre, été exclus du Parlement et des fonctions gouvernementales, les premiers jusqu'en 1829, et ces derniers jusqu'en 1858.

their chief object. If there is any class of people who are not interested, or who do not think themselves interested, in the security of property and the maintenance of order, that class ought to have no share of the powers which exist for the purpose of securing property and maintaining order. But why a man should be less fit to exercise those powers because he wears a beard, because he does not eat ham, because he goes to the synagogue on Saturdays instead of going to the church on Sundays, we cannot conceive.

The points of difference between Christianity and Judaism have very much to do with a man's fitness to be a bishop or a rabbi. But they have no more to do with his fitness to be a magistrate, a legislator, or a minister of finance, than with his fitness to be a cobbler. Nobody has ever thought of compelling cobblers to make any declaration on the true faith of a Christian[1]. Any man would rather have his shoes mended by a heretical cobbler than by a person who had subscribed all the thirty-nine articles[2], but had never handled an awl. Men act thus, not because they are indifferent to religion, but because they do not see what religion has to do with the mending of their shoes. Yet religion has as much to do with the mending of shoes as with the budget and the army estimates. We have surely had several signal proofs within the last twenty years that a very good Christian may be a very bad Chancellor of the Exchequer[3].

But it would be monstrous, say the persecutors, that Jews should legislate for a Christian community. This is a palpable misrepresentation. What is proposed is, not that the Jews should legislate for a Christian community, but that a legislature composed of Christians and Jews should legislate for a community composed of Christians

1. *On the true faith of a Christian*, expression contenue dans le serment de fidélité que devait autrefois prêter tout candidat aux fonctions publiques, civiles ou militaires. En 1858, lors de l'émancipation des Israélites, cette expression fut supprimée.

2. Voyez note 8, page 110.

3. *Chancellor of the Exchequer*, Chancelier de l'Échiquier, ministre des finances.

and Jews. On nine hundred and ninety-nine questions out of a thousand, on all questions of police, of finance, of civil and criminal law, of foreign policy, the Jew, as a Jew, has no interest hostile to that of the Christian, or even to that of the Churchman [1]. On questions relating to the ecclesiastical establishment [2], the Jew and the Churchman may differ. But they cannot differ more widely than the Catholic and the Churchmann, or the Independent [3] and the Churchman. The principle that Churchmen ought to monopolize the whole power of the state would at least have an intelligible meaning. The principle that Christians ought to monopolize it has no meaning at all. For no question connected with the ecclesiastical institutions of the country can possibly come before Parliament, with respect to which there will not be as wide a difference between Christians as there can be between any Christian and any Jew.

In fact, the Jews are not now excluded from political power. They possess it; and as long as they are allowed to accumulate large fortunes, they must possess it. The distinction which is sometimes made between civil privileges and political power is a distinction without a difference. Privileges are power. Civil and political are synonymous words, the one derived from the Latin, the other from the Greek. Nor is this mere verbal quibbling. If we look for a moment at the facts of the case, we shall see that the things are inseparable, or rather identical.

That a Jew should be a judge in a Christian country would be most shocking. But he may be a juryman. He may try issues of fact [4]; and no harm is done. But if he should be suffered to try issues of law, there is an end of [5] the constitution. He may sit in a box plainly dressed,

1. *Churchman*, membre de l'Eglise anglicane. Pour les Anglais, *Church*, sans épithète, c'est l'Eglise anglicane.
2. *The ecclesiastical establishment*, l'Eglise officielle.
3. Les Indépendants sont une des sectes religieuses si nombreuses en Angleterre.

4. *Issues of fact*, questions de fait. Plus loin : *issues of law*, questions de droit. Le sens propre de *issue*, dans la langue du droit, est *conclusions*.

5. *There is an end of*, c'en est fait de.

and return. verdicts. But that he should sit on the bench[1] in a black gown and white wig, and grant new trials[2], would be an abomination not to be thought of among baptized people. The distinction is certainly most philosophical.

What power in civilised society is so great as that of the creditor over the debtor? If we take this away from the Jew, we take away from him the security of his property. If we leave it to him, we leave to him a power more despotic by far than that of the king and all his cabinet.

It would be impious to let a Jew sit in Parliament. But a Jew may make money; and money may make members of Parliament. Gatton and Old Sarum[3] may be the property of a Hebrew. An elector of Penryn will take ten pounds from Shylock rather than nine pounds nineteen shillings and eleven pence three farthings from Antonio. To this no objection is made. That a Jew should possess the substance of legislative power, that he should command eight votes on every division[4] as if he were the great Duke of Newcastle himself, is exactly as it should be. But that he should pass the bar and sit down on those mysterious cushions of green leather[5], that he should cry "hear"[6] and "order,"[7] and talk about being on his legs[8], and being, for one[9], free to say this and to say that, would be a profanation sufficient to bring ruin on the country.

That a Jew should be privy councillor to a Christian king would be an eternal disgrace to the nation. But the

---

1. *The bench*, le tribunal.
2. *Grant new trials*, accorde l'appel.
3. Voyez note 6, page 18.
4. *On every division*, à chaque vote (de la Chambre). Au lieu de voter en déposant un bulletin dans une urne, les députés anglais se partagent en deux camps; d'où le nom de *division*.
5. *Cushions of green leather*, dont sont garnies les banquettes des députés à la Chambre des Communes.
6. *Hear* (écoutez!) peut, suivant le ton, être une marque d'approbation ou de blâme.

7. *Order*, à l'ordre! exclamation poussée quand un orateur se laisse aller à prononcer des paroles contraires aux convenances ou aux règlements de la Chambre.
8. Dans la langue du Parlement, *to be on one's legs* signifie avoir la parole, parce que les députés, ordinairement assis sur les banquettes de « cuir vert », se lèvent, à leur place, pour prononcer un discours.
9. *For one*, quant à lui.

Jew may govern the money-market[1], and the money-market may govern the world. The minister may be in doubt as to his scheme of finance till he has been closeted with the Jew. A congress of sovereigns may be forced to summon the Jew to their assistance. The scrawl of the Jew on the back of a piece of paper may be worth more than the royal word of three kings, or the national faith of three new American republics. But that he should put Right Honourable[2] before his name would be the most frightful of national calamities. . , . .

If it is our duty as Christians to exclude the Jews from political power, it must be our duty to treat them as our ancestors treated them, to murder them, and banish them, and rob them. For in that way, and in that way alone, can we really deprive them of political power. If we do not adopt this course, we may take away the shadow, but we must leave them the substance. We may do enough to pain and irritate them; but we shall not do enough to secure[3] ourselves from danger, if danger really exists. Where wealth is, there power must inevitably be.

The English Jews, we are told, are not Englishmen. They are a separate people, living locally in this island, but living morally and politically in communion with their brethren who are scattered over all the world. An English Jew looks on a Dutch or a Portuguese Jew as his countryman, and on an English Christian as a stranger. This want of patriotic feeling, it is said, renders a Jew unfit to exercise political functions.

The argument has in it something plausible; but a close examination shows it to be quite unsound. Even if the alleged facts are admitted, still the Jews are not the only people who have preferred their sect to their country. The feeling of patriotism, when society is in a healthful state, springs up by a natural and inevitable association, in the minds of citizens who know that they owe all their

---

1. *Money-market*, marché financier.
2. Titre dont on fait précéder le

nom des *privy councillors*.
3. *To secure*, mettre à l'abri.

comforts and pleasures to the bond which unites them in one community. But, under a partial and oppressive government, these associations cannot acquire that strength which they have in a better state of things. Men are compelled to seek from their party that protection which they ought to receive from their country, and they, by a natural consequence, transfer to their party that affection which they would otherwise have felt for their country. The Huguenots of France called in the help of England against their Catholic kings. The Catholics of France called in the help of Spain against a Huguenot king. Would it be fair to infer, that at present the French Protestants would wish to see their religion made dominant by the help of a Prussian or English army? Surely not. And why is it that they are not willing, as they formerly were willing, to sacrifice the interests of their country to the interests of their religious persuasion? The reason is obvious : they were persecuted then, and are not persecuted now. The English Puritans, under Charles the First, prevailed on the Scotch to invade England. Do the Protestant Dissenters of our time wish to see the Church[1] put down by an invasion of foreign Calvinists? If not, to what cause are we to attribute the change? Surely to this, that the Protestant Dissenters are far better treated now than in the seventeenth century. Some of the most illustrious public men that England ever produced were inclined to take refuge from the tyranny of Laud in North America[2]. Was this because Presbyterians[3] and Independents[4] are incapable of loving their country? But it is idle to multiply instances. Nothing is so offensive to a man who knows any thing of history or of human nature as to hear those who exercise the powers of government accuse any sect

1. *The Church*, l'Eglise anglicane. Voyez note 6, page 153.
2. *To take refuge etc... America*, à chercher, dans l'Amérique du Nord, un refuge contre la tyrannie de Laud.
3. *Presbyterians*, Presbytériens; secte protestante qui rejette l'autorité des évêques et considère le *presbyter*, prêtre, comme investi d'une autorité spirituelle suffisante.
4. *Independents*. Voyez note 3, page 153.

of foreign attachments. If there be any proposition universally true in politics it is this, that foreign attachments are the fruit of domestic misrule. It has always been the trick of bigots to make their subjects miserable at home, and then to complain that they look for relief abroad; to divide society, and to wonder that it is not united; to govern as if a section of the state were the whole, and to censure the other sections of the state for their want of patriotic spirit. If the Jews have not felt towards England like [1] children, it is because she has treated them like a step-mother. There is no feeling which more certainly developes itself in the minds of men living under tolerably good government than the feeling of patriotism. Since the beginning of the world, there never was any nation, or any large portion of any nation, not cruelly oppressed, which was wholly destitute of that feeling. To make it therefore ground of accusation against a class of men, that they are not patriotic, is the most vulgar legerdemain of sophistry. It is the logic which the wolf employs against the lamb. It is to accuse the mouth of the stream of poisoning the source. . . . . .

The English Jews are, as far as we can see, precisely what our government has made them. They are precisely what any sect, what any class of men, treated as they have been treated, would have been. If all the red-haired people in Europe had, during centuries, been outraged and oppressed, banished from this place, imprisoned in that, deprived of their money, deprived of their teeth, convicted of the most improbable crimes on the feeblest evidence [2] dragged at horses' tails, hanged, tortured, burned alive, if, when manners became milder, they had still been subject to debasing restrictions and exposed to vulgar insults, locked up in particular streets in some countries, pelted and ducked by the rabble in others, excluded everywhere from magistracies and honours, what would be the patriotism of gentlemen with

1. *Felt... like* (senti... comme), eu les sentiments de.

2. *Evidence*, témoignage.

red hair? And if, under such circumstances, a proposition were made for admitting red-haired men to office, how striking a speech might an eloquent admirer of our old institutions deliver against so revolutionary a measure! "These men," he might say, "scarcely consider themselves as Englishmen. They think a red-haired Frenchman or a red-haired German more closely connected with them than a man with brown hair born in their own parish. If a foreign sovereign patronises red hair, they love him better than their own native king. They are not Englishmen : they cannot be Englishmen : nature has forbidden it : experience proves it to be impossible. Right to political power they have none[1]; for no man has a right to political power. Let them enjoy personal security; let their property be under the protection of the law. But if they ask for leave to exercise power over a community of which they are only half members, a community the constitution of which is essentially dark-haired, let us answer them in the words of our wis ancestors, "*Nolumus leges Angliæ mutari*[2]."

But, it is said, the Scriptures declare that the Jews are to be restored to their own country; and the whole nation looks forward to that restoration. They are, therefore, not so deeply interested as others in the prosperity of England. It is not their home, but merely the place of their sojourn[3], the house of their bondage[4]. This argument, which first appeared in the Times newspaper, and which has attracted a degree of attention proportioned not so much to its own intrinsic force as to the general talent with which that journal is conducted, belongs to a class of sophisms by which the most hateful persecutions may easily be justified. To charge men with practical consequences which they themselves deny is disingenuous in controversy; it is atrocious in government.

---

1. *Right to political power they have none* = they have no right to political power.

2. En latin : Nous ne voulons pas qu'on change les lois de l'Angleterre.

3. Voy. plus loin, note 1, page 161.

4. Expression employée plusieurs fois dans la Bible, où elle s'applique particulièrement à la captivité des Hébreux en Egypte.

. . . .

It is altogether impossible to reason from the opinions which a man professes to his feelings and his actions; and in fact no person is ever such a fool as to reason thus, except when he wants a pretext for persecuting his neighbours. A Christian is commanded, under the strongest sanctions, to be just in all his dealings. Yet to how many of the twenty-four millions of professing Christians in these islands would any man in his senses lend a thousand pounds without security? A man who should act, for one day, on the supposition that all the people about him were influenced by the religion which they professed, would find himself ruined before night; and no man ever does act on that supposition in any of the ordinary concerns of life, in borrowing, in lending, in buying, or in selling. But when any of our fellow-creatures are to be oppressed, the case is different. Then we represent those motives which we know to be so feeble for good as omnipotent for evil. Then we lay to the charge of our victims all the vices and follies to which their doctrines, however remotely, seem to tend. We forget that the same weakness, the same laxity, the same disposition to prefer the present to the future, which make men worse than a good religion, make them better than a bad one. . . . .

People are now reasoning about the Jews as our fathers reasoned about the Papists. The law which is inscribed on the walls of the synagogues prohibits covetousness. But if we were to say that a Jew mortgagee[1] would not foreclose[2] because God had commanded him not to covet his neighbour's house, every body would think us out of our wits. Yet it passes for an argument to say that a Jew will take no interest in the prosperity of the country in which he lives, that he will not care how bad its laws and police may be, how heavily it may be taxed, how

---

1. *Mortgagee*, créancier hypothécaire.
2. *Foreclose* (terme de droit :) faire enlever à un débiteur le droit de racheter une hypothèque.

often it may be conquered and given up to spoil, because God has promised that, by some unknown means, and at some undetermined time, perhaps ten thousand years hence, the Jews shall migrate to Palestine. Is not this the most profound ignorance of human nature? Do we not know that what is remote and indefinite affects men far less than what is near and certain? The argument too applies to Christians as strongly as to Jews. The Christian believes as well as the Jew, that at some future period the present order of things will come to an end. Nay, many Christians[1] believe that the Messiah will shortly establish a kingdom on the earth, and reign visibly over all its inhabitants. Whether this doctrine be[2] orthodox or not we shall not here inquire. The number of people who hold it is very much greater than the number of Jews residing in England. Many of those who hold it are distinguished by rank, wealth, and ability. it is preached from pulpits, both of the Scottish and of the English church. Noblemen and members of Parliament have written in defence of it. New wherein[3] does this doctrine differ, as far as its political tendency is concerned, from the doctrine of the Jews? If a Jew is unfit to legislate for us because he believes that he or his remote descendants will be removed to Palestine, can we safely open the House of Commons to a fifth-monarchy man[4], who expects that before this generation shall pass away, all the kingdoms of the earth will be swallowed up in one divine empire?

Does a Jew engage less eagerly than a Christian in any competition which the law leaves open to him? Is he less

---

1. Les Millénaires, qui croient que le Christ régnera personnellement mille ans sur la terre. Cette croyance repose sur un passage de l'Apocalypse : « Je vis aussi des trônes et des personnes qui s'assirent dessus... Je vis encore les âmes de ceux qui avaient eu la tête coupée pour le témoignage qu'ils avaient rendu à Jésus... ; et elles entrèrent dans la vie, et elles régnèrent avant Jésus-Christ pendant mille ans. » xx, 4.

2. Voyez note 6, page 96.

3. *Now wherein*, or, en quoi.

4. *Fifth-monarchy man* (homme de la cinquième monarchie), millénaire, parce que le règne personnel de Jésus constituerait la cinquième monarchie universelle, les quatre autres ayant été l'assyrienne, la perse, la macédonienne et la romaine. Ce nom de *fifth-monarchy men* se donne surtout aux millénaires du temps de Cromwell.

active and regular in his business than his neighbours? Does he furnish his house meanly, because he is a pilgrim and sojourner[1] in the land? Does the expectation of being restored to the country of his fathers make him insensible to the fluctuations of the stock-exchange? Does he, in arranging his private affairs, ever take into the account[2] the chance of his migrating to Palestine? If not, why are we to suppose that feelings which never influence his dealings as a merchant, or his dispositions as a testator, will acquire a boundless influence over him as soon as he becomes a magistrate or a legislator?

There is another argument which we would not willingly treat with levity, and which yet we scarcely know how to treat seriously. Scripture, it is said, is full of terrible denunciations against the Jews. It is foretold that they are to be wanderers. Is it then right to give them a home? It is foretold that they are to be oppressed. Can we with propriety suffer them to be rulers? To admit them to the rights of citizens is manifestly to insult the Divine oracles.

We allow that to falsify a prophecy inspired by Divine Wisdom would be a most atrocious crime. It is, therefore, a happy circumstance for our frail species, that it is a crime which no man can possibly commit. If we admit the Jews to seats in Parliament, we shall, by so doing, prove that the prophecies in question, whatever they may mean, do not mean that the Jews shall be excluded from Parliament.

In fact it is already clear that the prophecies do not bear the meaning put upon them by the respectable persons whom we are now answering. In France and in the United States the Jews are already admitted to all the rights of citizens. A prophecy, therefore, which should mean that the Jews would never, during the course of

---

1. *A pilgrim and sojourner*, expression biblique : *sojourner* désigne un étranger simplement de passage dans un pays.

2. *Does he... take into the account* (met-il dans le compte), tient-il compte de.

their wanderings, be admitted to all the rights of citizens in the places of their sojourn, would be a false prophecy. This, therefore, is not the meaning of the prophecies of Scripture.

But we protest altogether against the practice of confounding prophecy with precept, of setting up predictions which are often obscure against a morality which is always clear. If actions are to be considered as just and good merely because they have been predicted, what action was ever more laudable than that crime which our bigots are now, at the end of eighteen centuries, urging us to avenge on the Jews, that crime which made the earth shake and blotted out the sun from heaven? The same reasoning which is now employed to vindicate the disabilities imposed on our Hebrew countrymen will equally vindicate the kiss of Judas and the Judgment of Pilate. "The Son of man goeth, as it is written of him; but woe to that man by whom the Son of man is betrayed"[1]. And woe to those who, in any age or in any country, disobey his benevolent commands under pretence of accomplishing his predictions. If this argument justifies the laws now existing against the Jews, it justifies equally all the cruelties which have ever been committed against them, the sweeping edicts of banishment and confiscation, the dungeon, the rack, and the slow fire. How can we excuse ourselves for leaving property to people who are to "serve their enemies in hunger, and in thirst, and in nakedness, and in want of all things"[2]; for giving protection to the persons of those who are to "fear day and night, and to have none assurance of their life"[3]; for not seizing on the children of a race whose "sons and daughters are to be given unto another people"[4].

We have not so learned the doctrines of Him who commanded us to love our neighbour as ourselves, and

---

1. Saint Marc, xiv, 21.
2. Seconde Épître de saint Paul aux Corinthiens, xi, 27.
3. Deutéronome, xxviii, 66. — *None*, archaïque pour *no*.
4. Deutéronome, xxviii, 32.

who, when he was called upon [1] to explain what He meant
by a neighbour, selected as an example a heretic and an
alien. Last year, we remember, it was represented by a
pious writer in the John Bull newspaper [2], and by some
other equally fervid Christians, as a monstrous indecency,
that the measure for the relief of the Jews should be
brought forward in Passion week. One of these humour-
ists ironically recommended that it should be read a
second time on Good Friday [3]. We should have had no
objection ; nor do we believe that the day could be com-
memorated in a more worthy manner. We know of no
day fitter for terminating long hostilities, and repairing
cruel wrongs, than the day on which the religion of mercy
was founded. We know of no day fitter for blotting out
from the statute-book the last traces of intolerance than
the day on which the spirit of intolerance produced the
foulest of all judicial murders, the day on which the list
of the victims of intolerance, that noble list wherein Socrates and More are enrolled [4], was glorified by a yet
greater and holier name [5].

Bacon [6].

He was now [7] satisfied [8] that he had little to hope from
the patronage of those powerful kinsmen whom he had
solicited during twelve years with such meek pertinacity;
and he began to look towards a different quarter. Among
the courtiers of Elizabeth [9] had lately appeared a new

1. *Called upon*, invité.
2. *The John Bull newspaper*, le journal " *le John Bull*". — *John Bull* est le sobriquet des Anglais, sobriquet qu'ils se sont d'ailleurs donné eux-mêmes. Le personnage de John Bull parut pour la première fois en 1712 dans une satire d'Arbuthnot.
3. *Good Friday*, le Vendredi Saint.
4. *Enrolled*, inscrits.
5. Cet Essai est de janvier 1831. Le 17 avril 1833, Macaulay soutenait la même thèse dans un admirable discours prononcé à la Chambre des Communes.
6. Extrait de l'Essai sur *Bacon*.
7. Vers 1593, après avoir échoué dans une tentative d'opposition au gouvernement, en sa qualité de député du Middlesex à la Chambre des Communes.
8. *Satisfied*, certain.
9. La reine Elisabeth, qui régna de 1558 à 1603.

favourite[1], young, noble, wealthy, accomplished, eloquent, brave, generous, aspiring; a favourite who had
obtained from the grey-headed queen such marks of regard as she had scarce vouchsafed to Leicester in the
season of the passions; who was at once the ornament of
the palace and the idol of the city; who was the common
patron[2] of men of letters and of men of the sword; who
was the common refuge of the persecuted Catholic and of
the persecuted Puritan. . . . .

Nothing in the political conduct of Essex entitles him
to esteem; and the pity with which we regard his early
and terrible end[3] is diminished by the consideration, that
he put to hazard the lives and fortunes of his most attached
friends, and endeavoured to throw the whole country
into confusion, for objects purely personal. Still, it is
impossible not to be deeply interested for a man so brave,
high-spirited, and generous; for a man who, while he
conducted himself towards his sovereign with a boldness
such as was then found in no other subject, conducted
himself towards his dependents with a delicacy such
as has rarely been found in any other patron. Unlike
the vulgar herd of benefactors, he desired to in-
spire, not gratitude, but affection. He tried to make
those whom he befriended feel towards him as towards
an equal. His mind, ardent, susceptible, naturally disposed to admiration of all that is great and beautiful,
was fascinated by the genius and the accomplishments of
Bacon. A close friendship was soon formed between
them, a friendship destined to have a dark, a mournful,
a shameful end. . . . .

The fortunes of Essex had now reached their height,
and began to decline. He possessed indeed all the qualities which raise men to greatness rapidly. But he had
neither the virtues nor the vices which enable men to retain greatness long. His frankness, his keen sensibility

1. Robert Devereux, comte d'Essex.   la reine, il fut condamné à mort et
2. *Patron*, protecteur.   exécuté (1601).
3. Convaincu de conspiration contre

to insult and injustice, were by no means agreeable to a
sovereign naturally impatient of opposition, and accustomed, during forty years, to the most extravagant
flattery, and the most abject submission. The daring
and contemptuous manner in which he bade defiance to
his enemies excited their deadly hatred. His administration in Ireland[1] was unfortunate, and in many respects
highly blamable. Though his brilliant courage and his
impetuous activity fitted him admirably for such enter-
prises as that of Cadiz[2], he did not possess the caution,
patience, and resolution necessary for the conduct of a
protracted war, in which difficulties were to be gradually
surmounted, in which much discomfort was to be endured,
and in which few splendid exploits could be achieved.
For the civil duties of his high place he was still
less qualified. Though eloquent and accomplished, he
was in no sense a statesman. The multitude indeed still
continued to regard even his faults with fondness. But
the Court had ceased to give him credit, even for the
merit which he really possessed. The person on whom,
during the decline of his influence, he chiefly depended, to
whom he confided his perplexities, whose advice he
solicited, whose intercession he employed, was his friend
Bacon. The lamentable truth must be told. This friend,
so loved, so trusted, bore a principal part in ruining the
Earl's fortunes, in shedding his blood, and in blackening
his memory.

But let us be just to Bacon. We believe that, to the
last[3], he had no wish to injure[4] Essex. Nay, we believe
that he sincerely exerted himself to serve Essex, as long
as he thought that he could serve Essex without injuring
himself. The advice which he gave to his noble benefactor was generally most judicious. He did all in his
power to dissuade the Earl from accepting the Govern-

1. En 1599, Essex commandait une expédition contre l'Irlande.

2. En 1591, au cours de la guerre avec l'Espagne, les Anglais s'emparèrent de Cadix, grâce au courage impétueux d'Essex.

3. *To the last* (sous-entendu : *moment*), jusqu'à la fin.

4. *Injure*, nuire à.

ment of Ireland. "For," says he, "I did as plainly see his overthrow chained as it were [1] by destiny to that journey, as it is possible for a man to ground a judgment upon future contingents." The prediction was accomplished. Essex returned in disgrace. Bacon attempted to mediate between his friend and the Queen; and, we believe, honestly employed all his address for that purpose. But the task which he had undertaken was too difficult, delicate, and perilous, even for so wary and dexterous an agent. He had to manage two spirits equally proud, resentful, and ungovernable. At Essex House [2], he had to calm the rage of a young hero incensed by multiplied wrongs and humiliations, and then to pass to Whitehall for the purpose of soothing the peevishness of a sovereign, whose temper, never very gentle, had been rendered morbidly irritable by age, by declining health, and by the long habit of listening to flattery and exacting implicit obedience. It is hard to serve two masters. Situated as Bacon was, it was scarcely possible for him to shape his course [3] so as not to [4] give one or both of his employers reason to complain. For a time he acted as fairly as, in circumstances so embarrassing, could reasonably be expected. At length he found that, while he was trying to prop the fortunes of another, he was in danger of shaking his own. He had disobliged both the parties whom he wished to reconcile. Essex thought him wanting in zeal as a friend : Elizabeth thought him wanting in duty as a subject. The Earl looked on him as a spy of the Queen; the Queen as a creature of the Earl. The reconciliation which he had laboured to effect appeared utterly hopeless. A thousand signs, legible to eyes far less keen than his, announced that the fall of his patron was at hand. He shaped his course accordingly. When Essex was brought before the council to

---

1. *As it were*, pour ainsi dire.

2. Les demeures princières étaient souvent ainsi désignées par le nom du maître et le mot *house*. *Hôtel* joue le même rôle en français.

3. *To shape his course*, se comporter, agir. *Course* ici signifie : ligne de conduite.

4. *So as... to*, de façon à.

answer for his conduct in Ireland, Bacon, after a faint attempt to excuse himself from taking part against his friend, submitted himself to the Queen's pleasure, and appeared at the bar in support of the charges. But a darker scene was behind.   The unhappy young nobleman, made reckless by despair, ventured on a rash and criminal enterprise[1], which rendered him liable to the highest penalties of the law.   What course was Bacon to take?   This was one of those conjunctures which show what men are.   To a high-minded man, wealth, power, court-favour, even personal safety, would have appeared of no account, when opposed to friendship, gratitude, and honour.   Such a man would have stood by the side of Essex at the trial, would have " spent all his power, might, authority, and amity" in soliciting[2] a mitigation of the sentence, would have been a daily visitor at the cell, would have received the last injunctions and the last embrace on the scaffold, would have employed all the powers of his intellect to guard from insult the fame of his generous though erring friend.   An ordinary man would neither have incurred the danger of succouring Essex, nor the disgrace of assailing him.   Bacon did not even preserve neutrality.   He appeared as counsel for the prosecution[3].   In that situation, he did not confine himself to what would have been amply sufficient to procure a verdict[4].   He employed all his wit, his rhetoric, and his learning, not to insure a conviction[5], — for the circumstances were such that a conviction was inevitable, — but to deprive the unhappy prisoner of all those excuses which, though legally of no value, yet tended to diminish the moral guilt of the crime, and which, therefore, though they could not justify the peers in[6] pronouncing an acquittal, might incline the Queen to grant a pardon.   The

----

1. Voyez note 3, page 164.

2. *In soliciting*, à solliciter.

3. *Counsel for the prosecution* (avocat pour la poursuite), désigne ordinairement l'avocat du demandeur. Ici le demandeur étant la reine, *counsel* *for the prosecution* équivaut à : ministère public.

4. *Procure a verdict*, obtenir un verdict (de culpabilité). Voyez plus loin : *obtaining a verdict*.

5. *Conviction*, condamnation.

6. *Justify... in*, autoriser... à.

Earl urged as a palliation of his frantic acts that he was surrounded by powerful and inveterate enemies, that they had ruined his fortunes, that they sought his life, and that their persecutions had driven him to despair. This was true; and Bacon well knew it to be true. But he affected to treat it as an idle pretence. He compared Essex to Pisistratus who, by pretending to be in imminent danger of assassination, and by exhibiting self-inflicted wounds, succeeded in establishing tyranny at Athens [1]. This was too much for the prisoner to bear. He interrupted his ungrateful friend by calling on him [2] to quit the part of an advocate, to come forward as a witness, and to tell the Lords whether, in old times, he, Francis Bacon, had not, under his own hand [3], repeatedly asserted the truth of what he now represented as idle pretexts. It is painful to go on with this lamentable story. Bacon returned a shuffling answer to the Earl's question, and, as if the allusion to Pisistratus were not sufficiently offensive, made another allusion still more unjustifiable. He compared Essex to Henry Duke of Guise, and the rash attempt in the city [4] to the day of the barricades [5] at Paris. Why Bacon had recourse to such a topic it is difficult to say. It was quite unnecessary for the purpose of obtaining a verdict. It was certain to produce a strong impression on the mind of the haughty and jealous princess on whose pleasure the Earl's fate depended. The faintest allusion to the degrading tutelage in which the last Valois had been held by the House of Lorraine was sufficient to harden her heart against a man who in rank, in military reputation, in popularity among the citizens of the capital, bore some resemblance to the Captain of the League.

Essex was convicted. Bacon made no effort to save him, though the Queen's feelings were such that he

1. Au sixième siècle avant Jésus-Christ.

2. *Calling on him*, l'invitant, le sommant.

3. *Hand*, signature.

4. C'est le 8 février 1601 qu'Essex essaya de soulever contre la reine la population de la Cité.

5. La journée des Barricades, 12 mai 1588.

might have pleaded his benefactor's cause, possibly with success, certainly without any serious danger to himself. The unhappy nobleman was executed. His fate excited strong, perhaps unreasonable feelings of compassion and indignation. The Queen was received by the citizens of London with gloomy looks and faint acclamations. She thought it expedient to publish a vindication of her late proceedings. The faithless friend who had assisted in taking [1] the Earl's life was now employed to murder the Earl's fame. The Queen had seen some of Bacon's writings and had been pleased with them. He was accordingly selected to write " A Declaration of the Practices and Treasons attempted and committed by Robert Earl of Essex ", which was printed by authority. In the succeeding reign, Bacon had not a word to say in defence of this performance, a performance abounding in expressions which no generous enemy would have employed respecting a man who had so dearly expiated his offences. His only excuse was, that he wrote it by command, that he considered himself as a mere secretary, that he had particular instructions as to the way in which he was to treat every part of the subject, and that, in fact, he had furnished only the arrangement and the style . . . .

The real explanation of all this is perfectly obvious ; and nothing but a partiality amounting to a ruling passion could cause any body to miss it. The moral qualities of Bacon were not of a high order. We do not say that he was a bad man. He was not inhuman or tyrannical. He bore with meekness his high civil honours [2], and the far higher honours gained by his intellect. He was very seldom, if ever, provoked into treating any person with malignity and insolence. No man more readily held up the left cheek to those who had smitten the right [3]. No man was more expert at the soft answer

---

1. *In taking*, à prendre.
2. Allusion à ce passage de Shakespeare, où *faculties* = power, *meek* = meekly, et où *to bear* signifie exercer :

> This Duncan
> Hath borne his faculties so meek...
> (*Macbeth*, I, vii, 16.)

3. Allusion biblique : " *Whosoever*

which turneth away wrath[1]. He was never charged, by any accuser entitled to the smallest credit, with licentious habits. His even temper, his flowing courtesy[2], the general respectability of his demeanour, made a favourable impression on those who saw him in situations which do not severely try the principles. His faults were — we write it with pain — coldness of heart, and meanness of spirit. He seems to have been incapable of feeling strong affection, of facing great dangers, of making great sacrifices. His desires were set on things below. Wealth, precedence, titles, patronage[3], the mace[4], the seals[5], the coronet[6], large houses, fair gardens, rich manors, massy services of plate, gay hangings, curious cabinets, had as great attractions for him as for any of the courtiers who dropped on their knees in the dirt when Elizabeth passed by, and then hastened home to write to the King of Scots that her Grace[7] seemed to be breaking[8] fast. For these objects he had stooped to every thing, and endured every thing. For these he had sued in the humblest manner, and, when unjustly and ungraciously repulsed, had thanked those who had repulsed him, and had begun to sue again. For these objects, as soon as he found that the smallest show of independence in Parliament[9] was offensive to the Queen, he had abased himself to the dust before her, and implored forgiveness in terms better suited to a convicted

shall smite thee on thy right cheek, turn to him the other also". (St MATTHEW, v, 39.)

1. Allusion biblique : "*A soft answer turneth away wrath ; but grievous words stir up anger.*" (*Proverbs*, xv, 1.) — *Turneth* = turns.

2. *His flowing courtesy.* — Ici *flowing* = smooth. Il semble y avoir là un souvenir d'un passage de l'historien Clarendon cité par Macaulay dans son *Essai sur Hampden* : "*He (Hampden) preserved his own natural cheerfulness and vivacity, and, above all, a flowing courtesy to all men*".

3. *Patronage*, influence.

4. *The mace*, la masse, que l'on porte devant certains hauts dignitaires.

5. *The seals*, les sceaux. En 1607, Bacon fut nommé *Lord Keeper* ou *Keeper of the Great Seal*. Aujourd'hui c'est le *Lord Chancellor* qui est investi des fonctions de garde des sceaux.

6. *Coronet*, petite couronne, représentant tout titre de noblesse inférieur à celui de souverain. En 1618, Bacon reçut le titre de *Baron Verulam*, et. en 1621, celui de *Viscount St-Albans*.

7. *Her Grace*, Sa Majesté (Elisabeth).

8. *To be breaking*, perdre ses forces, dépérir.

9. Voyez note 7, page 163.

thief than to a knight of the shire[1]. For these he joined, and for these he forsook, Lord Essex. He continued to plead his patron's cause with the Queen as long as he thought that by pleading that cause he might serve himself. Nay, he went further; for his feelings, though not warm, were kind; he pleaded that cause as long as he thought that he could plead it without injury to himself. But when it became evident that Essex was going headlong to his ruin, Bacon began to tremble for his own fortunes. What he had to fear would not indeed have been very alarming to a man of lofty character. It was not death. It was not imprisonment. It was the loss of court favour. It was the being left behind by others in the career of ambition. It was the having leisure to finish the *Instauratio Magna*[2]. The Queen looked coldly on him. The courtiers began to consider him as a marked[3] man. He determined to change his line of conduct, and to proceed in a new course with so much vigour as to make up for lost time. When once he had determined to act against his friend, knowing himself to be suspected, he acted with more zeal than would have been necessary or justifiable if he had been employed against a stranger. He exerted his professional talents to shed the Earl's blood, and his literary talents to blacken the Earl's memory. . . .

In a few weeks was signally brought to the test the value of those objects for which Bacon had sullied his integrity, had resigned his independence, had violated the most sacred obligations of friendship and gratitude, had flattered the worthless, had persecuted the innocent, had tampered with judges, had tortured prisoners, had plundered suitors, had wasted on paltry intrigues all the powers of the most exquisitely constructed intellect that has ever been bestowed on any of the children of men. A sudden and terrible reverse was at hand. A

1. *Knight of the shire* (chevalier du comté), député représentant un comté au Parlement.
2. *Instauratio Magna* (la Grande Renaissance), titre général de l'œuvre philosophique de Bacon.

3. *Marked*, ici : taré.

Parliament had been summoned. After six years of silence the voice of the nation was again to be heard. .

A committee of the lower House [1] had been appointed to inquire into the state of the Courts of Justice. On the fifteenth of March the chairman of that committee, Sir Robert Philips, member for [2] Bath, reported that great abuses had been discovered. "The person", said he, "against whom these things are alleged is no less than the Lord Chancellor [3], a man so endued with all parts, both of nature and art, as that [4] I will say no more of him, being not able to say enough". Sir Robert [5] then proceeded to state, in the most temperate manner, the nature of the charges. A person of the name of Aubrey had a case [6] depending in Chancery [7]. He had been almost ruined by law-expenses, and his patience had been exhausted by the delays of the court. He received a hint from some of the hangers-on of the Chancellor that a present of one hundred pounds would expedite matters. The poor man had not the sum required. However, having found out an usurer who accommodated him with it at high interest, he carried it to York House [8]. The Chancellor took the money, and his dependents assured the suitor that all would go right. Aubrey was, however, disappointed; for, after considerable delay, a "killing decree" [9] was pronounced against him. Another suitor of the name of Egerton complained that he had been induced by two of the Chancellor's jackals [10] to make his Lordship a present of

1. *The lower House* (la chambre inférieure), la Chambre des Communes.

2. *Member for*, député de.

3. C'est en 1618 que Bacon fut nommé *Lord Chancellor*, titre qui correspond à celui de notre Ministre de la Justice. Comme ce dernier, le *Lord Chancellor* est en même temps garde des sceaux. Du temps de Bacon les deux fonctions étaient distinctes. Voyez note 5. page 170.

4. *As that*, ancien pour *that*.

5. *Sir Robert.* — Voyez note 1, page 89.

6. *Case*, procès.

7. *Chancery*, la cour de Chancellerie, qui est, après le Parlement, la plus haute cour de justice en Angleterre.

8. *York House*, demeure de Bacon. Elle était située dans le Strand. C'était la résidence officielle des chanceliers et des gardes des sceaux.

9. *A killing decree*, un jugement défavorable.

10. *Jackals*, chacals, c'est-à-dire rabatteurs. On croyait autrefois que le chacal aidait le lion à découvrir sa proie.

four hundred pounds, and that, nevertheless, he had not been able to obtain a decree in his favour. The evidence to [1] these facts was overwhelming. Bacon's friends could only entreat the House to suspend its judgment, and to send up the case to the Lords, in a form less offensive than an impeachment.

On the nineteenth of March the King sent a message to the Commons, expressing his deep regret that so eminent a person as the Chancellor should be suspected of misconduct. His Majesty declared that he had no wish to screen the guilty from justice, and proposed to appoint a new kind of tribunal, consisting of eighteen commissioners, who might be chosen from among the members of the two Houses, to investigate the matter. The Commons were not disposed to depart from their regular course of proceeding. On the same day they held a conference with the Lords, and delivered in [2] the heads [3] of the accusation against the Chancellor. At this conference Bacon was not present. Overwhelmed with shame and remorse, and abandoned by all those in whom he had weakly put his trust, he had shut himself up in his chamber from the eyes of men. The dejection of his mind soon disordered his body. Buckingham, who visited him by the King's order, " found his Lordship very sick and heavy [4] ". It appears from a pathetic letter which the unhappy man addressed to the Peers on the day of the conference, that he neither expected nor wished to survive his disgrace. During several days he remained in his bed, refusing to see any human being. He passionately told his attendants to leave him, to forget him, never again to name his name, never to remember that there had been such a man in the world. In the mean time, fresh instances of corruption were every day brought to the knowledge of his accusers. The number of charges rapidly increased from two to twenty-three.

---

1. *Evidence to*, témoignage à l'appui de.
2. *Delivered in*, remirent, déposèrent.
3. *Heads* (têtes), points, chefs.
4. *Heavy* (lourd), accablé.

The Lords entered on the investigation of the case with laudable alacrity.   Some witnesses were examined at the bar of the House.   A select committee was appointed to take the depositions of others; and the inquiry was rapidly proceeding, when, on the twenty-sixth of March, the King adjourned the Parliament for three weeks.

This measure revived Bacon's hopes.   He made the most[1] of his short respite.   He attempted to work on the feeble mind of the King.   He appealed to all the strongest feelings of James, to his fears, to his vanity, to his high notions of prerogative.   Would the Solomon of the age[2] commit so gross an error as to encourage the encroaching spirit of Parliaments?   Would God's anointed, accountable to God alone, pay homage to the clamorous multitude?   "Those", exclaimed Bacon, "who now strike at the Chancellor will soon strike at the Crown.   I am the first sacrifice.   I wish I may be the last".   But all his eloquence and address were employed in vain. . . . .

On the seventeenth of April the Houses reassembled, and the Lords resumed their inquiries into the abuses of the Court of Chancery[3].   On the twenty-second, Bacon addressed to the Peers a letter, which the Prince of Wales[4] condescended to deliver.   In this artful and pathetic composition, the Chancellor acknowledged his guilt in guarded and general terms, and, while acknowledging, endeavoured to palliate it.   This, however, was not thought sufficient by his judges.   They required a more particular confession, and sent him a copy of the charges. On the thirtieth, he delivered a paper in which he admitted, with few and unimportant reservations, the truth of the accusations brought against him, and threw

1. *He made the most*, il tira le plus grand parti.
2. *The Solomon of the age*, le Salomon du siècle, surnom donné au roi Jacques Ier à cause de son érudition.
3. Voyez note 7, page 172.
4. *The Prince of Wales*, le Prince de Galles. — Depuis la conquête du pays de Galles, à la fin du treizième siècle. les fils aînés des rois d'Angleterre ont toujours porté ce titre. Celui dont il est question ici régna quelques années plus tard sous le nom de Charles Ier.

himself entirely on the mercy of his peers. " Upon advised consideration of the charges ", said he, " descending into my own conscience, and calling my memory to account so far as[1] I am able, I do plainly and ingenuously confess that I am guilty of corruption, and do renounce all defence ".

The Lords came to a resolution[2] that the Chancellor's confession appeared to be full and ingenuous, and sent a committee to inquire of him whether it was really subscribed by himself. The deputies, among whom was Southampton, the common friend, many years before, of Bacon and Essex, performed their duty with great delicacy. Indeed the agonies[3] of such a mind and the degradation of such a name might well have softened the most obdurate natures. " My Lords ", said Bacon, " it is my act, my hand, my heart. I beseech your Lordships to be merciful to a broken reed "[4]. They withdrew; and he again retired to his chamber in the deepest dejection. The next day, the sergeant-at-arms[5] and the usher of the House of Lords came to conduct him to Westminster Hall, where sentence was to be pronounced. But they found him so unwell that he could not leave his bed; and this excuse for his absence was readily accepted. In no quarter does there appear to have been the smallest desire to add to his humiliation.

The sentence was, however, severe, the more severe, no doubt, because the Lords knew that it would not be executed, and that they had an excellent opportunity of exhibiting, at small cost, the inflexibility of their justice, and their abhorrence of corruption. Bacon was condemned to pay a fine of forty thousand pounds, and to be imprisoned in the Tower[6] during the King's pleasure.

---

1. *So far as*, autant que.
2. *Came to a resolution*, décidèrent.
3. *Agonies*, angoisses.
4. Expression biblique : " *A bruised reed shall he not break* ", ISAIAH, XLII, 3.
5. *Sergeant-at-arms*, sergent d'armes, officier attaché à la Chambre des Lords, et chargé d'exécuter les sentences prononcées par cette chambre quand elle siège comme cour suprême de justice.
6. *The Tower*, la Tour de Londres, située sur la rive gauche de la Tamise. La Tour, qui date de Guillaume le Conquérant, fut longtemps forteresse, palais royal et prison ; elle sert aujourd'hui d'arsenal.

He was declared incapable of holding any office in the State or of sitting in Parliament; and he was banished for life from the verge of the court. In such misery and shame ended that long career of worldly wisdom and worldly prosperity . . . .

The chief peculiarity of Bacon's philosophy seems to us to have been this, that it aimed at things altogether different from those which his predecessors had proposed to themselves. This was his own opinion. . . . . . .

The more carefully his works are examined, the more clearly, we think, it will appear that this is the real clue to his whole system, and that he used means different from those used by other philosophers, because he wished to arrive at an end altogether different from theirs.

What then was the end which Bacon proposed to himself? It was, to use his own emphatic[1] expression " fruit." It was the multiplying of human enjoyments and the mitigating of human sufferings. . . . .

Two words form the key of the Baconian doctrine, Utility and Progress. The ancient philosophy disdained to be useful, and was content to be stationary. It dealt largely in[2] theories of moral perfection, which were so sublime that they never could be more than theories; in attempts to solve insoluble enigmas; in exhortations to the attainment of unattainable frames of mind. It could not condescend to the humble office of ministering to the comfort of human beings. All the schools contemned that office as degrading; some censured it as immoral. Once indeed Posidonius, a distinguished writer of the age[3] of Cicero and Cæsar, so far forgot himself as to[4] enumerate, among the humbler blessings which mankind owed to philosophy, the discovery of the principle of the arch, and the introduction of the use of metals. This eulogy was considered as an affront, and was taken up with proper spirit[5]. Seneca vehemently disclaims these insulting compliments. Phi-

---

1. *Emphatic*, énergique.
2. *It dealt largely in*, elle s'occupait beaucoup de.
3. *Age*, siècle, époque.

4. *So far... as to* (assez loin... pour), au point de.

5. *Proper spirit*, la vigueur voulue.

losophy, according to him, has nothing to do with teaching men to rear arched roofs over their heads. The true philosopher does not care whether he has an arched roof or any roof. Philosophy has nothing to do with teaching men the uses of metals. She teaches us to be independent of all material substances, of all mechanical contrivances. The wise man lives according to nature. Instead of attempting to add to the physical comforts of his species, he regrets that his lot was not cast[1] in that golden age when the human race had no protection against the cold but the skins of wild beasts, no screen from the sun but a cavern. To impute to such a man any share in the invention or improvement of a plough, a ship, or a mill, is an insult. " In my own time", says Seneca, " there have been inventions of this sort, transparent windows, tubes for diffusing warmth equally through all parts of a building, short-hand, which has been carried to such a perfection that a writer can keep pace with the most rapid speaker. But the inventing of such things is drudgery for the lowest slaves; philosophy lies deeper. It is not her office to teach men how to use their hands. The object of her lessons is to form the soul . . . .

" We shall next be told, " exclaims Seneca, " that the first shoemaker was a philosopher." For our own part, if we are forced to make our choice between the first shoemaker, and the author[2] of the three books On Anger, we pronounce for the shoemaker. It may be worse to be angry than to be wet. But shoes have kept[3] millions from being wet; and we doubt whether Seneca ever kept any body from being angry . . . .

The spirit which appears in the passage of Seneca to which we have referred tainted the whole body of the ancient philosophy from the time of Socrates downwards, and took possession of intellects with which that of Seneca cannot for a moment be compared. It pervades the dia-

---

1. *His lot was not cast* (son sort n'ait pas été jeté), il ne lui ait pas été donné de vivre.

2. Sénèque.

3. *Kept*, empêché.

logues of Plato. It may be distinctly traced in many parts of the works of Aristotle. Bacon has dropped hints from which it may be inferred that, in his opinion, the prevalence of this feeling was in a great measure to be attributed to the influence of Socrates. Our great countryman evidently did not consider the revolution which Socrates effected in philosophy as a happy event and constantly maintained that the earlier Greek speculators[1], Democritus in particular, were, on the whole, superior to their more celebrated successors. . . . . .

Assuredly if the tree which Socrates planted and Plato watered is to be judged of by its flowers and leaves, it is the noblest of trees. But if we take the homely test of Bacon, if we judge of the tree by its fruits, our opinion of it may perhaps be less favourable. When we sum up all the useful truths which we owe to that philosophy, to what do they amount? We find, indeed, abundant proofs that some of those who cultivated it were men of the first order of intellect. We find among their writings incomparable specimens both of dialectical and rhetorical art. We have no doubt that the ancient controversies were of use, in so far as[2] they served to exercise the faculties of the disputants; for there is no controversy so idle that it may not be of use in this way. But, when we look for something more, for something which adds to the comforts or alleviates the calamities of the human race, we are forced to own ourselves disappointed. We are forced to say with Bacon that this celebrated philosophy ended in nothing but disputation, that it was neither a vineyard nor an olive-ground, but an intricate wood of briers and thistles, from which those who lost themselves in it brought back many scratches and no food.

We readily acknowledge that some of the teachers of this unfruitful wisdom were among the greatest men that the world has ever seen . . . .
But in truth the very admiration which we feel for the

***

1. *Speculators*, penseurs.　　|　2. *In so far as*, en tant que.

eminent philosophers of antiquity forces us to adopt the opinion that their powers were systematically misdirected. For how else could it be that such powers should effect so little for mankind? A pedestrian may show as much muscular vigour on a treadmill[1] as on the highway road. But on the road his vigour will assuredly carry him forward; and on the treadmill he will not advance an inch. The ancient philosophy was a treadmill, not a path. It was made up of revolving questions, of controversies which were always beginning again. It was a contrivance for having much exertion and no progress. We must acknowledge that more than once, while contemplating the doctrines of the Academy[2] and the Portico[3], even as they appear in the transparent splendour of Cicero's incomparable diction[4], we have been tempted to mutter with the surly centurion in Persius, "Cur quis non prandeat hoc est[5]?" What is the highest good, whether pain be an evil, whether all things be fated, whether we can be certain of any thing, whether we can be certain that we are certain of nothing, whether a wise man can be unhappy, whether all departures from right be equally reprehensible, these, and other questions of the same sort, occupied the brains, the tongues, and the pens of the ablest men in the civilised world during several centuries. This sort of philosophy, it is evident, could not be progressive. It might indeed sharpen and invigorate the minds of those who devoted themselves to it; and so might the disputes of the orthodox Lilliputians and the heretical · Blefuscudians[6] about

1. *Treadmill*, instrument en usage dans les prisons anglaises et qui consiste en une roue cylindrique que le prisonnier doit faire tourner en posant, comme s'il marchait, les pieds sur des planchettes dont cette roue est munie et qui forment une sorte d'escalier sans fin.

2. *The Academy*, l'Académie, l'école de Platon, ainsi appelée parce qu'elle était installée dans les jardins d'un certain Academus.

3. *The Portico*, le Portique. — Le philosophe grec Zénon (troisième siècle av. J.-C.), fondateur de l'école stoïcienne, réunissait souvent ses élèves sous un portique d'Athènes ; d'où le nom de *Portique* donné à cette école.

4. *Diction*, style.

5. *Cur quis non prandeat hoc est?* (PERSE, *Sat.*, III, 85.) Cela est-il une raison pour ne pas manger ?

6. *Lilliputians, Blefuscudians*, Lilliputiens, Blefuscudiens, habitants des îles de Lilliput et de Blefuscu,

the big ends and the little ends of eggs. But such disputes could add nothing to the stock of knowledge. The human mind accordingly, instead of marching, merely marked time. It took as much trouble as would have sufficed to carry it forward; and yet remained on the same spot. There was no accumulation of truth, no heritage of truth acquired by the labour of one generation and bequeathed to another, to be again transmitted with large additions to a third. Where this philosophy was in the time of Cicero, there it continued to be in the time of Seneca, and there it continued to be in the time of Favorinus. The same sects were still battling, with the same unsatisfactory arguments, about the same interminable questions. There had been no want of ingenuity, of zeal, of industry. Every trace of intellectual cultivation was there, except a harvest. There had been plenty of ploughing, harrowing, reaping, threshing. But the garners contained only smut and stubble.

The ancient philosophers did not neglect natural science; but they did not cultivate it for the purpose of increasing the power and ameliorating the condition of man. The taint of barrenness had spread from ethical to physical speculations. Seneca wrote largely[1] on natural philosophy, and magnified the importance of that study. But why? Not because it tended to assuage suffering, to multiply the conveniences of life, to extend the empire of man over the material world; but solely because it tended to raise the mind above low cares, to separate it from the body, to exercise its subtilty in the solution of very obscure questions. Thus natural philosophy was considered in the light merely of a mental exercise. It was made subsidiary to the art of disputation; and it consequently proved altogether barren of useful discoveries.

There was one sect which, however absurd and perni-

---

pays imaginaires décrits dans les *Voyages de Gulliver*, de Swift. Les Lilliputiens orthodoxes cassaient leurs œufs par le petit bout; les autres par le gros bout. De là des controverses et des guerres sanglantes.

1. *Largely,* abondamment.

cious some of its doctrines may have been, ought, it should seem, to have merited an exception from the general censure which Bacon has pronounced on the ancient schools of wisdom. The Epicurean, who referred all happiness to bodily pleasure, and all evil to bodily pain, might have been expected to exert himself for the purpose of bettering his own physical condition and that of his neighbours. But the thought seems never to have occurred to any member of that school. Indeed their notion, as reported by their great poet[1], was, that no more improvements were to be expected in the arts which conduce to the comfort of life . . . .

This contented despondency, this disposition to admire what has been done, and to expect that nothing more will be done, is strongly characteristic of all the schools which preceded the school of Fruit and Progress. Widely as the Epicurean and the Stoic differed on most points, they seem to have quite agreed in their contempt for pursuits so vulgar as to be useful. The philosophy of both was a garrulous, declaiming, canting, wrangling philosophy. Century after century they continued to repeat their hostile war-cries, Virtue and Pleasure; and in the end it appeared that the Epicurean had added as little to the quantity of pleasure as the Stoic to the quantity of virtue.

When learning began to revive in the West, similar trifles occupied the sharp and vigorous intellects of the Schoolmen. There was another sowing of the wind, and another reaping of the whirlwind[2]. The great work of improving the condition of the human race was still considered as unworthy of a man of learning. Those who undertook that task, if what they effected could be readily comprehended, were despised as mechanics[3]; if not, they were in danger of being burned as conjurors. . . . . . .

Words, and more words, and nothing but words, had been all the fruit of all the toil of all the most renowned

---

1. Lucrèce, poète latin du deuxième siècle.

2. Allusion biblique : " *They have*

sown the wind, and they shall reap the whirlwind ". Hosea, vii. 7.

3. *Mechanics*, artisans.

sages of sixty generations.   But the days of this sterile exuberance were numbered[1].

Many causes predisposed the public mind to a change. The study of a great variety of ancient writers, though it did not give a right direction to philosophical research, did much towards destroying that blind reverence for authority which had prevailed when Aristotle ruled alone. The rise of the Florentine sect of Platonists, a sect to which belonged some of the finest minds of the fifteenth century, was not an unimportant event.   The mere substitution of the Academic[2] for the Peripatetic philosophy[3] would indeed have done little good.   But any thing was better than the old habit of unreasoning servility.   It was something to have a choice of tyrants. " A spark of freedom ", as Gibbon has justly remarked, " was produced by this collision of adverse servitude ".

Other causes might be mentioned.   But it is chiefly to the great reformation of religion that we owe the great reformation of philosophy.   The alliance between the Schools[4] and the Vatican had for ages been so close that those who threw off the dominion of the Vatican could not continue to recognise the authority of the Schools. Most of the chiefs of the schism treated the Peripatetic philosophy with contempt, and spoke of Aristotle as if Aristotle had been answerable for all the dogmas of Thomas Aquinas . . . . , .

. . . Scarcely any text was more frequently cited by the reformers than that in which St. Paul cautions the Colossians not to let any man spoil them by philosophy[5].   Luther, almost at the outset of his career, went so far as to declare that no man could be at once

1. *Numbered*, comptés, dans le sens de : proches de leur fin.

2. *The Academic philosophy*. (la philosophie académique), la philosophie de l'Académie ou de Platon. Voyez note 2. page 179.

3. *The Peripatetic philosophy*, la philosophie péripatéticienne, c'est-à-dire la philosophie d'Aristote, ainsi appelée parce que le maître enseignait tout en se promenant avec ses élèves : (en grec. *pateo*, je me promène ; *peri*, autour).

4. *The Schools*, les écoles du moyen âge où s'enseignait la philosophie dite scolastique.

5. " *Beware lest any man spoil you through philosophy and vain deceit* ". *The Epistle to the Colossians*, ii, 8.

a proficient in the school of Aristotle and in that of
Christ. Zwingle, Bucer, Peter Martyr, Calvin, held
similar language. In some of the Scotch universities,
the Aristotelian system was discarded for that of Ramus.
Thus, before the birth of Bacon, the empire of the schol-
astic philosophy had been shaken to its foundations.
There was in the intellectual world an anarchy resembling that which in the political world often follows the
overthrow of an old and deeply rooted government.
Antiquity, prescription, the sound of great names, had
ceased to awe mankind. The dynasty which had reigned
for ages was at an end; and the vacant throne was left
to be struggled for by pretenders. . . . .

At this time Bacon appeared. It is altogether incorrect to say, as has often been said, that he was the first
man who rose up against the Aristotelian philosophy
wehn in the height of its power. The authority of that
philosophy had received a fatal blow long before he was
born. Several speculators [1], among whom Ramus is the
best known, had recently attempted to form new sects...

The part which Bacon played in this great change was
the part, not of Robespierre, but of Bonaparte. The
ancient order of things had been subverted. Some
bigots still cherished with devoted loyalty the remem-
brance of the fallen monarchy and exerted themselves to
effect a restoration. But the majority had no such
feeling. Freed, yet no knowing how to use their freedom, they pursued no determinate course, and had found
no leader capable of conducting them.

That leader at length arose. The philosophy which he
taught was essentially new. It differed from that of the
celebrated ancient teachers, not merely in method, but
also in object. Its object was the good of mankind, in
the sense in which the mass of mankind always have
understood and always will understand the word good...

The difference between the philosophy of Bacon and

_____

1. *Speculators*, penseurs. Plus loin : *speculative men.*

that of his predecessors cannot, we think, be better illustrated than by comparing his views on some important
subjects with those of Plato. We select Plato, because
we conceive that he did more than any other person
towards giving to the minds of speculative men [1] that
bent which they retained till they received from Bacon
a new impulse in a diametrically opposite direction.

It is curious to observe how differently these great men
estimated the value of every kind of knowledge. . .

On the greatest and most useful of all human inventions, the invention of alphabetical writing, Plato did not
look with much complacency. He seems to have
thought that the use of letters had operated on the
human mind as the use of the go-cart in learning to
walk, or of corks in learning to swim, is said to operate
on the human body. It was a support which, in his
opinion, soon became indispensable to those who used it,
which made vigorous exertion first unnecessary, and
then impossible. The powers of the intellect would, he
conceived, have been more fully developed without this
delusive aid. Men would have been compelled to exercise the understanding and the memory, and, by deep
and assiduous meditation, to make truth thoroughly
their own. Now, on the contrary, much knowledge is
traced on paper, but little is engraved in the soul.
A man is certain that he can find information at a moment's notice when he wants it. He therefore suffers it
to fade from his mind. Such a man cannot in strict-
ness [2] be said to know any thing. He has the show without the reality of wisdom. These opinions Plato has
put into the mouth of an ancient king of Egypt. But it
is evident from the context that they were his own ; and
so they were understood to be by Quinctilian. Indeed
they are in perfect accordance with the whole Platonic
system.

Bacon's views, as may easily be supposed, were

1. *Speculative men*, penseurs. | 2. *In strictness*, rigoureusement.

widely different.   The powers of the memory, he obser-
ves, without the help of writing, can do little towards
the advancement of any useful science.   He acknow-
ledges that the memory may be disciplined to such a
point as to be able to perform very extraordinary feats.
But on such feats he sets little value.   The habits of his
mind, he tells us, are such that he is not disposed to
rate highly any accomplishment, however rare, which is
of no practical use to mankind.   As to these prodigious
achievements of the memory, he ranks them with the
exhibitions of rope-dancers and tumblers.   " The two
performances ", he says, " are of much [1] the same sort.
The one is an abuse of the powers of the body; the other
is an abuse of the powers of the mind.   Both may perhaps excite our wonder; but neither is entitled to our
respect. "

To Plato, the science of medecine appeared to be of
very disputable advantage.   He did not indeed object to
quick cures for acute disorders, or for injuries produced
by accidents.   But the art which resists the slow sap of
a chronic disease, which repairs frames enervated by
lust, swollen by gluttony, or inflamed by wine, which
encourages sensuality by mitigating the natural punishment of the sensualist, and prolongs existence when the
intellect has ceased to retain its entire energy, had no
share of his esteem.   A life protracted by medical skill
he pronounced to be a long death.   The exercise of the
art of medicine ought, he said, to be tolerated, so far
as [2] that art may serve to cure the occasional distempers
of men whose constitutions are good.   As to those who
have bad constitutions, let them die; and the sooner the
better.   Such men are unfit for war, for magistracy, for
the management of their domestic affairs, for severe
study and speculation.   If they engage in any vigourous
mental exercise, they are troubled with giddiness and
fulness [3] of the head, all which they lay to the account

1. *Of much*, à peu près de.   3. *Fulness*, congestion.
2. *So far as*, dans la mesure où.

of philosophy. The best thing that can happen to such wretches is to have done with life at once. He quotes mythical authority in support of this doctrine : and reminds his disciples that the practice of the sons of Æsculapius, as described by Homer, extended only to the cure of external injuries.

Far different was the philosophy of Bacon. Of all the sciences, that which he seems to have regarded with the greatest interest was the science which, in Plato's opinion, would not be tolerated in a well regulated community. To make men perfect was no part of Bacon's plan. His humble aim was to make imperfect men comfortable. The beneficence his philosophy resembled the beneficence of the common Father, whose sun rises on the evil and the good, whose rain descends for the just and the unjust[1]. In Plato's opinion man was made for philosophy : in Bacon's opinion philosophy was made for man; it was a means to[2] an end; and that end was to increase the pleasures and to mitigate the pains of millions who are not and cannot be philosophers. That a valetudinarian who took great pleasure in being wheeled along his terrace, who relished his boiled chicken and his weak wine and water, and who enjoyed a hearty laugh over the Queen of Navarre's tales[3], should be treated as a *caput lupinum*[4] because he could not read the Timæus[5] without a headache, was a notion which the humane spirit of the English school of wisdom altogether rejected. Bacon would not have thought it beneath the dignity of a philosopher to contrive an improved garden chair for such a valetudinarian, to devise some way of rendering his medicines more palatable, to invent repasts which he might enjoy, and pil-

---

1. Allusion biblique : " *Your Father which is in heaven... maketh his sun to rise on the evil and on the good and sendeth rain on the just and on the unjust.*" (St MATTHEW, v, 45).

2. *To*, pour arriver à.

3. Les Contes de la Reine de Navarre, dont le titre principal est *l'Heptaméron*. Marguerite de Valois, reine de Navarre, était sœur de François Ier.

4. *Caput lupinum* (en latin, tête de loup), loup dont la tête est mise à prix.

5. *The Timæus*, le Timée, dialogue de Platon.

lows on which he might sleep soundly; and this though
there might not be the smallest hope that the mind of
the poor invalid would ever rise to the contemplation of
the ideal beautiful and the ideal good. As Plato had
cited the religious legends of Greece to justify his contempt for the more recondite parts of the art of healing,
Bacon vindicated the dignity of that art by appealing to
the example of Christ, and reminded men that the great
Physician of the soul did not disdain to be also the
physician of the body.

When we pass from the science of medicine to that of
legislation, we find the same difference between the systems of these two great men. Plato, at the commencement of the Dialogue on Laws, lays it down as a fundamental principle that the end of legislation is to make
men virtuous. It is unnecessary to point out the extravagant conclusions to which such a proposition leads.
Bacon well knew to how great an extent the happiness
of every society must depend on the virtue of its members; and he also knew what legislators can and what
they cannot do for the purpose of promoting virtue.
The view which he has given of the end of legislation,
and of the principal means for the attainment of that
end, has always seemed to us eminently happy, even
among the many happy passages of the same kind with
which his works abound.

... The end is the well-being of the people. The means
are the imparting of moral and religious education; the
providing of every thing necessary for the defence
against foreign enemies; the maintaining of internal
order; the establishing of a judicial, financial, and com-
mercial system, under which wealth may be rapidly
accumulated and securely enjoyed.

Even with respect to the form in which laws ought to
be drawn, there is a remarkable difference of opinion
between the Greek and the Englishman. Plato thought
a preamble essential; Bacon thought it mischievous.
Each was consistent with himself. Plato, considering

the moral improvement of the people as the end of legislation, justly inferred that a law which commanded and
threatened, but which neither convinced the reason, nor
touched the heart, must be a most imperfect law. He
was not content with deterring from theft a man who
still continued to be a thief at heart, with restraining a
son who hated his mother from beating his mother.
The only obedience on which he set much value was the
obedience which an enlightened understanding yields to
reason, and which a virtuous disposition yields to precepts of virtue. He really seems to have believed that,
by prefixing to every law an eloquent and pathetic
exhortation, he should, to a great extent[1], render penal
enactments superfluous. Bacon entertained no such
romantic hopes; and he well knew the practical inconveniences of the course which Plato recommended.

... To sum up the whole, we should say that the aim of
the Platonic philosophy was to exalt man into a god.
The aim of the Baconian philosophy was to provide man
with what he requires while he continues to be man. The
aim of the Platonic philosophy was to raise us far above
vulgar wants. The aim of the Baconian philosophy was
to supply our vulgar wants. The former aim was noble;
but the latter was attainable. Plato drew a good bow;
but, like Acestes in Virgil, he aimed at the stars; and
therefore, though there was no want of strength or skill,
the shot was thrown away[2]. His arrow was indeed
followed by a track of dazzling radiance, but it struck
nothing.

Bacon fixed his eye on a mark which was placed on the
earth, and within bow-shot, and hit it in the white[3].
The philosophy of Plato began in words and ended in
words, noble words indeed, words such as were to be
expected from the finest of human intellects exercising
boundless dominion over the finest of human languages.

1. *To a great extent*, dans une
grande mesure.
2. *Thrown away*, perdu.

3. *The white*, le blanc, le centre de
la cible qui était peint en blanc.

The philosophy of Bacon began in observations and ended in arts.

The boast of the ancient philosophers was that their doctrine formed the minds of men to a high degree of wisdom and virtue. This was indeed the only practical good which the most celebrated of those teachers even pretended to effect; and undoubtedly, if they had effected this, they would have deserved far higher praise than if they had discovered the most salutary medicines or constructed the most powerful machines. But the truth is that, in those very matters in which alone they professed to do any good to mankind, in those very matters for the sake of which they neglected all the vulgar interests of mankind, they did nothing, or worse than nothing They promised what was impracticable; they despised what was practicable; they filled the world with long words and long beards; and they left it as wicked and as ignorant as they found it.

An acre in Middlesex is better than a principality in Utopia. The smallest actual good is better than the most magnificent promises of impossibilities. The wise man of the Stoics would, no doubt, be a grander object than a steam-engine. But there are steam-engines. And the wise man of the Stoics is yet to be born. A philosophy which should enable a man to feel perfectly happy while in agonies of pain would be better than a philosophy which assuages pain. But we know that there are remedies which will assuage pain; and we know that the ancient sages liked the toothache just as little as their neighbours. A philosophy which should extinguish cupidity would be better than a philosophy which should devise laws for the security of property. But it is possible to make laws which shall, to a very great extent, secure property. And we do not understand how any motives which the ancient philosophy furnished could extinguish cupidity. We know indeed that the philosophers were no better than other men. From the testimony of friends as well as of foes, from the confessions of Epictetus and

Seneca, as well as from the sneers of Lucian and the fierce invectives of Juvenal, it is plain that these teachers of virtue had all the vices of their neighbours, with the additional vice of hypocrisy.   Some people may think the object of the Baconian philosophy a low object, but they cannot deny that, high or low, it has been attained.   They cannot deny that every year makes an addition to what Bacon called " fruit."   They cannot deny that mankind have made, and are making, great and constant progress in the road which he pointed out to them.   Was there any such progressive movement among the ancient philosophers?   After they had been declaiming eight hundred years, had they made the world better than when they began?   Our belief is that, among the philosophers themselves, instead of a progressive improvement there was a progressive degeneracy . . . .

Ask a follower of Bacon what the new philosophy, as it was called in the time of Charles the Second, has effected for mankind, and his answer is ready; " It has lengthened life; it has mitigated pain : it has extinguished diseases; it has increased the fertility of the soil; it has given new securities to the mariner; it has furnished new arms to the warrior; it has spanned great rivers and estuaries with bridges of form unknown to our fathers; it has guided the thunderbolt innocuously from heaven to earth; it has lighted up the night with the splendour of the day; it has extended the range of the human vision; it has multiplied the power of the human muscles; it has accelerated motion; it has annihilated distance; it has facilitated intercourse, correspondence, all friendly offices, all despatch of business; it has enabled man to descend to the depths of the sea, to soar into the air, to penetrate securely into the noxious recesses of the earth, to traverse the land in cars which whirl along without horses, and the ocean in ships which run ten knots an hour against the wind.   These are but a part of its fruits, and of its first fruits.   For it is a philosophy which never rests, ... which is never perfect.   Its law is progress. A point which yesterday was invisible is its goal to-day, and will be its starting-post to-morrow".

We have sometimes thought that an amusing fiction might be written, in which a disciple of Epictetus and a disciple of Bacon should be introduced as fellow-travellers. They come to a village where the small-pox has just begun to rage, and find houses shut up, intercourse suspended, the sick abandoned, mothers weeping in terror over their children. The Stoic assures the dismayed population that there is nothing bad in the small-pox, and that to a wise man disease, deformity, death, the loss of friends are not evils. The Baconian takes out a lancet and begins to vaccinate. They find a body of miners in great dismay. An explosion of noisome vapours has just killed many of those who were at work; and the survivors are afraid to venture into the cavern. The Stoic assures them that such an accident is nothing but a mere ἀποπρόηγμενον [1]. The Baconian, who has no such fine word at his command, contents himself with devising a safety-lamp. They find a shipwrecked merchant wringing his hands on the shore. His vessel with an inestimable cargo has just gone down, and he is reduced in a moment from opulence to beggary. The Stoic exhorts him not to seek happiness in things which lie without [2] himself, and repeats the whole chapter of Epictetus προς τοὺς τὴν ἀποριαν δεδοικότας [3]. The Baconian constructs a diving-bell, goes down in it, and returns with the most precious effects from the wreck. It would be easy to multiply illustrations of the difference between the philosophy of thorns and the philosophy of fruit, the philosophy of words and the philosophy of works . . . .

It is painful to turn back from contemplating Bacon's philosophy to contemplate his life. Yet without so turning back it is impossible fairly to estimate his powers. He left the University [4] at an earlier age than that at

---

1. *Apoproégmenon*, terme de la philosophie stoïcienne : chose qui n'est pas préférée.

2. *Without*, en dehors de.

3. *Pros toùs tèn aporian dedoikótas* (en grec) : contre ceux qui craignent la misère.

4. Bacon resta à Trinity College

which most people repair thither. While yet a boy [1] he was plunged into the midst of diplomatic business. Thence he passed to the study of a vast technical system of law, and worked his way up [2] through a succession of laborious offices [3] to the highest post [4] in his profession. In the mean time he took an active part in every Parliament; he was an adviser of the Crown : he paid court with the greatest assiduity and address to all whose favour was likely to be of use to him; he lived much in society; he noted the slightest peculiarities of character and the slightest changes of fashion. Scarcely any man has led a more stirring life than that which Bacon led from sixteen to sixty. Scarcely any man has been better entitled to be called a thorough man of the world. The founding of a new philosophy, the imparting of a new direction to the minds of speculators [5], this was the amusement of his leisure, the work of hours occasionally stolen from the Woolsack [6] and the Council Board [7]. This consideration, while it increases the admiration with which we regard his intellect, increases also our regret that such an intellect should so often have been unworthily employed. He well knew the better course, and had, at one time, resolved to pursue it. "I confess, " said he in a letter written when he was still young, " that I have as vast contemplative ends as I have moderate civil ends. " Had his civil ends continued to be moderate, he would have been, not only the Moses, but the Joshua of philosophy. He would have fulfilled a large part of his own magnificent predictions. He would have

Cambridge, de l'âge de treize ans à l'âge de seize ans.

1. *While yet a boy* = while *he was yet a boy* (alors qu'il était encore jeune garçon), encore adolescent.

2. *Worked his way up... to* (se fit, par son travail, un chemin jusqu'à), atteignit, par son travail, à.

3. *Laborious offices,* fonctions pénibles.

4. Celui de Lord Chancellor, en 1618. Voyez note 3, page 172.

5. *Speculators,* penseurs.

6. *The Woolsack* (le sac de laine), nom que l'on donne au siège du Lord Chancellor à la Chambre des Lords. Sous le règne d'Elisabeth, une loi interdisant l'exportation de la laine fut votée et contribua à la prospérité commerciale du pays. En souvenir, on donna un sac de laine comme siège aux juges de la Chambre des Lords.

7. Il était membre du *Privy Council* (conseil privé).

led his followers, not only to the verge, but into the heart
of the promised land. He would not merely have pointed
out, but would have divided the spoil. Above all, he
would have left, not only a great, but a spotless name.
Mankind would then have been able to esteem their illustrious benefactor. We should not then be compelled to
regard his character with mingled contempt and admiration, with mingled aversion and gratitude. We should
not then regret that there should be so many proofs of
the narrowness and selfishness of a heart, the benevolence of which was yet large enough to take in all races
and all ages. We should not then have to blush for the
disingenuousness of the most devoted worshipper of
speculative truth, for the servility of the boldest champion
of intellectual freedom. We should not then have seen
the same man at one time far in the van, and at another
time far in the rear of his generation. We should not
then be forced to own that he who first treated legislation
as a science was among the last Englishmen who used
the rack, that he who first summoned philosophers to the
great work of interpreting nature was among the last
Englishmen who sold justice. And we should conclude
our survey of a life placidly, honourably, beneficently
passed, " in industrious observations, grounded conclusions, and profitable inventions and discoveries"[1], with
feelings very different from those with which we now turn
away from the checkered spectacle of so much glory and
so much shame.

1. Extrait d'une lettre de Bacon à Lord Burleigh.

APPENDICE

Voici la donnée de l'intrigue principale du *Merchant of Venice* de Shakespeare. (Pour l'intrigue secondaire, voyez, au Lexique, Bassanio.)

Le juif Shylock, usurier de Venise, a pris en haine le négociant Antonio, parce que celui-ci prête de l'argent sans intérêt, diminuant ainsi les bénéfices des prêteurs, et montre en toutes circonstances son mépris pour Shylock et ses coreligionnaires. Un jour un ami d'Antonio, nommé Bassanio, le prie de lui prêter trois mille ducats pour pouvoir épouser la belle héritière Portia. Antonio, qui n'avait pas à ce moment une somme aussi forte, voulant néanmoins rendre service à son ami, a recours à Shylock, qui voit là une occasion de se venger. « Pour vous prouver que je vaux mieux que vous ne croyez, lui dit-il, je vous prêterai l'argent sans intérêt. Mais, pour la forme, et en manière de plaisanterie, vous me signerez un billet par lequel vous me donnerez le droit, si l'argent ne m'est pas rendu tel jour à telle heure, d'enlever, d'une partie quelconque de votre corps, une livre de chair. » Antonio signe. Quelque temps après, à la suite de la perte de plusieurs navires, il se trouve dans l'impossibilité de payer Shylock. Celui-ci exige l'exécution du billet. Devant le tribunal, il reste sourd à tous les appels faits à sa pitié, et Antonio est condamné à livrer une livre de sa chair à son créancier. Shylock, triomphant, aiguise déjà son couteau. Antonio se croit perdu ; mais son avocat (qui n'est autre que Portia travestie) fait remarquer que le billet parle de chair et non de sang. Or la loi punit de confiscation de tous ses biens le juif qui verse une seule goutte de sang chrétien. Antonio est sauvé par cet argument inattendu.

LEXIQUE

A

Abydos (*abaï'doss*), Abydos, ville d'Asie Mineure. — Voyez BYRON.

Acestes (*acess'tiz*), Acestes, personnage de l'*Énéide*.

Achilles (*akil'iz*), Achille, héros de l'*Iliade*.

Adam (*ad'eumm*), Adam.

Addison (*ad'içeunn*), Joseph, 1672-1719, un des plus grands prosateurs anglais. Ses articles ou essais, publiés dans le journal *The Spectator* (1711-1712), sont demeurés classiques.

Adonais (*adoné'iss*). — Voyez SHELLEY.

Adriatic (*adriat'ic*), Adriatique.

Æneid (*ini'id*), *Énéide*, poème de Virgile.

Æschylus (*ess'kileuss*), Eschyle (525-456 av. J.-C.), le plus illustre des tragiques grecs, auteur du *Prométhée enchaîné*.

Æsculapius (*esskioulé'pieuss*), Esculape, dieu de la médecine dans la mythologie grecque.

Ainsworth (*ennss'oueurth*), romancier anglais (1805-1882). — Voyez SHEPPARD (Jack).

Alastor (*alas'teur*). — Voyez SHELLEY.

Albemarle (*albimârl'*) Lord, amiral anglais (1725-1786).

Albigenses (*albidjenn'ciz*) the, les Albigeois.

Alexander (*alegzann'deur*), Alexandre.

Alfieri (*alfié'ri*), poète dramatique italien (1749-1803).

Algernon Sydney (*al'djeur-neunn sid'ni*), homme politique anglais (1622-1683); occupa diverses hautes situations sous la République; se réfugia sur le continent lors de la Restauration de 1660, et revint en 1667. Impliqué dans une conspiration, il fut condamné à mort et exécuté.

Alnaschar (*alnass'kâr*).

Alps (*alpss*), Alpes.

Amelia (*ami'lia*), Amélie. — Voyez FIELDING.

America (*amer'ica*), Amérique.

American (*amer'ikeunn*), Américain.

Andrews (*ann'drouz*). — Voyez FIELDING.

Anglican (*ann'glikeunn*), anglican, anglicane.

Anne (*anne*), reine d'Angleterre, 1702-1714.

Antonio (*annto'nio*). — Voyez l'Appendice.

Antony (*ann'toni*), Antoine.

Aquinas (*acoui'neuss*) THOMAS, saint Thomas d'Aquin, célèbre théologien du treizième siècle, professa à Paris et mérita, par son érudition et sa piété, le surnom *d'ange de l'école*.

Arblay (*ár'blé*) Madame d'. — FRANCES BURNEY (1752-1840), romancier anglais, épousa en 1793 un émigré français, le général d'Arblay. Ses principaux romans sont *Evelina* (1778) et *Cecilia* (1782).

Arbuthnot (*ár'beuthnott*) écrivain anglais (1667-1735), ami de Swift.

Argus (*ár'gueuss*). — Suivant la mythologie grecque, Argus avait cent yeux. Junon lui confia la garde

"

d'Io; mais Mercure réussit à l'endormir et lui trancha la tête.

Argyle (*árgaïl*), province d'Ecosse.

Arian (*é'rieunn*), Arien, partisan des théories d'Arius (quatrième siècle), qui niait la divinité du Christ.

Ariosto (*arioss'tó*), Arioste, poète italien (1474-1533), auteur du *Roland Furieux* et de plusieurs comédies.

Aristophanes (*aristof'euniz*), Aristophane, poète grec, auteur de comédies très satiriques et très licencieuses (cinquième siècle av. J.-C.).

Aristotelian (*aristotí'lieunn*), aristotélicien.

Aristotle (*ar'istoteul*), Aristote, célèbre philosophe grec du quatrième siècle avant Jésus-Christ.

Arragon (*ar'agueunn*), Aragon.

Artegal (*àr'téqueul*).

Artevelde (*àr'teveld*), Philip Van, drame en vers de sir Henry Taylor (1834).

Ascham (*ass'keumm*) Roger, 1515-1568, prosateur anglais; fut précepteur d'Elisabeth et de Lady Jane Grey. Ses principaux ouvrages sont : *Toxophilus* (1545), sur le tir à l'arc, et *The Schoolmaster* (1570), traité de pédagogie.

Asia (*é'jia*), Asie.

Asiatic (*éjiat'ic*), asiatique.

Athenian (*athí'nieunn*), Athénien.

Athens (*ath'ennz*), Athènes.

Atlantis (*atlann'tice*). — Voyez BACON.

Attila (*at'ila*), célèbre roi des Huns, qui se donnait à lui-même le surnom de *Fléau de Dieu* (cinquième siècle).

Aubrey (*o'bri*, o comme dans *or*).

Aulis (*o'liss*, o comme dans *or*), ville de l'ancienne Béotie, où est placée l'action de l'*Iphigénie* de Racine.

Aurora (*oró'ra*), Aurore, déesse de la mythologie grecque.

Austrian (*os'trieunn*), autrichien-ne.

Aylmer (*él'meur*) John, 1521-1594, fut évêque de Londres et précepteur de Lady Jane Grey.

B

Babington (*bab'igne-teunn*). — Voyez MACAULAY.

Bacchus (*bak'euss*).

Bacon (*bé'keunn*) Francis, 1561-1626, homme d'Etat, prosateur et philosophe anglais. Principales œuvres : *The Advancement of Learning*, 1605; le *Novum Organum*, 1620; *The New Atlantis*; des *Essays*.

Bacon, John, 1740-1799, sculpteur anglais.

Baconian (*bécó'nieunn*), de Bacon.

Bahar (*béhár*), province à l'Est du Bengale.

Bassanio (*bassá'nio*), personnage de la comédie de Shakespeare *The Merchant of Venice*. La riche héritière Portia, ne sachant auquel de ses adorateurs accorder sa main, a recours à un artifice. Elle prend trois cassettes : l'une, d'or, contenant une tête de mort; une seconde, d'argent, renfermant la figure d'un idiot; la troisième, de plomb, où elle met son portrait. Elle a décidé d'épouser celui qui choisirait cette dernière, et qui se trouve être Bassanio.

Bath (*bath'*), ville du comté de Somerset, célèbre par ses eaux minérales; d'où son nom de *bath*, bain.

Bayes (*béz*).

Beaconsfield (*bi'keunnzfild*).

Beauclerk (*bó'clárk*), 1739-1780, simple particulier, épris de littérature; fut l'ami de Johnson.

Bedford (*bed'feurde*).

Belisarius (*bélicé'rieuss*), Bélisaire. — Suivant une légende, Bélisaire, général de l'empereur Justinien (sixième siècle), aurait, aveugle, été réduit à la mendicité.

Ben (*benn*), diminutif de Benjamin.

Benedick (*benn'edic*), personnage de la comédie de Shakespeare : *Much Ado about Nothing*.

Bengal (*benngol'*, *o* comme dans *or*), le Bengale.

Bengalee (*benngoli*), habitant du Bengale.

Beppo (*bep'ó*). — Voyez BYRON.

Bernard (*beur'neurde*).

Bessus (*bess'euss*). Soldat lâche et fanfaron, personnage de *King and no King*, tragédie de Beaumont et Fletcher (*bô'monnt, fletch'eur*), auteurs dramatiques contemporains de Shakespeare.

Bethel (*beth'el*).

Betty (*bett'i*) Master, le *jeune Betty*, acteur anglais (1791-1874), remarquable surtout par sa précocité qui lui fit donner le nom sous lequel il est connu.

Beulah (*biou'la*). Dans la Bible, c'est le nom donné par Isaïe à la terre d'Israël. Le Maistre de Sacy rend Beulah par : *la terre habitée*. Dans le *Pilgrim's Progress*, la terre de Beulah est la terre du repos où les pèlerins attendent la mort qui doit les conduire dans la Cité céleste.

Blackwall (*black'ouol*, *o* comme dans *or*), faubourg à l'est de Londres, sur la rive gauche de la Tamise. C'est un quartier de Docks.

Blefuscudians (*bléfeusskiou'dieunnz*).

Bobadil (*bob'adil*). — Le capitaine Bobadil, aventurier fanfaron, est un personnage de *Every Man in his Humour*, comédie de Ben Jonson.

Bolt Court (*bólt*). — C'est dans Bolt Court, qui donne dans Fleet Street, que Johnson passa les dernières années de sa vie.

Bonaparte (*bô'napárte*).

Borgia (*bor'dja*).

Boswell (*boz'ouel*) James, 1740-1795, célèbre par sa biographie de Johnson : *The Life of Samuel Johnson* (1791).

Bourbon (*bour'beunn*).

Boyse (*boïce*).

British (*brit'iche*), britannique.

Brutus (*brout'euss*), Romain célèbre, qui prit part au meurtre de César (44 av. J.-C.). C'est un des principaux personnages du *Julius Cæsar* de Shakespeare.

Bucer (*biou'seur*) Martin, 1491-1551, un des plus ardents apôtres du protestantisme en Allemagne. Il termina sa vie en Angleterre.

Buckingham (*beuk'igneum*). Le fameux Georges Villiers, duc de Buckingham, favori de Jacques 1er et de Charles 1er, et qui fut assassiné en 1628.

Bunyan (*beun'ieunn*) John, 1628-1688, simple chaudronnier anglais; fut de bonne heure absorbé par les idées religieuses; arrêté en 1660 pour ses opinions, il resta en prison jusqu'en 1672. Malgré une éducation des plus rudimentaires, il est l'auteur de plusieurs volumes, dont l'un, *The Pilgrim's Progress* (le voyage du Pèlerin) est un chef-d'œuvre.

Burgundy (*beur'gueunndi*), Bourgogne.

Burke (*beurke*) Edmund, 1729-1797, homme d'État, écrivain et orateur anglais. Quelques-uns de ses discours sont classiques, entre autres celui qu'il prononça au cours du procès de Warren Hastings.

Burleigh (*beur'li*) William CECIL, Lord, 1520-1598, homme d'État anglais; fut pendant quarante ans premier ministre d'Elisabeth.

Burlington (*beur'ligne-teunn*).

Burney (*beur'ni*). — Voyez ARBLAY.

Byron (*baï'reunn*), 1788-1824. Illustre poète anglais. — Principales œuvres : *Childe Harold* (1812, 1816, 1818), *The Giaour* (1813), *The Bride of Abydos* (1813), *The Corsair* (1814), *Lara* (1814), *The Siege of Corinth* (1816), *Parisina* (1816), *Beppo* (1818), *Don Juan* (1819-1824), *Manfred* (1817), *Cain* (1821), *Heaven and Earth* (1822).

C

Cadiz (*ké'diz*), Cadix.

Cæsar (*ci'zeur*), César.

Cain (*kéne*), Caïn.

Caius (*ké'yeuss*).

Calcutta (*calkeut'a*).

Calvin (*cal'vinn*).

Calvinist (*cal'vinist*).

Cambridge (*kém'bridj*), ville d'Angleterre, siège d'une université.

Canning (*ca'nigne*) George, 1770-1827, homme d'État et orateur anglais.

Canterbury (*cann'teurbéri*) Cantorbéry, ville d'Angleterre. — Voyez CHAUCER.

Carlyle (*cár'laïle*), célèbre écrivain anglais, 1795-1881.

Carthage (*kár'thedj*).

Cassius (*ca'chieuss*), personnage du *Julius Cæsar* de Shakespeare.

Castilian (*casti'lieunn*), castillan.

Catherine (*cath'eurinn*).

Catholic (*cath'olic*).

Catiline (*cat'ilaïne*), Catilina, le fameux agitateur romain, dont la conspiration contre la république (63 av. J.-C.) fut déjouée par les efforts et l'éloquence de Cicéron.

Cave (*kév*). — *St. John's Gate* (la porte de Saint-Jean) est tout ce qui reste d'un vieux prieuré des chevaliers de Saint-Jean. Cave, fondateur du *Gentleman's Magazine*, et dont Johnson a écrit la biographie, habitait au-dessus de cette porte.

Cecil (*cess'il* ou *ci'cil*). — Voyez BURLEIGH.

Cecilia (*cecil'ia*). — Voyez ARDLAY.

Cenci (*tchenn'tchi*). — Voyez SHELLEY.

Chalmers (*tchá'meurz*) Thomas, 1780-1847, prêtre de l'Église écossaise; fut professeur de philosophie et de théologie.

Champagne (*chammpéne'*).

Charing-Cross (*tché'rigne cross*), carrefour situé à l'extrémité ouest du Strand; c'est le centre conventionnel de Londres. La croix (*cross*) qui a donné son nom à ce carrefour a disparu.

Charlemont (*tchárl'meunnt*).

Charles (*tchárlz*).

Chatham (*tchat'eumm*), William PITT, earl of, 1708-1778, homme d'État et orateur anglais; était au pouvoir pendant la guerre de Sept Ans; fut premier ministre en 1766.

Chaucer (*tcho'seur*, o comme dans *or*) Geoffrey, 1340-1400, poète anglais, auteur d'un nombre considérable d'ouvrages, dont le plus connu est intitulé : *The Canterbury Tales*, les Contes de Cantorbéry.

Chesterfield (*tchess'teurfild*) Lord, 1694-1773, orateur et écrivain anglais; est surtout célèbre par l'élégance de ses manières et par ses lettres à son fils.

Childe Harold (*tchaïld har'euld*). — Voyez BYRON.

Christ (*craïste*).

Christian (*criss'tieunn*), chrétien-ne.

Christianity (*cristiann'ili*), Christianisme.

Christopher (*crist'ofeur*), Christophe.

Churchill (*tcheurtch'ill*) Charles, 1731-1764, poète satirique. C'est surtout dans son poème *The Ghost* (le Revenant), qu'il tourne Johnson en ridicule, à propos du fameux *Cock Lane Ghost*, revenant de Cock Lane.

Cicero (*ciss'ero*), Cicéron (106-143 av. J.-C.), homme d'État et orateur romain.

Clarendon (*clar'enndeunn*), 1608-1674, homme d'État et historien anglais; fut le conseiller de Charles Ier et de Charles II; il fut exilé par le Parlement en 1667. Il a écrit une histoire de la guerre civile entre Charles Ier et le Parlement : *A History of the Rebellion*.

Clarissa Harlowe (*clariss'a*

hâr'lo). — Voyez Richardson.

Clarkson (*clark'seunn*), 1760-1846, philanthrope anglais; combattit la traite des nègres.

Claude (*clod, o comme dans or*).

Clement (*clem'eunnt*) the Seventh, pape de 1523 à 1534.

Cleopatra (*cliopë'tra*), Cléopâtre.

Clive (*claïv*) Robert, 1725-1774, homme d'Etat et général anglais. Tout jeune il partit pour l'Inde (1743) en qualité de commis de la Compagnie des Indes Orientales. En 1744, la guerre ayant éclaté aux Indes entre les colons anglais et les colons français, il prit du service dans l'armée de la Compagnie, et fit preuve de capacités militaires qui lui valurent, après divers succès, le commandement de l'expédition dirigée, en 1756, contre Surajah Dowlah. Il le battit à Plassey (1757). Il fut à deux reprises gouverneur du Bengale (1758 et 1765). C'est le vrai fondateur de la puissance anglaise aux Indes.

Cock Lane (*coq léne*). — Le revenant de Cock Lane est resté célèbre en Angleterre. En 1762, des bruits mystérieux s'entendaient tous les jours dans une maison de cette rue habitée par un nommé Parsons (*pâr'seunnz*) et sa fille. Bien des gens, Johnson entre autres, crurent à un revenant. Il fut démontré que Parsons était un mystificateur. L'expression a *Cock Lane ghost* est devenue synonyme de : histoire invraisemblable.

Colossians (*coloch'ieunnz*), Colossiens, habitants de Colosses, ville de Phrygie.

Comines (*prononcez comme en français*), Commines, historien français, 1445-1509.

Comus (*cô'meuss*). — Voyez Milton.

Congreve (*conn'grïv*) William, 1670-1729, auteur dramatique anglais.

Constantine(*conn'steunntaïne*),

Constantin le Grand, empereur romain, 306-337.

Corinth (*cor'innth*), Corinthe.

Coriolanus (*coriolé'neuss*), Coriolan, général romain du cinquième siècle avant Jésus-Christ. — Irrité de l'ingratitude de sa patrie, il passa au camp de l'ennemi, et Rome n'échappa à sa vengeance que grâce à l'intervention de sa mère. — Coriolan est le héros du drame de Shakespeare : *Coriolanus*.

Corsica (*cor'sica*), la Corse.

Coventry (*keuv'enntry*), ville d'Angleterre.

Cressida (*cress'ida*).

Crisp (*crispe*).

Croker (*crô'keur*), auteur de l'édition de la vie de Johnson à propos de laquelle Macaulay écrivit cet essai.

Cromwell (*crom'ouel*) Olivier, 1599-1658, célèbre homme d'Etat anglais qui, simple fermier, prit une grande part à la Révolution qui coûta la vie à Charles Ier et aboutit à l'établissement de la République en 1649. Il fut nommé Protecteur de la République, *Lord Protector of the Commonwealth*.

Cyclops (*saï'clopce*), dans la mythologie antique, géant qui n'avait qu'un œil au milieu du front. Les Cyclopes étaient forgerons de Vulcain.

Cymbeline (*cim'beline*). — Voyez Shakespeare.

D

Daniel Lambert (*dann'ieul lamm'beurte*), Anglais célèbre par sa corpulence; il avait atteint le poids de 739 livres anglaises. — Il mourut en 1809.

Dante (*dann'ti*), 1265-1321, illustre poète italien, auteur de la *Divine Comédie*.

Daun (*daoune*), général autrichien; commanda les troupes impériales pendant la guerre de Sept Ans.

David (*dé'vid*), le roi David, l'auteur des Psaumes.

Davila (*da'vila*), 1576-1631, historien italien, qui passa une partie de sa vie en France et servit sous Henri IV pendant la guerre civile. Il est l'auteur d'une Histoire des Guerres Civiles de France pendant la seconde moitié du seizième siècle.

Democritus (*democ'riteuss*), Démocrite, philosophe grec du cinquième siècle avant Jésus-Christ.

Demosthenes (*demoss'theniz*), Démosthène, illustre orateur grec (quatrième siècle av. J.-C.).

Denham (*den'eumm*) Sir John, 1615-1668, poète anglais.

Dickens (*dick'ennz*), célèbre romancier anglais, 1812-1870.

Domenichino (*doméniki'no*), le Dominiquin, célèbre peintre italien, 1581-1641.

Don Quixote (*donn kouix'ote*). Don Quichotte; le chef-d'œuvre de Cervantes est de 1605 et 1615.

Douw (*daou*) Gerard, célèbre peintre hollandais, 1613-1675.

Dresden (*drez'dn*), Dresde.

Dryden (*draï'dn*) John, 1631-1700, poète et auteur dramatique anglais.

Dudley (*deud'li*).

Duncan (*deunn'keunn*), personnage du *Macbeth* de Shakespeare.

Dunciad (*deunn'ciad*), poème satirique de Pope. — *Dunciad* est un mot fabriqué par l'auteur et qui vient de *dunce*, âne.

Dutch (*deutch*), hollandais.

E

Ebenezer (*ébéni'zeur*).

Eden (*i'dn*).

Edinburgh (*ed'innbro*), Édimbourg.

Edmund (*ed'meunnd*).

Edward (*ed'oueurd*).

Egerton (*edj'eurteunn*).

Egypt (*i'djipt*), Égypte.

Egyptian (*edjip'cheunn*), Égyptien.

Elizabeth (*eliz'eubeth*), Elisabeth, reine d'Angleterre de 1558 à 1603.

Elstow (*ell'stó*), localité du comté de Bedford.

England (*inn'gleunnd*), Angleterre.

English (*inn'gliche*), anglais.

Englishman (*inn'gliche-meunn*), Anglais.

Epictetus (*épicti'leuss*), Epictète, philosophe grec qui vécut à Rome au premier siècle.

Erskine (*eur'skinn*) John, 1721-1803, théologien écossais.

Essex (*ess'ex*).

Euphrates (*ioufré'tiz*).

Europe (*iou'ropp*).

European (*iouropi'eunn*), européen.

Evelina (*évélaï'na*). — Voyez ARBLAY.

F

Falconbridge (*fo'kn-bridj*, o comme dans *or*), personnage du *King John* de Shakespeare.

Falmouth (*fal'meuth*), ville d'Angleterre, dans le comté de Cornouailles.

Favorinus (*favori'neuss*), sophiste grec, mort en 135.

Ferguson (*feur'gueussn*) sir Adam, 1723-1816, philosophe et historien écossais.

Fielding (*fil'digne*) Henry, 1707-1754, célèbre romancier réaliste. Ses principaux romans sont : *Joseph Andrews* (1742), *Tom Jones* (1749) et *Amelia* (1751).

Flandres (*flann'deurz*), Flandre.

Flaxman (*flax'meunn*), célèbre sculpteur et dessinateur anglais, 1755-1826.

Fleet Street (*flîte strîte*), une des principales rues de Londres, elle fait suite au *Strand* en allant vers l'est.

Fleetwood (*flîte'woud*) Charles, mort en 1692, général des armées du Parlement.

Florence (*flor'eunnce*).

Florentine (*flor'enntinn* ou *flor'enntaïne*), florentin-e.

Fluellen (*flou-el'enn*).

Foote (*foutt*) Samuel, 1720-1777, auteur dramatique et acteur anglais; fut directeur du Haymarket Theatre.

Fox (*fox*) Charles James, 1749-1806, homme d'État et orateur anglais.

France (*frannce*).

Frances (*frann'cez*). Françoise.

Francis (*frann'ciss*), François.

Frank (*frannk*), diminutif de Francis.

Frederick (*fred'eric*) the Great, roi de Prusse, 1722-1786.

French (*frennch*), français.

Frenchman (*frennch'meunn*), Français.

Frenchmen (*frennch'menn*), Français.

Froissart (*froï'sárte*), chroniqueur français, 1327-1410.

G

Gama (*ga'ma*), Vasco de Gama, célèbre navigateur portugais, doubla le Cap de Bonne-Espérance en 1497 et fonda plusieurs colonies sur la côte orientale d'Afrique.

Ganges (*yann'djiz*), le Gange.

Garrick (*gar'ic*), illustre acteur anglais, 1716-1779.

Gatton (*gatt'n*).

Gay (*gué*) John, 1685-1732, poète et auteur dramatique anglais, connu surtout par ses *Fables* et son *Beggar's Opera* (Opéra du Gueux), 1728.

Genesis (*djenn'éciss*), la Genèse.

Genoa (*djenn'o-a*), Gênes.

Geoffrey (*djef'ri*), Geoffroy.

George (*djordj*), Georges.

Gerard (*djer'eurd*).

German (*djeur'meunn*), allemand.

Germany (*djeur'meuni*), Allemagne.

Giaour (*djaoueur*). — Voyez Byron.

Gibbon (*guib'n*) Edward, 1737-1794, célèbre historien anglais; son œuvre capitale est : *The History of the Decline and Fall of the Roman Empire*.

Gibraltar (*djibrol'tár*).

Gifford (*guif'eurde*) William, 1757-1826, critique et poète satirique.

Gihon (*gaï'honn*).

Gladstone (*glad'stonn*), né en 1809, illustre homme d'État anglais. Il débuta dans la politique en 1832 comme député conservateur. Vingt ans plus tard ses opinions avaient subi de telles modifications qu'il était passé du côté des libéraux, dont il ne tarda pas à devenir le chef. Il fut pour la première fois premier ministre en 1868. Ses concitoyens l'ont surnommé *The Grand Old Man*.

Goldsmith (*gôld'smith*) Olivier, 1728-1774, poète, romancier, auteur dramatique et historien anglais. Ses principales œuvres sont : *The Deserted Village*, 1770, poème; *The Good-Natured Man*, 1768, et *She Stoops to Conquer*, 1774, comédies; *The Vicar of Wakefield*, 1766, roman.

Gower (*gaou'eur*), 1325-1408, poète anglais.

Grandison (*grann'dissn*). — Voyez Richardson.

Grecian (*gri'cheunn*), grec.

Greece (*gri'ce*), Grèce.

Greek (*grik*), grec.

Gray (*gré*) Thomas, 1716-1771, poète anglais. Ses principales œuvres sont : *An Elegy written in a Country Churchyard*, 1751, et *The Bard*, 1757.

Grey (*gré*) Lady Jane, 1537-1554, arrière-petite-fille du roi Henri VIII d'Angleterre; elle eut pour précepteurs Aylmer et Ascham. En 1553, à la mort d'Édouard VI, elle fut proclamée reine, à la suite d'une conspiration; mais elle fut bientôt arrêtée, et exécutée à Tower Hill.

Grub Street (*greubb strite*), aujourd'hui *Milton Street*, fut longtemps habitée par une certaine bohème littéraire qui vivait au jour le jour de la production de misérables brochures, généralement sur des questions politiques ou religieuses.

Gulliver (*gueul'iveur*).

Guy Faux (*gaï fox*, o long comme dans *or*), celui des conjurés qui était chargé de mettre le feu aux poudres. En souvenir de cet attentat on brûle tous les ans un mannequin représentant le célèbre criminel.

H

Hailes (*hélz*) Lord, 1726-1792, auteur d'*Annals of Scotland*.

Hallam (*hal'eum*) Henry, 1777-1859, historien anglais, auteur de *A View of the State of Europe during the Middle Ages*, 1818; *The Constitutional History of England from the Accession of Henry VII to the Death of George II*, 1827.

Hamlet (*ham'lett*). — Voyez SHAKESPEARE.

Hampden (*hammp'denn*) John, 1594-1643, célèbre patriote anglais. Son refus de payer un impôt illégal fut un des incidents précurseurs de la Révolution de 1642.

Hampton (*hammp'teunn*), village des environs de Londres.

Hannibal (*hann'ibal*), Annibal, célèbre général carthaginois qui, après avoir vaincu les Romains pendant la deuxième guerre punique, fut enfin chassé d'Italie (deuxième siècle av. J.-C.).

Harry (*har'i*), diminutif de **Henry**. — Henry V, héros de la tragédie de Shakespeare ainsi intitulée.

Hastings (*héss'tign'z*), Warren, 1732-1818, fut, après Clive, un des fondateurs de l'Empire britannique des Indes. Homme d'État de premier ordre, il commit des fautes, des crimes même, et, en 1787, il fut mis en accusation et comparut devant la Chambre des Lords. Le procès dura jusqu'en 1795, et se termina par un acquittement, malgré les efforts des accusateurs, à la tête desquels se trouvait Burke.

Haymarket (*hé'mârkett*).

Hebrew (*hi'brou*), hébreu.

Hebrides (*heb'ridîz*).

Hector (*hec'teur*).

Helen (*hel'enn*), Hélène.

Helvetius (*pron. comme en français*), 1715-1771, philosophe français, auteur d'un livre intitulé *de l'Esprit*, où il donne l'intérêt personnel comme la source de toutes nos vertus.

Henry (*henn'ri*).

Hephzibah (*hef'zaïba*).

Hesperian (*hesspî'rieunn*), des Hespérides.

Hiddekel (*hid'ekel*).

Hierocles (*haïer'ocliz*), (cinquième siècle) auteur d'un recueil de plaisanteries.

Highland (*haï'lannd*).

Hodge (*hodj*).

Hogarth (*hô'gârth*), William, 1697-1764, peintre et graveur anglais.

Holland (*hol'annd*), Lord, homme d'État anglais, 1773-1840.

Holofernes (*holofeur'niz*), personnage de la comédie de Shakespeare, *Love's Labour's Lost*. C'est un maître d'école dont le langage ridicule est une caricature de l'euphuisme, préciosité particulière à l'Angleterre de cette époque.

Holwell (*hol'ouel*).

Homer (*hô'meur*), auteur présumé de l'*Iliade* et de l'*Odyssée*.

Hoole (*houle*) John, 1727-1803, poète anglais; a traduit la *Jérusalem Délivrée* du Tasse, et le *Roland Furieux* de l'Arioste.

Horace (*hor'euss*).

Hosea (*hôzî'a*), Osée.

Huguenot (*hiou'guenott*).

Hume (*hioume*), David, 1711-1776, philosophe et historien écossais, auteur d'une *History of England* (1754).

Hyde Park (*haïde pârke*) **Corner**,

le Coin de H. P., est le nom de l'entrée principale de cet admirable parc de Londres.

I

Iago (*i-â'gó*), personnage de l'*Othello* de Shakespeare, est le type de l'envieux venimeux et calomniateur.

Iliad (*il'ieuld*), *Iliade*.

India (*inn'dia*), l'Inde.

Indian (*inn'dieunn*), Indien.

Indies (*inn'diz*), les Indes.

Ionian (*aïó'nieunn*), Ionien.

Ireland (*aïr'lannd*), Irlande.

Irene (*aïri'ni*), *Irène*, tragédie de Johnson, jouée en 1749, et qui n'eut que neuf représentations.

Irish (*aï'riche*), Irlandais.

Isaac (*aï'zac*).

Isaiah (*aizé'ia*) Isaïe.

Islam (*iz'lam*).

Islington (*iz'ligne-teunn*), aujourd'hui faubourg de Londres; autrefois village indépendant de la capitale.

Isocrates (*aïsoc'ratiz*), Isocrate, orateur athénien, 436-338 av. J.-C.

Italian (*ital'ieunn*), Italien.

Italy (*it'eli*), Italie.

Ivanhoe (*aï'vannhó*).

Ivimey (*ivaï'mi*), auteur d'une biographie de Bunyan, 1809.

J

Jack (*djac*), diminutif de John.

Jacobin (*djac'ob'nn*).

James (*djémz*), Jacques.

Jane (*djéne*), Jeanne.

Jeremiah (*djerimaï'a*), Jérémie.

Jesus (*dji'zeuss*).

Jew (*djoû*), Juif.

Jewish (*djoü'iche*), juif.

Job (*djób*).

John (*djone*, o long comme dans *or*), Jean.

Johnson (*djone'seunn*), Samuel, 1709-1784, célèbre écrivain anglais, auteur de: *A Dictionary of the English Language* (1755); *Rasselas*, conte philosophique (1759); *The Lives of the English Poets* (1779-1781). Il doit sa réputation moins à ses œuvres qu'à sa biographie par Boswell.

Johnsonese (*djone'seunize*).

Jonathan (*djonn'athann*).

Jones (*djónnz*). — Voy. FIELDING.

Jonson (*djone'seunn*) Ben, 1573-1637, auteur dramatique contemporain de Shakespeare. Principales œuvres : *Court Masques* (Masques, divertissements pour la Cour); *The Alchemist, Catiline, Every Man in His Humour, Sejanus, Volpone.*

Joshua (*djoch'ou-a*), Josué, qui conduisit les Hébreux dans la Terre Promise, où Moïse n'entra pas.

Jourdain, le *Bourgeois gentilhomme* de Molière.

Juan (*djoü'eunn*).

Judaism (*djoü'dé-izm*), judaïsme.

Judas (*djou'deuss*).

Juliet (*djouliett'*), Juliette.

Julius (*djou'lieuss*), Jules.

Juvenal (*djou'veneul*), poète latin (42-123).

K

Kenilworth (*kenn'l-oueurth*). — Voy. SCOTT.

Kenrick (*kenn'ric*) William, 1720-1779, a écrit, entre autres choses, une *Review of Dr. Johnson's New Edition of Shakespeare.*

Kit Cat (*kitt catt*), célèbre club, ainsi nommé, croit-on, du nom du propriétaire *Christopher Cat* (*kit* est le diminutif de *Christopher*). — Addison fut le plus illustre des membres de ce club.

Koran (*kó'rann* ou *koráne'*).

L

Lalla Rookh (*lal'a rouk*). — Voy. MOORE.

Lara (*la'ra*). — Voy. BYRON.

Las Casas (*lass cass'ass*), célèbre dominicain, compagnon de Christophe Colomb ; il protégea les Indiens contre la tyrannie des Espagnols.

Latin (*lat'ine*).

Laud (*lod*, *o* long comme dans *or*), archevêque de Cantorbéry sous Charles Ier, dont il fut premier ministre. Il tenta d'imposer à ses compatriotes un système de religion qui souleva contre lui de telles haines que, lors de la Révolution, il fut arrêté et exécuté.

Lawrence (*lo'rennce*, *o* long comme dans *or*), Sir Thomas, 1769-1830, célèbre peintre de portraits.

Lear (*lire*). — Voy SHAKE-SPEARE.

Leicester (*less'teur*), Robert Dudley, comte de ; fut, jusqu'à sa mort (1588), le favori de la reine Elisabeth.

Leonidas (*léonn'idass*), roi de Sparte, périt glorieusement en défendant le passage des Thermopyles contre les Perses (480 av. J.-C.).

Lilliput (*lil'ipeutt*), dans les *Voyages de Gulliver* de Swift, île imaginaire habitée par des hommes à peine hauts de six pouces.

Lilliputians (*lili̯ iou'cheunnz*), Lilliputiens.

Lisbon (*liz'beunn*), Lisbonne.

Livy (*liv'i*), Tite-Live, célèbre historien latin, contemporain de Jésus-Christ.

Lollards (*lol'eurdz*), hérétiques anglais du quatorzième siècle.

Lombard (*lomm'beurd*).

London (*leunn'deunn*), Londres.

Londoner (*leunn'de-neur*), Londonien.

Longwood (*lonng'woud*), habitation de Napoléon à Sainte-Hélène.

Lorenzo de Medici (*lorenn'dzo dé mé'dilchi*), 1492-1519, fils de Laurent le Magnifique et neveu du pape Léon X ; fut chef de la république de Florence.

Louis (*lou'îce*).

Lucian (*liou'chieunn*), Lucien, écrivain grec du deuxième siècle.

Luther (*lou'theur*), 1483-1546, fut un des principaux chefs de la Réforme en Allemagne.

Lysias (*lij'iass*), orateur athénien, 459-380 avant Jésus-Christ.

Lyttelton (*lil'eulleunn*) Lord, 1709-1773, poète, historien et homme politique anglais.

M

Mab (*mab*). — Voy. SHELLEY.

Macaulay (*maco'lé*, *o* long comme dans *or*), Thomas Babington, Voy. Introduction.

Macbeth (*macbeth'*). — Voy. SHAKESPEARE.

Machiavelli (*makiavel'i*), Machiavel, 1469-1527, homme d'État et écrivain italien. Ses principales œuvres sont : *Le Prince*, traité politique ; *Annales Florentines ; La Mandragore*, comédie.

Mackintosh (*mak'inntoche*) Sir James, 1765-1832, philosophe et historien écossais.

Madras (*madrass'*).

Mahometan (*méhom'eteunn*).

Mahometanism (*méhom'eta-nizm'*), mahométisme.

Mahratta (*marat'a*), Mahratte. Les Mahrattes étaient un peuple de l'Hindoustan de caractère très belliqueux.

Malvolio (*malvô'lio*).

Mandeville (*mann'de-vil*) Bernard, 1670-1733, écrivain anglais, d'origine hollandaise. Son œuvre principale est *The Fable of the Bees*, ou Recherches sur l'origine de la vertu morale (1714).

Manfred (*mann'fred*). — Voy. BYRON.

Marah (*mé'ra*), dans la Bible, source amère de la presqu'île de Sinaï.

Marengo (*marenn'go*).

Mark (*mârk*), marc.

Marmion (*mâr'mieunn*). — Voy. SCOTT.

Mars (*márss*).

Martin (*már'tinn*).

Massillon (*pron. comme en français*), 1663-1742, célèbre prédicateur français; fut évêque de Clermont.

Matthew (*math'iou*), Mathieu.

Maurice (*mor'iss*) **of Saxony**, Maurice de Saxe, 1521-1553; fut d'abord l'allié de Charles Quint contre la France; puis l'allié des Français contre Charles Quint.

Mecca (*mek'a*), La Mecque, ville d'Arabie, patrie de Mahomet.

Medea (*medi'a*), Médée, magicienne de l'antiquité mythologique, héroïne d'une tragédie d'Euripide, poète grec du cinquième siècle avant Jésus-Christ.

Medici (*méd'itchi*).

Merovingian (*merovinn'-djieunn*), Mérovingien.

Messiah (*messaï'a*), Messie.

Michael Angelo (*maï'kel ann' djélo*), Michel-Ange, illustre peintre, sculpteur, architecte et poète italien, 1475-1564.

Middlesex (*mid'eulsex*). comté d'Angleterre où se trouve la Cité de Londres.

Milan (*milane'* ou *mil'eunn*).

Mile End (*maïl ennd*), aujourd'hui faubourg à l'est de Londres, était autrefois une localité indépendante.

Milton (*mil'teunn*) John, 1608-1674, illustre poète et prosateur anglais. Ses principaux poèmes sont : *Comus*, 1634; *Paradise Lost*, 1667; *Paradise Regained*, 1671; *Samson Agonistes*, 1671. Ses ouvrages en prose (en latin et en anglais) sont surtout des ouvrages de controverse politique ou religieuse.

Minerva (*mineur'va*), Minerve.

Missolonghi (*missôlonng'ghi*), ville de Grèce (située à l'entrée nord du golfe de Corinthe) où mourut Byron.

Mogul (*môgueul'*), le Grand Mogol, empereur de l'empire des Mogols, qui, fondé en 1526, fut morcelé en 1707; le dernier empereur Mogol fut déposé en 1857.

Mohawk (*mó'hok*, *o* long comme dans *or*). Les Mohawks sont une tribu d'Indiens de l'Amérique du Nord.

Montgomery (*monntgom'eri*) Robert, 1771-1854, poète anglais.

Moore (*mour*) Thomas, 1779-1852, poète anglais, d'origine irlandaise, célèbre par ses *Irish Melodies*, 1806. Parmi ses autres œuvres le poème de *Lalla Rookh*, 1817, est le plus populaire. Moore est l'auteur d'une biographie de Byron au sujet de laquelle Macaulay a écrit son essai.

Moorshedabad (*mourchidabad'*) Mourched-Abad, ville située à quelque distance au nord de Calcutta.

Moravia (*moré'via*), Moravie.

More (*mór*) Sir Thomas, grand chancelier du roi Henri VIII; il fut décapité en 1535 pour avoir refusé de se séparer de l'église de Rome. Il occupe un rang honorable parmi les écrivains anglais. On connaît surtout son *Utopia*, Utopie, description d'une république idéale qui est restée le type des chimères sociales et politiques.

Moses (*mó'zez*), Moïse.

Mucius (*miou'chieuss*), Mucius Scævola. En 507 avant Jésus-Christ, Rome était assiégée par les Etrusques. Mucius pénétra dans la tente du roi ennemi et, croyant le tuer, égorgea un de ses serviteurs. Pour se punir de son erreur il se brûla lui-même la main droite.

Murillo (*miouril'o*), célèbre peintre espagnol, 1618-1682.

Murray (*meur'é*).

Mussulman (*meuss'eulmeunn*), musulman.

N

Nabob (*né'bob*), nabab.

Naples (*né'plz*).

Navarre (*ne-vár'*).

Nephelococcygia (*néfélócoxid'jia*), ville des Coucous dans les nuages, cité imaginaire dont il est question dans les *Oiseaux*, comédie d'Aristophane.

Nero (*ni'ro*). Néron.

Newburg (*niouber'i*).

New England (*niou inn'gleunnd*), nom donné à la partie nord-est des Etats-Unis.

Newton (*niou'teunn*), Isaac, 1642-1727, illustre savant anglais; a découvert les lois de la gravitation universelle.

Niobe (*naï'obi*), Niobé, dans la mythologie antique, personnifie la douleur maternelle. Ayant offensé Diane et Apollon, ceux-ci firent périr tous ses enfants.

Nollekens (*nol'ekennz*), 1737-1823, sculpteur anglais.

Norman (*nor'meunn*), Normand.

Northumbrian (*northeumm'bri-eunn*), du comte de Northumberland.

O

Œdipus (*éd'ipeuss*), Œdipe, personnage de la mythologie grecque, héros de deux tragédies de Sophocle : *Œdipe Roi* et *Œdipe à Colone.*

Old Sarum (*óld se'reumm*).

Oliver (*ol'iveur*), Olivier.

Orissa (*óriss'a*), province au sud-ouest du Bengale..

Orléans (*or lieunnz*).

Othello (*óthel'o*). — Voy. SHAKESPEARE.

Otranto (*ólrann'lo*). — Voy. WALPOLE.

P

Paddington (*pad'igne-teunn*), faubourg au nord-ouest de Londres.

Paine (*pénc*), Tom, écrivain anglais qui, avant émigré aux Etats-Unis en 1774, contribua à l'indépendance américaine. En 1792 il fut élu membre de la Convention Française.

Palestine (*pal'estaïne*).

Pall Mall (*pell mell*), rue de Londres.

Pamela (*pam'ela*). — Voy. RICHARDSON.

Pantheon (*pann'thi-eunn*).

Paoli (*paô'li*).

Papist (*pap'ist*), papiste, catholique romain,

Paris (*par'iss*).

Parisian (*parij'eunn*), Parisien.

Parisina (*parizi'na*). — Voy. BYRON.

Parnell (*pâr'nel*) Thomas, 1679-1717, poète anglais, dont un petit poème, *The Hermit*, a seul conservé quelque popularité.

Parolles (*parol'ez*), personnage comique de la comédie de Shakespeare *All's well that ends well.*

Paternoster (*pat'eurnost'eur*).

Paul (*pol*, o long comme dans *or*).

Penryn (*pennrinn'*), bourg du comté de Cornouailles, qui, réuni à Falmouth, envoie deux députés au Parlement.

Pericles (*per'icliz*), Périclès, un des plus illustres généraux et hommes d'Etat de la Grèce ancienne. Il dut surtout sa célébrité à la protection éclairée qu'il accorda aux lettres et aux arts.

Persius (*peur'chieuss*), Perse, poète satirique latin (34-62).

Peter (*pi'teur*), Pierre.

Peter Martyr (*pi'teur mâr'teur*), 1455-1526, historien d'origine italienne, dont la vie se passa en grande partie en Espagne, où il fut au service de la reine Isabelle.

Pharaoh (*fé'rô*), Pharaon.

Pharisees (*far'iciz*). Pharisiens, secte qui, chez les Juifs, affectaient une grande rigueur dans l'observance des pratiques religieuses.

Phidias (*fid'iass*), illustre sculpteur grec (cinquième siècle av. J.-C.).

Philips (*fil'ips*).

Piccadilly (*pic'adili*), rue de Londres.

Pilate (*paï'lett*).

Pisistratus (*piciss'trateuss*).

Pison (*paï'seunn*).

Pistol (*pis'teul*), personnage comique que l'on rencontre, en compagnie du célèbre Falstaff (*fol'staff'*), dans deux pièces de Shakespeare : *The Merry Wives of Windsor* et la seconde partie de *Henry IV*.

Pitt (*pitt*). — Voy. CHATHAM.

Pius (*paï'euss*) **the Fifth**, Pie V, pape de 1566 à 1572.

Plato (*plé'to*). Platon, 429-327 avant Jésus-Christ, illustre philosophe grec, disciple de Socrate. Sa philosophie, purement idéaliste, est exposée dans un nombre assez considérable d'ouvrages sous forme de dialogues.

Platonic (*platonn'ic*), platonicien, platonique.

Platonist (*plé'tonist*), Platonicien.

Plunkett (*pleunn'kett*) Lord, 1765-1854, orateur et magistrat anglais.

Pole (*pôl*), 1550-1558, prélat anglais catholique romain. À la suite d'un conflit avec Henri VIII, il fut arrêté et décapité.

Poole (*poûle*).

Pope (*pôpe*) Alexander, 1688-1744, poète anglais, dont l'influence littéraire eut quelque analogie avec celle de Boileau. Ses principaux poèmes sont : *l'Essay on Criticism*, 1711; *The Rape of the Lock*, 1712; *The Dunciad*, 1742, et une traduction de l'*Iliade* et de l'*Odyssée*.

Portia (*por'chia*), personnage du *Merchant of Venice* de Shakespeare.

Portuguese (*por'liouguize*), Portugais.

Posidonius (*possido'nieuss*).

Presbyterian (*prezbili'rieunn*).

Prometheus (*promi'thi-euss*). Prométhée ayant dérobé le feu du ciel fut cloué, sur l'ordre de Jupiter, au sommet du Caucase, et là il continua, malgré ses souffrances, à braver le roi des dieux.

Prussian (*preuch'eunn*), prussien.

Pry (*praïe*), personnage d'une comédie de John Poole, jouée pour la première fois en 1825. Pry est un oisif qui tue le temps à se mêler des affaires d'autrui.

Ptolemy (*tol'emi*), Ptolémée astronome et géographe grec, (deuxième siècle av. J.-C.).

Punic (*piou'nic*).

Puritanism (*piou'ritanizm*).

Pyrgopolynices (*peurgópolinaï'ciz*), Pyrgopolynice, héros de la comédie de Plaute (poète latin, 250-184 av. J.-C.), *Miles gloriosus*, le Soldat fanfaron.

Q

Quentin Durward (*couenn'tinn deur'oueuerde*). — Voy. SCOTT.

Quinctilian (*couinnti'ieunn*), Quintilien, 42-120, écrivain latin, auteur d'ouvrages sur l'art oratoire.

Quirinal (*couir'ineul*).

R

Rachel (*ré'tchel*).

Ramus (*ré'meuss*), de son vrai nom Pierre La Ramée, philosophe français, 1502-1572, périt dans le massacre de la Saint-Barthélemy.

Ranke (*rann'ki*), 1795-1886, historien allemand.

Raphaël (*raf'ael*), célèbre peintre italien, 1483-1520.

Rasselas (*rass'e-lass*), conte philosophique de Johnson.

Red Riding Hood (*red raï'digne houd*), Le Petit Chaperon Rouge, littéralement : le capuchon rouge pour aller à cheval. Le *riding-hood* était un manteau à capuchon porté autrefois par les femmes.

Rembrandt (*remm'brannt*) célèbre peintre hollandais du dix-septième siècle, dont les tableaux présentent de merveilleux effets de lumière.

Rhine (*raïne*), Rhin.

Richard (*ritch'eurd*).

Richard the Third. — Richard III roi d'Angleterre de 1483 à 1485. Mélange d'audace et de perfidie, son caractère a été admirablement dépeint par Shakespeare.

Richardson (*ritch'ardseunn*), Samuel, 1689-1761, célèbre romancier anglais, auteur de *Pamela*, 1741 ; *Clarissa Harlowe*, 1751, et *Sir Charles Grandison*, 1754.

Robert (*rob'eurte*).

Robertson (*rob'eurtseunn*) William, 1721-1793, historien écossais. Ses principaux ouvrages sont : *A History of Scotland*, 1759; *A History of the Reign of the Emperor Charles V*, 1769; *A History of America*, 1777.

Roman (*rô'meunn*), Romain.

Rome (*rôme*).

Romeo (*rom'eo*). — Voy. SHA-KESPEARE.

Rosa (*rô'za*).

Rosalind (*roz'alinnd*) — Voy. SHELLEY.

Rothley Temple (*roth'lé temm'-peul*).

Rupert (*roŭ'peurte*).

S

St. Albans (*sénnt ol'beunnz*). — Voy. BACON.

St. Bartholomew (*sénnt bár-thol'omiou*) Saint-Barthélemy.

St. Denis (*prononcez comme en français*).

St. Paul (*sénnt pol, o long comme dans or*).

St. Vitus (*sénnt vaï'teuss*), Saint-Gui.

Salvator (*salvé'teur*).

Samson Agonistes (*samm'seunn agonis'tiz*). — Voy. MILTON.

Samuel (*sam'iou-el*).

Satan (*sé'teunn*).

Savage (*sav'édj*), Richard, 1698-1743, poète anglais, dont le nom est sauvé de l'oubli par Johnson qui lui a donné une place dans ses *Lives of the English Poets*.

Saxon (*sax'eunn*).

Saxony (*sax'e-ni*), Saxe.

Scotch (*scotch*), écossais.

Scotchman (*scotch'meunn*), Écossais.

Scotland (*scot'lannd*), Écosse.

Scott (*scott*) Sir Walter, 1771-1832, célèbre poète et romancier écossais, un des écrivains les plus populaires de toute la littérature anglaise. Ses principaux poèmes sont : *Marmion*, 1808, et *The Lady of the Lake*, 1810. Parmi ses très nombreux romans historiques nous citerons : *Waverley*, 1814; *Ivanhoe*, 1820; *Kenilworth*, 1821; *Quentin Durward*, 1823.

Scriblerus (*scribli'reuss*) **Club**, fondé par Swift en 1714 ; il compta Pope parmi ses membres.

Sejanus (*sidjé'neuss*). — Voy. JONSON.

Seneca (*senn'éca*), Sénèque, célèbre philosophe latin; il fut précepteur et ministre de Néron.

Shaftesbury (*chafts'berri*), 1671-1713, moraliste anglais.

Shakespeare (*chék'spire*) William, 1564-1616. Illustre auteur dramatique anglais. Ses principales œuvres sont : *Midsummer Night's Dream* (1591), *The Two Gentlemen of Verona* (1592), *Romeo and Juliet* (1591-1593), *Richard II* (1593), *Richard III* (1594), *King John* (1595), *The Merchant of Venice* (1596), *The Taming of the Shrew* (1597), *Henry IV* (1597), *The Merry Wives of Windsor* (1598), *Henry V* (1599), *Much Ado about Nothing* (1600), *As you Like it* (1600), *Twelfth Night* (1601), *All's Well that Ends well* (1601), *Julius Cæsar* (1601), *Hamlet* (1602), *Measure for Measure* (1603), *Othello* (1604), *Troilus and Cressida* (1604), *Macbeth* (1605), *King Lear* (1605), *Antony and Cleopatra* (1606), *Coriolanus* (1607), *The Tempest* (1610), *Cymbeline* (1610), *Winter's Tale* (1611).

Shallow (*chal'o*).

Shelley (*chel'i*), 1792-1822, poète anglais, un des plus grands poètes lyriques. Principales œuvres : *Queen Mab* (1813), *Alastor* (1816), *The Revolt of Islam* (1818), *Rosalind and Helen* (1818), *The Cenci* (1819), *Prometheus Unbound* (1819), *Adonais* (1821).

Sheppard (*chep'eurde*) **Jack,** pièce tirée d'un roman d'Ainsworth (1805-1882), et dont le héros, qui donne son nom au roman et à la pièce, fut un bandit célèbre au commencement du dix-huitième siècle.

Shylock (*chaï'loc*), personnage du *Merchant of Venice* de Shakespeare. — Voy. l'Appendice.

Siamese Twins (*saï'amiz touinuz*) **The,** les Jumeaux Siamois, connus en France sous le nom de *Frères Siamois.* Leurs corps étaient réunis par un cartilage qui reliait leurs foies. Morts en 1872.

Siddons (*sid'eunns*) Mrs., 1755-1831, célèbre tragédienne anglaise dont le triomphe fut son interprétation de *Lady Macbeth.*

Sismondi (*cissmonn'di*), historien génevois (1773-1842), auteur d'une *Histoire des Républiques Italiennes,* d'une *Histoire des Français,* etc.

Smithfield (*smith'fild*), place de de Londres où, sous le règne de Marie Tudor, un grand nombre d'hérétiques furent brûlés.

Smollett (*smol'ett*) 1721-1771, romancier et historien anglais.

Socinian (*socinn'ieunn*), Socinien, partisan de la doctrine des deux Socin, hérésiarques italiens du seizième siècle. Les Sociniens niaient la divinité de Jésus-Christ, tout en considérant son origine comme miraculeuse.

Socrates (*soc'ratiz*), Socrate, célèbre philosophe grec (cinquième siècle av. J.-C.).

Solomon (*sol'omeunn*), Salomon.

Somers (*seumm'eurz*), 1652-1716, homme d'Etat anglais.

Somersetshireman (*seum'eursetchir'mann*), homme du comté de Somerset.

Sophocles (*sof'ocliz*), Sophocle, illustre poète dramatique grec, auteur d'*Œdipe Roi,* d'*Antigone,* etc.

Southampton (*saouthammp' teunn*), le comte de S. fut l'ami de Shakespeare.

Southey (*saouth'i,* ou *seuth'i*), 1774-1843, poète anglais.

Spain (*spéne*), Espagne.

Spaniard (*spann'ieurde*), Espagnol.

Spenser (*spenn'seur*).

Stadthouse (*state haouss*).

Strabo (*stré'bo*), Strabon, géographe grec du cinquième siècle avant Jésus-Christ.

Strand (*strannd*), rue de Londres.

Stratford-on-Avon (*straff'feurde onn é'veunn*), petite ville du comté de Warwick où Shakespeare naquit en 1564.

Sunderland (*seunn'deurlannd*), 1641-1702, homme d'Etat anglais.

Surajah Dowlah (*soura'dja daou'la*).

Surrey (*seur'i*), comté au sud de Londres.

Swedenborgian (*souidn-bor'dji-eunn*). Swedenborgien, partisan des doctrines religieuses de Swedenborg, célèbre philosophe suédois (1688-1772).

Swift (*souift*) Jonathan, 1667-1749, célèbre écrivain anglais, auteur des Voyages de Gulliver, *Gulliver's Travels,* 1726.

Switzerland (*souitz'eurlannd*), la Suisse.

Sydney. — Voy. ALGERNON SYDNEY.

T

Tacitus (*lass'iteuss*), Tacite, célèbre historien latin (55-135).

Talus (*té'leuss*).

Tamerlane (*tameurléne*), Tamerlan, célèbre conquérant tartare du quatorzième siècle.

Tavislock (*tav'isloc*).

Taylor (*té'leur*).

Temple (*temm'peul*), Sir William, 1628-1699, homme d'Etat et écrivain anglais.

Thames (*temmz*), Tamise.

Theodosius (*thi-odō'chieuss*), Théodose le Grand, 379-395.

Thermopylæ (*theurmop'ili*), les Thermopyles, défilé de la Grèce ancienne où, en 480 avant Jésus-Christ, un millier de Grecs, commandés par Léonidas, soutinrent un combat héroïque contre l'immense armée des Perses.

Thomas (*tom'euss*).

Thrale (*thréle*) Mrs., 1741-1821, célèbre par son amitié pour le Dr. Johnson.

Thraso (*thré'sô*), Thrason, militaire fanfaron, personnage de l'*Eunuque*, comédie de Térence, poète latin, 194-158 avant Jésus-Christ.

Threadneedle (*thred'nidl*) **Street**, rue de la Cité de Londres, au commencement de laquelle se trouvent la Bourse et la Banque.

Timæus (*taïmi'euss*).

Tokay (*tôké*).

Tom (*tom*), diminutif de **Thomas**.

Tower Hill (*taou'eur hil*), située dans le voisinage de la Tour de Londres, fut longtemps le lieu d'exécution des condamnés politiques.

Toxophilus (*toxof'ileuss*). — Voy. **Ascham**.

Trent (*trennt*), Trente, ville d'Autriche.

Troilus (*trô'ileuss*). — Voy. **Shakespeare**.

Troy (*troï*), Troie.

Turcaret (*pron. comme en français*), personnage d'une comédie de Le Sage, 1708. C'est un financier grossier et vaniteux.

Turkish (*teur'kiche*), turc.

Tuscan (*teuss'keunn*), toscan.

Tyre (*taïre*), Tyr.

U

Ugolino (*iougoli'no*).

Ulm (*oulm*).

United States (*iounaï'led stélz*), États-Unis.

Utopia (*ioulô'pia*).

V

Valencia (*valenn'chia*), Valence.

Vane (*véne*), 1612-1662, homme d'État puritain; fut décapité à la Restauration.

Vatican (*val'ikeunn*).

Venise (*venn'ice*), Venise.

Venus (*vi'neuss*).

Verona (*verô'na*), Vérone.

Versailles (*veursélz*).

Verulam (*ver'ouleumm*). — Voy. **Bacon**.

Virgil (*veur'djil*), Virgile.

Virginia (*veurdji'nia*), Virginie, jeune Romaine que son père poignarda pour la soustraire au déshonneur (cinquième siècle av. J.-C.).

Volpone (*volpône*). — Voy. **Jonson**.

Voltaire (*pron. comme en français*).

W

Wakefield (*ouék'fild*). — Voy. **Goldsmith**.

Wales (*ouélz*), Galles.

Waller (*ouol'eur*) Edmund, 1605-1687, poète anglais.

Walpole (*ouol'pôle*) Horace, 1717-1797, écrivain anglais dont on lit encore un roman, *The Castle of Otranto*.

Walter (*ouol'teur*).

Warren (*ouor'enn*). — Voy. **Hastings**.

Warwick (*ouor'ic*).

Warverley (*oué'veurli*). — Voy. **Scott**.

Wesley (*oues'li ou ouez'li*) John, 1703-1791, fondateur de la secte des *Methodists*.

Westminster (*ouest'minnsteur*), **Abbey**. — Voisine des Chambres du Parlement, l'Abbaye de W. est peut-être le plus célèbre des monuments anglais; car, outre sa valeur architecturale, elle renferme la tombe d'une foule d'Anglais illustres, hommes d'État, poètes, généraux, etc.

Whitehall (*houaïte holl*, o long comme dans *or*), palais des rois d'Angleterre à Londres.

Whitfield (*houitt'filde*).

Wilkes (*ouilx*), 1727-1797, célèbre agitateur anglais. Expulsé du Parlement à cause d'un ouvrage à scandale, il fut à diverses reprises élu député du comté de Middlesex, et, chaque fois, expulsé de nouveau de la Chambre.

William (*ouil'ieum*), Guillaume.

Windsor (*ouinn'zeur*).

Wolfe (*woulf*), général anglais, fut tué le 13 septembre 1759 à la bataille de Québec où il vainquit Montcalm, qui, mortellement blessé, mourut le lendemain.

Wolsey (*woul'zi*), célèbre cardinal, ministre de Henri VIII, est un des principaux personnages du *Henry VIII* de Shakespeare.

Wordsworth (*oueurdz'oueurth*) William, 1770-1850, célèbre poète anglais; contribua à délivrer la poésie anglaise du style conventionnel du dix-huitième siècle.

X

Xeres (*zer'ess*).

Y

York (*yórke*).

Z

Zecharia (*zekeuraï'a*), Zacharie.

Zeuxis (*ziouk'ciss*), peintre grec du cinquième siècle avant Jésus-Christ.

Zwingle (*zvinn'glé*), 1484-1531, propagateur du protestantisme en Suisse.

TABLE DES MATIÈRES

SAINT-CLOUD. — IMPRIMERIE BELIN FRÈRES.

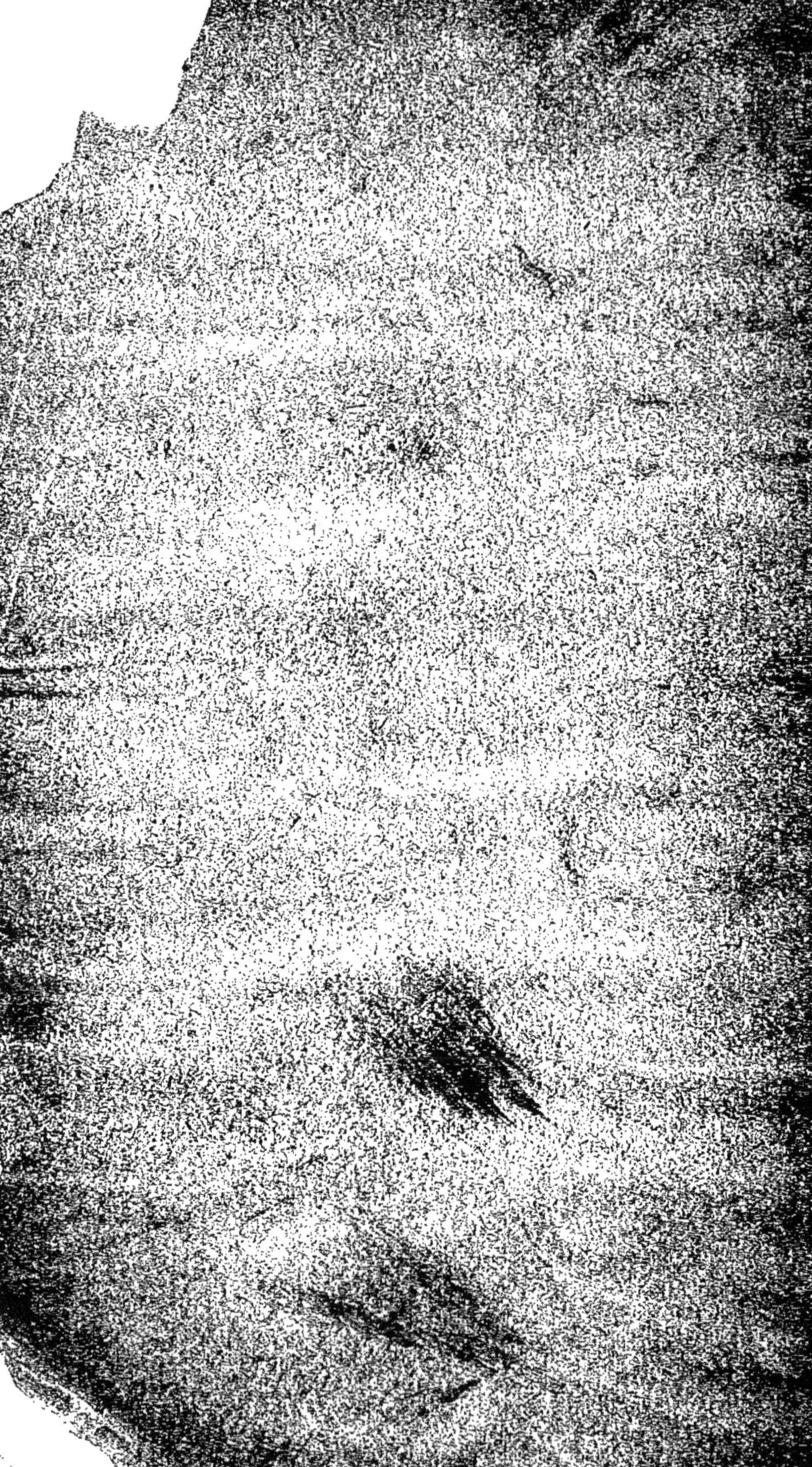